Democracy and Interest Groups

Democracy and Interest Groups

Enhancing Participation?

Grant Jordan
Professor of Politics
University of Aberdeen, UK

and

William A. Maloney
Professor of Politics
University of Newcastle, UK

First published 2007 by
PALGRAVE MACMILLAN
Houndmills, Basingstoke, Hampshire RG21 6XS and
175 Fifth Avenue, New York, N.Y. 10010
Companies and representatives throughout the world

PALGRAVE MACMILLAN is the global academic imprint of the Palgrave
Macmillan division of St. Martin's Press, LLC and of Palgrave Macmillan Ltd.
Macmillan® is a registered trademark in the United States, United Kingdom
and other countries. Palgrave is a registered trademark in the European
Union and other countries.

ISBN-13: 978–0–333–76333–9 hardback
ISBN-10: 0–333–76333–5 hardback

This book is printed on paper suitable for recycling and made from fully
managed and sustained forest sources.

A catalogue record for this book is available from the British Library.

A catalog record for this book is available from the Library of Congress.

10   9   8   7   6   5   4   3   2   1
16   15   14   13   12   11   10   09   08   07

Printed and bound in Great Britain by
Antony Rowe Ltd, Chippenham and Eastbourne

Contents

List of Figures and Tables

Figures

Tables

Acknowledgements

The research for this book was funded under the ESRC Democracy and Participation Programme (1215252038). In the preparation of this text we benefited from the comments and advice of many colleagues at: several Democracy and Participation Programme meetings; departmental seminars in Aberdeen, Dublin, Mannheim and Paris; and at the following annual conferences – American Political Science Association (2003), Meeting of Midwest Political Science Association (2003), the Joint Sessions of the European Consortium for Political Research (2004) and the Political Studies Association (2002). Specifically we wish to thank Jan van Deth, Frank Baumgartner, Martin Elff, Joan Font Fàbregas, Mark Franklin, Wyn Grant, Peter John, David Lowery, Robert McMaster, Michael Marsh, Neil Mitchell, Linda Stevenson, Stephanie Stuck, Eric Uslaner, Sonja Zmerli and the anonymous reviewer of this book appointed by Palgrave. Our data collection depended on utilizing eligible participants identified in the large Citizen Audit survey orchestrated by Paul Whiteley, Patrick Seyd and Charles Pattie and we are very grateful for their full support and unhesitating cooperation. Without in any way diminishing our gratitude to the above colleagues, we must give special mention to Sigrid Roßteutscher. We would also like to acknowledge research support from Emma Clarence, particularly with regard to data collection, and to Jennifer Lees-Marshment in the development of the *Beliefs and Actions* Project from which this research is drawn. Finally, we are particularly grateful to Sara Davidson. Her explorations on public opinion arrived at the same destination as us from our group direction. We were delighted that she agreed to join us in Chapter 3. As always, we accept full responsibility for the text below, while co-authors naturally retain the traditional right to point to each other.

Grant Jordan, Aberdeen
William A. Maloney, Newcastle

1
Looking for Democracy: The Democratic Contribution of Membership-based Interest Groups

Beyond 'direct' democracy lies an infinite wealth of possible forms in which the 'people' may partake in the business of ruling or influence or control those who actually do the ruling (Schumpeter, 1943: 247).

Democracy without organization is inconceivable... But direct democracy falls down in the face of increasing numbers. The individual plain man, swallowed up in a sea of highly differentiated human beings, finds it necessary to organize with others of a like mind so that by concerted action they may bend the state to their will. Political parties are one result of this process. But political parties invariably include adherents whose wills are hopelessly at variance upon all but a very few questions... It is this situation which has engendered the pressure group (Odegard, 1928: Preface).

It is a fundamental property – and perhaps defect – of democracy that citizens may watch laws being made, and when they do so they often compare democracy to its image and then reject the actual process with righteous disdain, even outrage, opaquely dismissing it as bickering and correctly, but uncomprehendingly, labelling it 'politics as usual'. Effectively, however, politics as usual is the same as democracy in action (Mueller, 1999: 248).

Introduction: The (growing) importance of groups to democratic politics?

The traditional 20th century perspective on political parties was that 'they' were central to the study of Anglo-American political participation:

> By every democratic principle the parties, as mobilizers of majorities, have claims on the public more valid and superior to those asserted by pressure groups which merely mobilize minorities (Schattschneider, 1942: 193).

Schattschneider's confidence in the merit of party-based activity is now widely questioned. There is a perception that parties are 'damaged goods' as participatory vehicles. Interest groups are regarded as filling this void. But an exaggerated respect accorded to parties as democratically useful institutions may have been replaced by a too uncritical faith in groups. That groups were in the foreground of the picture of democracy was central to the pluralist approach of the 1960s. (And Skocpol (2003) documents the centrality of groups in the 19th-century US – also described, of course, in Tocqueville's *Democracy in America*.) However, the mid-(20th)-century pluralist celebration of groups was not imbued with the current assumption that activity *within* groups is important: now there is a strong expectation that groups should offer opportunities for face-to-face interaction to enhance social integration and democracy itself. (Though Tocqueville ([1848] 1966: 522) offered the very modern observation, 'One may think of political associations as great free schools to which all citizens come to be taught the general theory of association.') In summary, the modern support for the democratic contribution of groups appears to be twofold. Groups are seen as democratically valuable in offering more effective representation (than parties) and hence securing overall public policy that better 'fits' citizens' preferences. Secondly, the political and social experiences *within* groups are viewed as democratically relevant. Accordingly interest groups have become central (again) to the study of political science and the practice of politics.[1]

The valourization of a group-mobilized democracy of active individuals became prominent in the US in the 1980s, expanded there, and has been reinvented elsewhere. For example, as Cigler and Loomis (1986: 1) note, in the early 1960s there was an interest group proliferation while '(US) political parties' abilities to perform key electoral and policy-related activities' continued to decline. Later (1991: 10) they argued that 'a participation revolution has occurred . . . large numbers of citizens have become active in an ever increasing number of protest groups, citizens' organizations, and special interest groups'. Approximately at the same time as the explosion in the number and membership levels of groups, British political parties began to experience a haemorrhaging in the level of both membership and intra-organizational activity. Now group membership (in aggregate) dwarfs that of parties. In the last 50 years Labour Party membership declined from 1 million to 200,000 or under (*Times*, May 24, 2005), and the Conservative Party from 3 million to circa 300,000 in 2002 (see also Scarrow, 2000). Meanwhile membership of the National Trust for England and Wales has soared (2.8 million), and Royal Society for the Protection of Birds (RSPB) increased to 1.02 million. Even relative 'newcomers' such as the Countryside Alliance appear to involve larger numbers of citizens than the governing parties. The Alliance has over 100,000 ordinary members and a further 250,000 associate members. Hall (2002: 25) suggests that the average number of associational memberships in Britain grew by 44% between 1959 and 1990: partly as a result of rising educational levels and the increasing density of the group universe.

Mair (2005: 8) sums up by noting that 'citizens are voting in fewer numbers and with less sense of partisan consistency, and they are also increasingly reluctant to commit themselves to parties, whether in terms of identification or membership'. However, he (2005: 8) also notes that they are 'becoming involved in other areas of social and political behaviour'. Mair quotes the Pattie *et al.* (2004: 107) point that the focus on the fall in participation in conventional political institutions – rather than broader activity – has led to an exaggerated sense of the 'public exit from civic behaviour'.

The Directory of British Associations (CBD, 2006) records 7755 organizations and Figure 1.1 shows the start-up dates for 6168 groups. Forty eight per cent of current groups (2963) were created in the 1966–1995 period.[2] The explosion from the 1960s seems normal in all politically mature systems. In the US, in 1929, Herring (cited in Truman, 1951: 57) estimated that a 'conservative estimate' of the number of groups with representatives in Washington was 'well over five hundred'. By 1956 the *Encyclopaedia of Associations* reckoned that the number of Washington DC-based organizations was just under 5000, by 1970 it was over 10,000 and by 1997 it had risen to 22,901 (Putnam, 2000: 49).[3] Walker (1991: 79) shows that almost half of the US citizen sector[4] groups surveyed in 1985 were created in the 1960–1983 period. Finally, Rauch (1994: 39) estimated that in the US between 1970 and 1990 'an average of about ten new groups were formed every week'.[5]

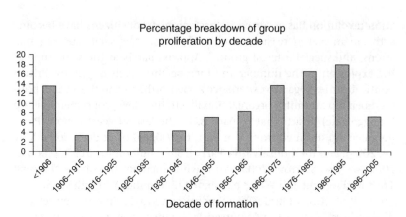

Figure 1.1 The formation date of British Associations as reported in the 2006 Directory of British Associations (percentage per decade for groups with known dates of origin).
Source: CBD (2006).

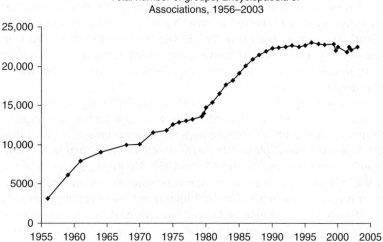

Figure 1.2 The total number of US groups listed in the Encyclopaedia of Associations, 1956–2003.
Source: Baumgartner (2005).

The best US data – Baumgartner (2005) – also highlights the same trend of expansion from the 1960s followed by a plateau (and possibly even a fall) (Figure 1.2).

Dalton (2006: 49) shows Great Britain, France and Germany recording about 6–8% participation in public interest groups according to the World Values Survey 1999–2002. (However, the US data show an increase from the 1993 figure of 18% to a remarkable high of 33% by 1999.) These burgeoning numbers appear to demonstrate that in an increasingly segmented and niche-driven world, more and more organizations are catering for ever more specialized tastes and, of course, providing potential opportunities for wider citizen participation.[6]

In the light of these sorts of mutually reinforcing sources, a widespread view has emerged that the mobilization of a large number of groups offsets the undesirable consequences of reduced party activity, and provides a renewal of patterns of civic and political engagement (e.g. remedying declines in political trust and low and diminishing electoral turnout). Accordingly, participation, by any means, is seen as good. Or as John Stuart Mill would put it, 'any participation, even in the smallest public function, is useful' (quoted in Parry *et al.*, 1992: 433). Verba and Nie (1972: 184) argue that group proliferation will

> increase the propensity of the individual to be a participant because they give him an opportunity for training in participation within the organization that can be transferred to the political realm . . . (quoted in Leighley, 1996: 449).

Verba and Nie (1972: 1) asserted, 'If democracy is interpreted as rule by the people then . . . the more participation there is in decisions, the more democracy there is.' This is an unusually blunt version of the belief that democracy rests on the engagement of the many. But the thrust of Skocpol (2003: 73) is that civic voluntarism is not new, but has flourished as part of representative democratic governance and was, and is not, a substitute for it.

Norris (2002: 19) makes the point that *modernization theory* as supplied by Bell, Inglehart, Dalton and others identify a new style of activist citizen politics. She notes that such activities are choice-based rather than loyalty-centred – in other words action is more likely to be found in organizations that reflect values and preferences rather than traditional interests. In line with this identification of group activity, Walker (1991) noted that by the 1960s there was a political atmosphere that encouraged group emergence. Arguably, creating and supporting groups is now an intuitive and routinized reaction – or the *default instinct* – of those facing a political 'threat'.

If this general tendency exists then the task for group entrepreneurs has, in at least one way, become less challenging. They have no need to 'invent' the idea of group emergence – others expect the group proposal. Closures of hospitals, expansions of airports, the introduction of, or increases in, fees for public services (e.g. health care) are all likely catalysts of group formation. British news bulletins report protest after protest – for example the Community Charge/Poll Tax, 1990; Brent Spar, 1995; export of live animals (veal calves), 1995; Snowdrop Appeal (Dunblane massacre), 1996; second runway at Manchester airport, 1997; the banning of fox hunting, 1998 and 2004; petrol protest, 2000; the Iraq war, 2003; Fathers 4 Justice, 2004; Make Poverty History/G8 Summit protests, 2005; etc.). Ironically such reports are intercut by think pieces on the decline of participation and the 'democratic malaise'.

While the traditional view (outlined above) was that parties were the best representative agency available, more recently some have maintained that parties and groups are simply alternative means to the same end. Ryden (1996: 28) argues that '(parties and) groups mediate between the public and the elected. They allow individuals to participate and gain significance through association, while simultaneously narrowing, focusing, and defining the multiplicity of interests into discernible policy positions, which ultimately shape and guide governance.' However, others are not so charitable. The party/electoral channel of representation has increasingly been regarded as deficient. Lawson (1980) argued that major party decline is correlated with a failure of *linkage* between the parties and the political process. Groups have been successful because they have filled the linkage 'void'. In this respect the strength of parties tends to be inversely related to the strength of interest groups (Almond and Verba, 1963; Lawson and Merkl, 1988; Schattschneider, 1942; Schlozman and Tierney, 1986).[7] Loomis and Cigler (1991: 19) maintained that the traditional party system found it difficult to deal effectively with citizens' high expectations and a changing class structure. No matter how adroit parties have proven to be in assimilating new issues within their programmes, the public do not fall neatly into two, three or four partisan camps. There are too many issues cutting across constituencies. Groups with narrower niches better marry onto public demands. While Sorauf and Beck (1988; quoted in Thomas, 2004: 58) see 'party decline' as part of a maturation process – suggesting 'a natural cycle in the lives of parties' in which they are influential in the early years of democracy and then 'lose it in the much greater political literacy, wider political involvement, and newer political agendas of these societies and economies as they mature'. Norris (2002: 222) refers to the rise of 'critical citizens' who are 'less loyalist and deferential towards mass-branch parties'. This perspective sees dwindling membership as a problem for parties – *but not for democracy.* The observation or argument that groups have *replaced* parties as the most significant participatory vehicle is a crucial step in the debate, but this book while assuming that increased group mobilization and decreased party vitality has 'political consequences', seeks to explore the consequences rather than make a priori assumptions.

Groups as democratic transmission belts

The first sort of democratic virtue bestowed on groups lies in their provision of a responsive and direct form of 'particularised' linkage – groups are key democratic transmission belts. In this light, the breadth of support, on which successful parties rely, can be interpreted as a democratic weakness: strategically (in pursuit of vote maximization) parties cannot afford to reflect the narrow, and intensely held, concerns of individuals. In contrast, interest groups excel at capturing the *intensity of interest* of a fragmented public. Picking up the Sorauf and Beck (1988) point (above), large parties may be useful in mobilizing large numbers, but may do so in a way *ultimately* subversive of mature democracy. They over promise the likely scope for change in democratic contests and frequently seek to attract votes via the demonization of (party) political opponents. Political parties habitually attack each other – and appear surprised when public confidence and trust in parties as mechanisms declines. In more developed democracies, when citizens have witnessed patterns of alternating governments (and constrained degrees of change), they might be less easily convinced by party promises of dramatic change as a result of electoral success or the impending catastrophic consequences of defeat. These citizens may be less easily mobilized to vote or join parties. But as suggested by Norris (above) *a degree of sceptical distance from parties by the public can be seen a sign of a mature – rather than a failing – democracy.*

Responsiveness, accountability and *control* are some of the basic tenets of democratic politics. Citizens' demands and wishes should be taken into account by governments and they should have the opportunity to (s)elect or de-select political administrations. However, as Gray and Lowery (1996: 1) argue, elections are a primary, but inevitably *blunt*, democratic device – taking place infrequently and being unable to provide parties with 'detailed and nuanced signals about citizens' preferences'. They maintain that interest groups play an important secondary and supporting role as an effective 'channel of citizen communication and control'.

Berry (1984: 55) suggests that if one is politically active and willing to spend $100 to pursue one's political goals in a year then the interest group can be seen as a more prudent 'investment' – that is one can target the cash more effectively on one's personal priorities, be it protecting the wilderness or whales, consumer rights or whatever. Elsewhere he (1984: 43) maintains that 'The essence of the public interest philosophy is that party politics cannot be trusted. Parties are impure; they stand for compromise rather than hard-fought principles.' Accordingly, the increase in the number and size of campaigning groups (particularly public interest groups) has implied a shift in the main channels of politics (from parties to groups), and *allegedly* increased participatory democracy through organizations with more clearly articulated and deeply held views than 'broad-church' parties.

Generally the opening up of decision-making processes to a wider, diverse and larger number of groups is seen as contributing to democratic responsiveness. Many scholars in the US and the UK have argued that in the 1980s and 1990s the policy process became more open – characterized by issue network-type configurations rather than iron triangles/subgovernment/policy community-type arrangements; and with hitherto weakly represented interests gaining a foothold in the process, most notably public interest groups (see Berry, 1994; Browne, 1995; Gais *et al.*, 1984; Heclo, 1978; Levine and Thurber, 1986; and Salisbury *et al.*, 1992). The expanded group universe became, it is argued, broad enough to be a sort of *ersatz democracy*. Hudson (1995: 18) suggests, 'Since some interest group represents almost everyone's interests, the activities of interest-group leaders are an effective democratic channel for the expression of the public's wants and needs.'

Berry (1997: 8) suggests that groups help determine the political agenda and monitor policy developments. Not all problems are 'political issues being actively considered by government' – the agenda-building function of groups 'turns problems into issues'. And group expertise allows effective monitoring of policy outputs and enables these organizations to hold governments to account. Berry (1997: 7) also stresses groups' educative role – through 'their advocacy efforts, publications and publicity campaigns, interest groups can make people better aware of both policy problems and proposed solutions'. Similarly, Pierce *et al.* (1992: 18, 95, 107, 117) argue that interest groups meet individual's information needs and link 'citizens to policy processes'.

Their study of members of environmental groups in Canada and the United States found that the provision of information by groups was '*the* most important incentive to membership' and that environmental groups should be seen as 'social mechanisms linking micro level individual activity to macro level political processes'. From this perspective, groups help create and sustain a more informed citizenry.

Groups as locales for democratic development

McConnell (1969: 147–150) highlighted a number of 'benefits' that private associations deliver to the political system. Maintaining that a dense and diverse range of groups act as a barrier to the rise of totalitarian mass movements against the tyranny of government, he also suggested (pre-empting the concerns of social capital scholars[8]) that the internal aspects of membership engender mutual cooperation and accommodation, reciprocity and respect; inculcate members with pro-democratic values, attitudes and beliefs; provide 'order and stability' giving 'form and shape to relationships between citizens'; deliver opportunities for social and political participation; and are vehicles of self-government within which citizens are able to meaningfully participate in decisions which affect them. McConnell (1969: 150) concluded:

> As a consequence of all these considerations liberty itself is best served where a multitude of associations exist. Not only is the individual under such conditions unthreatened by mass movements and totalitarianism, he has the positive values of fellowship and meaning in his life without which liberty is a negative and empty thing.

Such views on the educative value of participation can be traced back to Tocqueville and John Stuart Mill. Famously the proponent of *Considerations on Representative Government* (1861), Mill would eventually be an important support for the work of Pateman in her influential *Participation and Democratic Theory* (1970). Writing on the benefit of local opportunities, Mill thought that participatory institutions fostered public-spirited motivations – 'we do not learn to read or write, to ride or swim, by merely being told to do it, so it is only by practising popular government on a limited scale, that the people will ever learn to exercise it on a larger' (Pateman, 1970: 31). This is compatible with Tocqueville's 'schools of democracy' where citizens learn democratic skills.

Fired by such sources, the social capital model sees groups as fundamental democratic devices. However, the question remains about the extent to which groups can in practice *deliver democracy*. In spite of the numerical explosion of groups, Rosenstone and Hansen (1993: 126) identify a decline in participation in political parties and groups: 'decreasing public involvement in voluntary organizations weakens an important link in the process by which citizens are moved to participate in government. Participation in governmental politics declines as participation in associational activity declines.' Putnam (2000), in line with Rosenstone and Hansen, argued that declines in participation have led to a diminution in stocks of social capital (the civic erosion or 'Bowling Alone' thesis). Accordingly, there is much controversy over whether there is greater or lesser group-centred participation and the corresponding implications. He (2002) argued that the US faces the paradoxical situation of a proliferation of groups and the simultaneous decline of *meaningful* citizen involvement. Putnam (1995a: 71) highlighted the decline in classic secondary associations and the rise of tertiary associations (or *protest business*-type groups [Jordan and Maloney, 1997]). He maintained that mass membership organizations (the American Association for Retired Persons (AARP), Greenpeace, etc.) may make an important contribution to the policy-making process, but they do not enhance political or social integration, and that the vast majority of members limit their involvement to signing a cheque, hardly any attend group meetings and there is no face-to-face interaction.

Thus the possible defect in the delivery of democracy through group activity relates to a decline in the widely perceived *positive* 'internal' effects of associationalism. *Protest businesses* are 'failing schools' of democracy. Accordingly the (democratic) contribution of groups in generating participatory habits is less effective than might be assumed because in practice groups have found that *less internal participation is actually an attractive quality in generating large-scale support*. People may join or support a group to *show* and financially support their preferences, but not to further them by personal activity (see Chapters 4–6). The tension in the literature between the image of 'exploding' group numbers and perceptions of declining citizen participation reflects differential consequences of changes along two dimensions – groups as vehicles and groups as locales. While there are more groups, fewer possess the internal characteristics requiring the sort of active citizen involvement that the social capital model deems essential.

If groups appear to be active at elite consultation level this may not extend far down the internal hierarchy of the organization. An ESRC report, 'Social Capital and the Participation of Marginalized Groups in Government' by Fevre *et al.* (2004) – based on Welsh fieldwork – found, 'Most grass roots members were much less interested in their organization's new role in the political process than the managers of these NGOs. Less than 1 in 5 thought that the Assembly had made a difference to their organization.' Group participation in political processes may be more important to group leaders than members. In the US context, Crenson and Ginsberg (2002: 147) argue that members are no longer crucial in affecting outcomes. 'The new politics of policy-making attempts to open itself "to all those who have ideas and expertise rather than to those who assert interest and preferences". Those admission requirements exclude the great mass of ordinary citizens.'

Inevitably, the picture is somewhat confused. Norris (2002: xi) rejected the civic erosion thesis, maintaining that caution should be exercised with regard to Golden Age visions of a time when all town hall meetings were packed, all voting booths overflowing, etc. (She also points out that decline is not the same as change.) The civic decline inter-pretation has also been challenged in the UK. Hall (2002: 25) argued that 'overall levels of associational memberships in Britain seem to have been at least as high in the 1980s and 1990s as they were in 1959, and perhaps somewhat higher'. Pattie *et al.* (2004: 51–52) found that civic commitment (a key social capital measure) was high, 'Seven in ten stated that they were willing to give blood; a similar number are willing to assist in a Neighbourhood Watch scheme; one in two are willing to assist in renovating a local park or amenity.' They also found that over 75% of their respondents engaged in one or more political actions (in the previous 12 months) and the mean number of individual actions was 3.6. When chequebook involvement (simply donating more) was excluded from the analysis, the mean remained high at 2.7. Pattie *et al.* (2004: 80) concluded that 'contrary to the claims of political apathy, people frequently participate in activities designed to influence political outcomes'; while Hall (2002: 25–27) noted that 'most recent studies of the voluntary sector in Britain conclude that it is extensive and vibrant'.[9] However, Pattie *et al.* (2004) also found that most political participation in Britain was of an individualistic (e.g. donating money, signing a petition, boycotting products or ethical shopping) rather than collective form (attending meetings, rallies or demonstration). For example, they (2004: 77–78; 98–99) found that donation was the most popular activity – 62% of the respondents had donated money and 30% had raised funds for a group. (Significantly, in this context, more British citizens were prepared to financially support voluntary associations than vote at the 2001 and 2005 General Elections – turnout was 59.4 and 61.2% respectively.)[10] In contrast, 41% never attend meetings and 51% never participate in decision-making. In summary, the picture is mixed. A significant proportion of UK citizens are group members (circa one-third), but active involvement is a minority sport – *chequebook* participation is the norm. Thus an expansion in the population of civic organizations – as a democratic remedy for electoral decline – can be re-evaluated less positively as the changing internal nature of modern civic organizations themselves can be seen as the occasion for further participatory retreat. (But Pattie *et al.* (2004) found that *civic commitment* remained high.) *It may be that group membership has become a devalued democratic currency as the role of the 'member' is reduced to that of financial donor?*

The political involvement of citizens through groups is seen by most observers as 'a good thing' (though the view appears now to be that this is a substitute for a 'higher' sort of direct personal participation). Yet Dahl (1961: 225) famously argued that 'Homo civicus is not, by nature, a political animal' and he (1961: 280) also queried the 'good thing' belief in many academic quarters:

> The sources of the myth about the primacy of politics in the lives of the citizens of a democratic order are ancient, manifold and complex... That initial bias has been reinforced by the human tendency to blur the boundaries between what is and what ought to be; by the inescapable fact that those who write about politics are deeply concerned with political affairs and sometimes find it difficult to believe that most other people are not.

Dahl (1961: 305) suggested that 'in liberal societies, politics is a sideshow in the great circus of life'. In this interpretation, the 'slack' in the system of underdeveloped participation can be seen as a signal of the limited extent of any alienation and a(n) (unintended but useful) means of preventing political overload in the system. Verba *et al.* (1995: 1) observed that political participation is at the heart of democracy; democracy is unthinkable without participation. Nevertheless, their study (1995: 97) found:

> politics is not at the heart of the day-to-day life of the American people. Beyond the domains of work and the family, which are the main concerns of most people, politics takes a secondary place to church and to other voluntary activities.

Challenged by the current emphasis on deliberation, democracy is now seen as requiring more personal involvement. Accordingly, as the picture book politics of an informed public deciding between competing party programmes has become less credible, more stress is placed on the pattern of interest group pressure as a *proxy* for public participation. And, of course, the activity of citizens within groups is perceived as crucial. However, the assumption that activity by groups and in groups are *in themselves* performance indicators of democratic health is questionable. *The idea that a citizen is necessarily better engaged with the political system while in-group membership needs to be subjected to a detailed examination.* Any thoughtful assessment of the relative contribution of groups and parties to democracy implies discussion about the types of group (and their differing roles); the consequences of expanded group numbers; the decline of parties; activity patterns within groups and parties; and conceptions of democracy.

Redeeming groups in 'democracy': Accepting 'warts and all'?

Positive approval of groups in a democracy is often undermined by an assumption that worthwhile democracy is locked onto non-group features – elections, parties and voting. However, choosing between candidates who stand on competing party programmes is simply *one* (naïve) version. The idea of democracy cannot be taken as a 'given'. It is endlessly reformulated and various versions highlight the positive and/or negative contribution of groups. For hundreds of years groups were generally seen as selfish challengers to the 'legitimate' policies proposed by (representative) governments with majority legitimation. Moreover there has been (from even earlier times), and still remains, a suspicion of *self-interest* in political life. Mansbridge (1990) notes that during the 1500 years that Christianity dominated Western thought there was a long-held philosophical view that self-interest should be limited, 'the notion that self-interest could serve as a legitimate foundation for political order found little support'. In the words of Mabbott (1958: 30) – discussing Rousseau's views on the participatory idea in the 18th century – citizens are called together to vote *not for what each wishes*, but *each for what all wish*. Individual self-interest is rejected: one participates to establish, and support, what is the overall view. For Rousseau participation is not about fighting for sectional advantage, but being prepared to abandon personal interest for the general good. Factions were condemned – even majority factions. Participants should try to establish the common good through discussion – not simply attempt to secure their prior preferences. The test of a proposed outcome should not be that one agrees with it, but whether it serves the general interest. An acceptable minority would not be pursuing self-interest, but would be offering what turned out to be a less popular version of the common good. Once the general will was established, the minority would be expected to support the dominant proposition. Of course, by contrast, today it is often assumed that participation simply means pursuing one's own interests, but some advocates of deliberative democracy have (once again) assumed that participation can be selfless.

A very different characterization of desirable participation that does not regard the pursuit of self-interest and the collective good as mutually incompatible is set out in Chapter II of *The Wealth of Nations*. Adam Smith famously argued that

> every individual... neither intends to promote the public interest, nor knows how much he is promoting it... he intends only his own gain, and he is in this, as in many other cases, led by an *invisible hand* to promote an end which was no part of his intention. Nor is it always the worse for the society that it was no part of it. By pursuing his own interest he frequently promotes that of the society more effectually than when he really intends to promote it (emphasis added).

Smith also noted that good did not emerge on the basis of altruism or philanthropy alone, 'It is not from the benevolence of the butcher, the brewer, or the baker that we expect our dinner, but from their regard to their own interest.' This is the essence of what Dahl (1996: 213) labels *modern individualism* 'each citizen is or should be moved by self-interest... [However, this] does not require one to deny that individuals may have an interest in protecting or advancing the ends of larger community to which they belong'. This perspective celebrates rather than condemns self-interested behaviour.

While classical democracy stressed the individual participation of citizens in the evolution and execution of policy, later versions of democracy became associated with majoritarian selection between competing manifestos: deferring to minorities was seen as eroding the grand legitimacy of the majority government. However, an interpretation of democracy more accommodating to groups emerged as early as the Federalist Papers. Madison ([1787] 2003: 71) (Federalist Paper: 10) maintained that the 'latent causes of faction are... sown in the nature of man... [and] The inference to which we are brought is that the *causes* of faction cannot be removed and that relief is only to be sought in the means of controlling its *effects'*. Madison ([1787] 2003) argued that the best check to the power of factions was essentially suffocation (*fighting fire with fire*) – using a multiplicity of interests to neutralize any too strong interest was preferable to trying to avoid interests completely (that remedy was a threat to liberty – even worse than the problem of interests). Tocqueville ([1848] 1966: 191, 524) also warned of the dangers of *unlimited* freedom of association and argued that at times it may be prudent to restrict it. However, Tocqueville's view was measured, he did not advocate 'strict limits to the rights of association', like Madison he believed the price was too high: 'To save a man's life, I can understand cutting off his arm. But I don't want anyone to tell me that he will be as dexterous without it.'[11] Hampsher-Monk (1992: 219) says that Madison made 'size and faction redeeming virtues, rather than a threat to the popular republic'.[12] While Crenson and Ginsberg (2002: 106) noted that, over time, 'Madison's remedy came to be regarded as a virtue in its own right. Competition among interest groups seemed to be the functional equivalent of party competition.'

In essence, Tocqueville ([1848] 1966) saw merit in associational proliferation. He argued that 'In no country in the world . . . has the principle of association been more successfully applied to a greater multitude of objects than in America.' However, he was not overly sentimental or romantic about associations. As Rosenblum (1998: 44) argues,

> He (Tocqueville) never doubted that 'individual interest will more than ever become the chief if not the only motive behind all actions'. The real question was 'how each man will interpret his individual interest', and what makes the pursuit of self-interest in America notably 'ordered, temperate, moderate, careful, and self-controlled'. 'Self-interest rightly understood', or 'refined and intelligent selfishness', follows from the understanding that increasing the prosperity of our district, the right to direct affairs, the hope of pressing through plans for improvements that enrich us and so on depend on cooperation.

Nevertheless hostility to groups persisted deep into the 20th century. David Truman's (1951) The *Governmental Process* began with a chapter on the 'The *Alleged* Mischiefs of Faction' (emphasis added). Truman (1951: 46) outlined – *and then altered* – the climate at the time, noting that some scholars saw groups as pathological to democracy. 'The "lobby" and the "pressure group" are familiar to many, but they are accepted in the way that the typhoid bacillus is, as an organism that is a feature of civilized existence but that must be eradicated if society is to develop and prosper'. Truman, like Madison, resisted the idea that factions should be restrained and set the tone for a (loosely labelled) pluralist decade tolerant of interest group activity. Interest groups were viewed as beneficial rather than inimical to democracy.

Dahl (1989: 177) refined the language used in discussions of the role of groups in democracy. He proposed that 'democracy' should refer to an ideal – while actual systems may be viewed as 'more' or 'less' democratic – hence his coining of the term 'polyarchy'. He argued that polyarchies can be thought of as systems in which the institutions necessary to the democratic process exist *above a certain threshold*. In the *real* world, polyarchy is the best *approximation* to democracy, but by *ideal* standards it will *always* be the runner-up. Thus for Dahl the question is not how democratic are democracies, but how democratic are polyarchies? He (1989: 223) maintains that in the West 'polyarchy' is often seen as unsatisfactory; if those who complain about polyarchical deficiencies had experience of polities that lacked such basic features, then polyarchy might seem highly desirable: '*warts and all*'.

Mueller (1992) also dissents from those who 'dress-up' democracy as a rather noble enterprise[13] and he cites the extravagant claim by President Kennedy, 'democracy is a difficult kind of government. It requires the highest qualities of self-discipline, restraint, a willingness to make commitments, and sacrifices for the general interest, and it also requires knowledge.' The problem with this kind of grand rhetoric is that once these qualities are demonstrated as being absent – by opinion polls or other means – then the system appears undemocratic. In fact, Mueller (1992: 990) believes that 'democracy is really quite easy – any dimwit can do it – and it can function remarkably well even when people exhibit little in the way of self-discipline, etc.' Mueller compares democracy to Ralph's Pretty Good Grocery in Garrison Keillor's Lake Woebegon books, 'If you can't get it at Ralph's, you can probably get along without it.' For Mueller the requirements of democracy, like those of the hardy citizens of Lake Woebegon, are minimal. This very relaxed interpretation of democracy finds self-interested group activity more palatable that Kennedy's pious characterization that stressed sacrifice. Finally, Mueller (1999: 247) controversially proposes, '*There are plenty of nonviolent methods for removing officeholders besides elections, and much of what goes on in a democracy comes from petition and pressure, not from elections and legislative voting*' (emphasis added). Pressure group activity is a large component of such non-electoral activity that might be relevant to this basement-level democracy.

Dahl's (1956: 3) general and minimal definition of democracy – *'processes by which ordinary citizens exert a relatively high degree of control over leaders'* – and his essential notion of a democracy as *'responsive'* means that (democracy or) polyarchy is not necessarily, or solely, achieved through the electoral process. Democracy comes close to contestation. It might in fact be better operationalized on a day-to-day basis by the group–government interface. Therefore, for some observers, groups are not a problem for democracy, they are its essence:

> the older idea of monistic democracy, in which autonomous political associations were thought to be unnecessary and illegitimate, was transformed into a pluralist political system in which autonomous associations were held to be not only legitimate but actually necessary to democracy on a large scale . . . political conflict came to be regarded as a normal, inevitable, even desirable part of the democratic order (Dahl, 1989: 30).

In this (pluralist) perspective government concessions to minorities (often groups) are seen as *adding value*. For Dahl there is more democracy in an endless process of concessions to minorities than majoritarian steamrolling. Following Mueller's (1992: 985) argument that citizens have the right to complain, petition, organize, protest, demonstrate, strike, publish, express a lack of confidence, etc. – government will tend to respond to the organized. This may not be a dignified form of democracy, but it may meet some basic requirements. Of course, there may also be problems of political inequality. The fundamental assumption is that *who participates matters!* Politicians and policy-makers will respond to the best-organized interests that advance the most coherent, compelling and convincing case, or those who mobilize the most resources or simply *shout the loudest*. ('The squeaking wheel gets the grease' belief.) If some voices are unraised or unheard the result is likely to be political inequality. Clearly the *persistent problem* for advanced democracies is that of inequality, most notably the continuing socio-demographic unrepresentativeness of participators. The democratic implications are clear. The fact that those most involved are drawn from a relatively small subset of the citizenry creates a *democratic paradox*. Arguably, those who stand to gain the most from involvement (disadvantaged groups) participate the least. In recent years, skewed participation has been further exacerbated by the recruiting strategies of many campaign groups (see Chapter 4 for a detailed discussion).

In spite of the political inequality argument sketched above, it is also important to note that *groups perform a surrogate function*. Groups act on behalf of a public that lack the resources (i.e. knowledge and expertise) and have the niche expertise to be able to effectively criticize government policy – on a continuous, not episodic, basis.[14] Much participation seeks *to* advance many causes that benefit constituencies and interests beyond the direct interests of participators. Imig (1994) talks of 'advocacy by proxy' to describe how individuals are mobilized to act on behalf of client groups (e.g. Make Poverty History). McCarthy and Zald (1973: 17–18) argued that many early civil rights groups in the US mainly recruited whites (cited in Baer and Bositis, 1993: 163) (see Chapter 7 for a more detailed discussion).

If government is accountable on a daily basis, it is to attentive groups. Consequently, for some, the quality of democratic politics in modern societies is *dependent* upon the performance of the interest group system.

Rejecting groups?

In spite of Truman, Dahl and others' defence, the group pathology view continued throughout the second half of the 20th century. Cupps (1977), for example, challenged the general assumption that the emergence of 'broadened' (unrestrained) participation offered by public interest groups has been universally beneficial to advanced democracies. He (1977: 478) argued that while there have been many benefits (e.g. increasing representativeness and responsiveness, heightened political efficacy, and checks on abuse of administrative discretion), 'there is a growing body of data to support the contention that public participation which is automatic, unrestrained, or ill-considered can be dangerously dysfunctional to political and administrative systems'. He (1977: 479–480) identified several fundamental problems with citizen participation through public interest groups:

> For purposes of simplicity and order, we may group into a few broad categories most of the problems of public participation as it is currently developing: the potential short sightedness of political responses to the citizen participation movement; problems of representation and legitimacy; problems associated with the style and tactics of public interest groups and their spokesmen (*sic*); and the absence of sophisticated cost–benefit analysis of citizen group policies and programs.

Accordingly, there are then at least three significant counter-arguments against the desirability of group dominance: *bias (inequality); capture* and *exclusion;* and *gridlock.*

Biases (inequality)

Olson's (1965) major contribution was to highlight that the rational position for a potential group member is to 'free-ride'. Whereas the (complacent) Truman view was that shared attitudes would lead to group mobilization and popular groups would in consequence be well resourced and would have policy success, Olson's thesis severed the link between attitudes and group membership. Groups with a smaller pool of potential members and those offering selective (material) incentives could more easily attain a viable membership level. Accordingly, the group population was likely to be biased in favour of groups that were easier to mobilize (e.g. business).

At one level there is a direct link between the number of interest groups and the 'thickness' of democracy, but as observed by Gray and Lowery (1996) group diversity is as important as density. Thus the growth in group numbers has perhaps aggravated the bias and a problem of pro-business advantage has emerged – more groups equal more business groupings. Accordingly, Lindblom (1988: 10) argued, in 'ostensibly democratic politics', business and other advantaged participants enjoyed a 'disproportionate influence' and the notion of competition of diverse groups is a sham.

However, there is an alternative school of thought that sees the growth of business representation as a reactive phenomenon and an indicator not of strength, but weakness. Walker (1991) and Berry (1993) argued that business mobilized in response to the expansion of the regulatory state and because a number of public interest groups enjoyed some notable political successes. The privileged position thesis may also exaggerate the capacity for business to act as a homogeneous unit. There are numerous areas where business finds it difficult to reach a common position. Indeed, there are many instances of intra-business conflict. But in any case the democratic quality of an interest group system seems to relate more to breadth than simple numbers (*diversity* rather than *density* in Gray and Lowery's language).

The general argument that the group system is 'good' because it increases participation has also been countered by the fact that the 'civic voluntarism' interpretation has established that participation is skewed towards citizens with higher status, income and educational attainment. In fact, Verba *et al.* (1997) argue that (social capital) debates about the decline in civic vitality and civic participation have missed (arguably) the most important issue – not simply 'the amount of civic activity but its distribution, not just how many people take part but who are they'. As Cupps (1977: 481) notes,

> the pursuit of policies ostensibly 'on behalf of the public' may simply serve to shroud the fact that the interest of one segment of the public are being pursued at the direct expense of others. There are those who argue that consumer, environmental, and other so-called 'public interest' issues are in reality middle and upper middle class concerns which are addressed for the most part at the expense of the poor, the aged, and urban and ethnic minorities.

Similarly, Baer and Bositis (1993: 163) argue that 'These organizations tend to reflect middle-class politics of the "haves".' More public interest groups need not inevitably mean wider citizen participation, it may mean more of the same?

'Capture' and exclusion

A related criticism of group-based democracy is that preferential rela-tionships emerge between certain interests and policy-making leads to a different style of bias. A number of approaches share a view that a clientelistic relationship emerges between parts of the civil service and 'their' groups. Richardson and Jordan's (1979: 74) policy community was defined as

> It is the relationships involved in committees, the *policy community* of departments and groups, the practices of co-option and the consen-sual style that perhaps better account for policy outcomes than do examinations of party stances, of manifestos or of parliamentary influence.

Baumgartner and Jones (1993) have used the term 'policy monopoly' to similarly describe how *pressure participants* (Jordan *et al.*, 2004) have an interest in creating and maintaining a particular set of images that support policy-making arrangements that reflect dominant ideas. In this sense the bias stems not from the power of certain groups, but from the policy-making logic that sees parts of the bureaucratic apparatus sharing general goals with specific types of interest. Accordingly, there could be different biases within various parts of the system with some sections of the machinery of government defining themselves as allies to some groups, but other government units acting in concert with very different interests.

Gridlock?

While the bias and exclusion ideas see policies favouring narrow interests, the gridlock proposition is that the aggregate density of the group system renders policy-making too difficult. The system is *inherently* stagnant: that is groups find it easier to obstruct than to generate new proposals. Walker (1991: 40) noted that the expanded interest group system has made the processes of passing legislation and evaluating public policies evermore conflictual (see Gais *et al.*, 1984). Salisbury (1992) highlighted the dysfunctional nature of *hyperpluralism*, and Euchner (1996: 12) characterized the US government as being 'like Gulliver tied down by Lilliputians'. Governmental gridlock was caused by the exponentially expanding interest group universe in which millions of dollars are spent pressing government to start, continue or expand programmes that favour a 'narrow band of clients'. The most sophisticated version of this argument was Olson's (1982) contention that stable societies accumulate special interests and that concessions won by these interests lead to reduced economic efficiency. The bias in the group system towards established and well-resourced groupings make innovation difficult and governmental accountability is blurred as inaction may result despite the best governmental efforts. In a similar view, Beer (1982: 1–2, 4) argued that the main problem of British politics was *numerical pluralism*:

> Repeatedly... the dictates of collective rationality have been disregarded and the self-defeating logic of short-run self-interest has won out... This rising pluralism so fragmented the decision-making system as to impair its power of acting for the long-term interests of its members.

Brittan (1973: 156) rejected Madison's countervailing thesis – he suggested that the group proliferation 'cure' is actually the problem – 'Unfortunately, one of the main troubles with a balance produced by self-cancelling interest groups is that it can have explosive inflationary potentialities.' Governments are portrayed as (group) appeasers and while each concession is relatively small the cumulative 'damage' is great. Not only will groups seek to redistribute scarce resources in favour of their clients (*rent seeking*), but the lobbying activities may lead to policy developments that 'corrupt' electoral choices. However, other observers might see untidy, self-interested democracy as essentially democratic nonetheless (see Mueller, 1992; 1999).

Only small warts?

Thus far this chapter has been tolerant of group involvement; accepted the many imperfections and flaws in the groups system; and shared Dahl's measured conclusion that without groups there is no democracy. It accepts the rather implicit proposition in Truman that groups 'saved' democracy in that empirical research found a public far from being as well informed and supportive to electorally based democracy as textbook assumptions required. In the pre-social capital era, groups contributed to the efficient functioning of democracy through their contribution to the design of effective and workable policy. Groups acted *on behalf* of concerned publics. They were taken into political account *despite* the fact they often had very few really active individuals. While interest group scholars are sometimes viewed as apologists for interest group activity, their defence is rarely blind and is predicated on an acceptance of rather limited participation – that may nonetheless be effective. As Walker (1991: 19) pointed out, the apparently tenuous links between citizens and their representatives are replaced by group links:

> Legislators may not communicate often with each individual voter, but they are in contact, almost every day, with professional advocates who claim to speak for the elderly, manufacturers of plastic pipe, teachers in the public schools, or some other specialized segment of the public.

Walker (1991: 13–14) concedes that interest groups might be imperfect democratic tools, but the issue is whether overall there is a net benefit:

> Despite its shortcomings as a sensitive register of the passions and desires of the American public, however, the interest-group system does allow for the expression of concern about emerging new problems, such as the growing menace of air pollution or the rising aspirations of black Americans for political equality . . . The interest-group system provides a mechanism in an increasingly complex society through which emerging issues and ideas can be offered up as possible new items on the national political agenda.

An example of the 'group as problem' critique is the case of Green-peace in the UK in 1995 effectively undermining an elaborate science-based justification for deep-sea disposal of the Brent Spar by Shell. For some critics this represented Good Science defeated by Better Political Campaigning. The Conservative's Oil Minister Tim Eggar concluded that 'Blackmail succeeded against well proven scientific effort. It was a victory, if you like, for single-issue politics at least in the short term' (see Jordan, 2001, for a more detailed analysis of the Brent Spar episode). The then Opposition (The Labour Party) backed Greenpeace. However, during the later (1991) GM food debate when the positions were reversed Tony Blair (now Prime Minister) complained that

> Standing in front of a stampede is never a nice business . . . Anyone who has dared to raise even the smallest hand in protest is accused of being either corrupt or a Dr Strangelove . . . There is no scientific evidence on which to justify a ban on GM . . . *we should resist the tyranny of pressure groups.* Just because an organization calls itself 'green' doesn't mean that we all have to do what it says or that we are destroying the environment.

Yet there is a strong counter view that group conflict is a part of the democratic toolkit. Berry (1984: 1) notes that interest groups push government to enact policies that benefit small constituencies at the expense of the general public: 'If the government does not allow people to pursue their self-interest, it takes away their political freedom.' While Skocpol (2003: 235) concludes, 'Conflict, tough argument, and close competition are good for democratic civil society and for electoral democracy.' Dahl (1984: 235) maintained that it is not accidental that among the first acts following a seizure of power by authoritarian leaders is the suppression of autonomous political organizations. He (1984: 238) went on to point out that although the power of groups may be a 'shocking outrage' to the vision of classical democracy, the most probable alternative to group proliferation is an authoritarian regime and thus he says from 'a democratic perspective the untidy systems of polyarchy and pluralism begin to look more charming'.

While there are complaints that the interest group system is narrow and exclusive, the impression of those at the receiving end of group pressure is often more about breadth and volume. Rosenthal (1998: 213) cites a Texas senator as baldly stating, 'They call me a tool of the special interests . . . Damn right, I'm the tool of the special interest. Every son of a bitch in my district has some special interest or another.' Rauch

(1994: 12) points out that the American Association of Retired Persons has over 30 million members:

> If you add the farmers and the veterans and oil workers and all the others... you see there is no longer anything special about 'special interests'. Today everyone is organized, and everyone is part of an interest group. We have met the special interests, and they are us.

Thus most groups could construct a plausible argument that they are acting on behalf of a wider community, or that the wider community will benefit from the changes, or goods and benefits they seek.

While flaws are self-evident in a group-centred version, the idea that individuals can personally make effective interventions in the process, or that government can be relied upon to make policies in isolation of informed pressure is also defective. Most citizens seeking to promote, defend or advance a cause look for a relevant group as an effective trans-mission belt. As Nagel (1987: 3–4) argues, 'While spontaneous popular action warms the heart of any good democrat, a moment's reflection shows that the people initiate little of what we normally call participa-tion... Acts of participation are stimulated by elites – if not by govern-ment, then parties, interest groups, agitators, and organizers' (cited in Rosenstone and Hansen, 1993: 10).

As already highlighted the possible adverse consequence of group activity/hyperactivity is well delineated. Although gridlock is a current complaint, it can be argued it is a deliberately built-in designed 'fault' – it was a means to limit an over-powerful government. Dahl (1956: 133), of course, sees merit in the group system:

> if there is anything to be said for the processes that actually distin-guish democracy (or polyarchy) from dictatorship... the distinction comes (close)... to being one between government by a minority and government by *minorities*. As compared with the political process of a dictatorship, the characteristics of polyarchy greatly extend the number, size, and diversity of the minorities whose preferences will influence the outcome of governmental decisions.

In this view, the appeasing of minority interests, rather than majorit-arian, imposition, *is* the essence of democracy. However, contemporary attitudes to groups are somewhat inconsistent. Schudson (1998: 280) noted that sociologists have drawn attention to civil society – all those myriad associations between the state and the household; they have emphasized the importance of the local, the face-to-face, and the many sites in which public conversations can take place. These, in the American idiom, are inherently good while the professionalized, staffed, nationalized, computerized operation of the thousands of associations that get typed as special interests are always bad. These two images of civic life have yet to be reconciled in American political and social thought.

Thus, in summary, the acceptance of groups as a benefit for democracy rests on two arguments. The first relates to the beneficial impact of interests on the policy process. The basic idea is that the more interests actively advance their concerns, the more government has to adjust policies to avoid opposition, and the more democracy there is. Groups may try to bias the system, but preventing that instinct may be worse than allowing it (Madison). This echoes Lindblom's (1988: 170) suggestion that the articulation of selfish interest is a sort of nervous system that reports pain, and that without the reaction, comment and protest by affected interests public policy-making would be damaged:

> We would not, however, survive without the pain that signals us to take our hand from hot stoves and teaches us to dodge falling objects... The bargaining network is the nervous system of the body politic.

As well as the argument that groups contribute to democracy in a policy-influencing way, a substantial second argument rests on the benefits associated with internal aspects of groups. This book focuses on this narrower aspect: that is it provides an in-depth examination of the wider benefit to the political system of member/supporter activity within interest groups. The book is not particularly sympathetic to the three main criticisms of interest group activity sketched above. Nevertheless, it queries the commonly alleged benefit of group activity: *the defence of groups as participatory institutions needs to be tested rather than assumed.* This is particularly the case among so-called 'New Politics' examples where normative beliefs among some of those using the terminology leads them to 'build-in' an expectation of internal democracy to their (implicit) definition. In fact, within social capital debates generally there is a strong expectation that groups should be open with transparent internal decision-making processes and an accountable and responsive leadership to enhance democracy itself.[15] While some observers defend groups as being 'little democracies' in which civic skills and social capital are generated; instead they may actually be venues of very little democracy. This is an empirical question at the core of this book.

Specifying the object: What is studied in interest group studies?

SIGNIFICANT amounts of power are wielded in American politics by those formations known as 'pressure groups'. Most people recognize...that these groups are critically important elements in the political process. The power such groups dispose is involved at every point in the institutions of government. Partly because the diversity of relationships between groups and government is bewildering, we have no inclusive working conception of the general political role of 'pressure groups' or, as I prefer to call them, interest groups (Truman, 1951: vii).

Membership-based groups

As discussed above, the democracy term has been identified as being less self-defining than is often assumed, so too with 'interest group'. The apparent ubiquity of interest groups is a consequence of their policy relevance – in shaping political agendas and in contributing to the drafting of the details of policy – and, of course, reflects their numerical proliferation and bewildering diversity. Accordingly, the task of recognition and labelling is tricky: for example, the recent discussion of a tax on carrier bags in Scotland in 2005 'flushed-out' organizations such as the UK Carrier Bag Consortium, the British Plastics Federation, the Packaging and Industrial Films Association and the British Polythene Industries plc and Simpac. Are all these bodies interest groups? As Gerring (2001: 38) notes there is a temptation 'just to get on with it' in social science research, but a 'blithely empirical approach to social science' only complicates matters when there is doubt about the cumulative nature of research after the use of idiosyncratic definitions and concepts (quoted in Thomas, 2005: 858).

Recognizing the interest group beast when it is seen may be easier than defining it in the abstract. The latter is trickier than it may initially appear. The broad-brush labelling of interest groups runs from organizations hierarchically, bureaucratically and professionally structured with large economic resources, to informal bodies in their nascent stage of development that may be resource poor and activist-based, to private companies, to public organizations, etc. Cammisa (1995: xv) argued that 'State and local governments emerged as important interest groups in response to increased federal grants in the 1960s'. She (1995: 21) further maintained that governments when acting as interest groups can be characterized as 'associations of public officials'. The state and local governments she found lobbying the federal government were lobbying on behalf of subnational governments. In this sense state and local governments are akin to public interest groups. Accordingly, the laissez-faire approach obscures differences between transnational organizations and the street-level local groups; and between participation in conventional or *ordinary* politics and participation in unconventional and *contentious* politics (see Euchner, 1996; Tarrow, 1994, 1998).

The British directory (CBD) cited above as listing 7755 organizations has a pragmatic and fairly arbitrary (if sensibly so) definition:

> national associations, societies, institutes and similar organizations... which have a voluntary membership. Regional and local organizations concerned with important industries and trades... as are local chambers of commerce and county agricultural, historical, natural history and similar organizations which are the principal sources of information and contacts in their areas.

So the CBD data is firmly biased to national-level bodies – though it also includes important regional and even local bodies. The introduction to the 16th edition (2002) notes that 'Excluded are friendly societies, building societies, benevolent societies in aid of specific trades or professions, advice centres, trusts...'

So the answer to the question – 'How many interest groups are there in the British Isles?' – is heavily dependent on definitions, particularly about the level of government formality-of-status action criteria used. Realistically political science has problems capturing ephemeral local bodies and at first sight it seems to have no interest in the proliferation of social and hobby clubs that exist. But of course such bodies of low immediate political salience may well be relevant to the social capital proposition and can become embroiled in the political arena on a temporary basis if their interests are challenged or threatened.

The CBD data has been checked across other databases for comprehensiveness (for the population it targets). It is easily the most inclusive and gives a highly respectable sense of scale to the question about national and major interests groups. Legitimate dissent from the ballpark figure offered would be definitionally rather than empirically based. The directory says special attention has been given to the inclusion of 'national federations of local organizations and of "controlling bodies" of various sports and interests . . . '. Significantly it notes that 'a complete listing of voluntary organizations in the British Isles, including all social, political, sports, young people's clubs and all specialised societies within major hobbies and interests would require a library of volumes the size of (the directory)'. Yet some gross guess might be attempted. Hall (2002) cites a Knapp and Saxon-Harold finding of a 27% growth in the number of voluntary organizations in the 1980s – reflecting the *creation* of 3000–4000 *each year*. He also cites Knight's survey of voluntary social service organizations in 14 localities which found that 3691 organizations were servicing just under one million people. Back-of-the-envelope arithmetic suggests that 'scaled-up' this equates to 200,000 voluntary organizations in the social service area (in the UK) alone. Thus the number of bodies that *could* be labelled 'interest groups' is (*hyper-*) dependent on the definition used. Common sense is not enough. The situation is also complicated by the fact that many organizations carry out several functions. Interest group-type activities may only be one relatively small activity, or one that can be identified on an episodic basis. Even more difficult for political science might be the cases of British Polythene Industries plc and Simpac mentioned above. They are part of the policy-making story. Are they part of the interest group world?

Truman (1951: 33) famously defined an interest group as 'any group that, on the basis of one or more shared attitudes, makes certain claims upon other groups in society for the establishment, maintenance, or enhancement of forms of behavior that are implied by the shared attitudes'. A standard conventional definition of an interest group would stress elements such as:

1. Seeking to influence policy on restricted range of issues.
2. Not wishing to govern.
3. With an individual-based membership.

Grant's (2000: 14) widely accepted definition is: 'an organization which seeks as one of its functions to influence the formulation and implementation of public policy, representing a set of authoritative decisions taken by the executive, the legislature, and the judiciary, and by local government and the European Union'. This definition is policy studies–oriented: it centres on the *policy influencing* role of groups.

This book adopts a more precise and limited interpretation of the group term and focuses on groups as participatory vehicles. By concentrating solely on the membership dimension, one is choosing to define a particular interpretation of 'group'. This is narrower than the Grant 'policy influence' version that implicitly includes corporations and other organizations that might seek to influence public policy; the latter might actually constitute a majority of organizations active in policy debates.

Much of the interest group literature is case study-based, and researchers have tended to work backwards to a definition fitting their particular focus. However, freed from a particular case study, researchers would probably present groups as *voluntary, democratically accountable* and *individual-based*. The starting point for this sort of definition would include most of the following features.

'Pure' interpretation of a membership-based interest group

1. It is organized *only* for a specific collective political end (e.g. banning or supporting hunting for sport).
2. Its goal is attainable; the group can be disbanded on realization of its aims.
3. It is a non-governmental body.
4. It does not seek to form a government, merely to influence public policy.
5. It has a formal, mostly voluntary, membership of private citizens (*not businesses*[16]).
6. The membership has some control over the leadership of the organization in connection with goals and means (internal democracy).
7. The membership funds the organization through subscriptions (while it may receive government or corporate patronage, membership funds should be a critical part of the groups' income).
8. It is organized to give expression to shared attitudes or pursue the shared interests (promotional/sectional) of a given constituency (the total pool of potential members).
9. As membership is seen to reflect a matching of group and individual goals, then it can be expected that members join groups with some long-term attachment.

Any organization with most of the sorts of qualities listed above would be defined as an interest group. Commonly cited examples invariably include Oxfam, Amnesty International, Trade Unions, Greenpeace – individual cases that (*roughly*) fit the 'pure' interpretation. Moreover, it is membership-based voluntary organizations (or to be more accurate, organizations that are *assumed* to have members) that are at the heart of the central debates in the group and voluntary association literatures – *the logic of collective action* and *social capital*. But Gray and Lowery (1996: 12) show that in 1990 only 22.78% of registered lobbying organizations in the states of the US were membership-based groups. Drawing on data on almost 3000 *social welfare* and *public affairs* groups established between the early 1960s and the late 1980s, Skocpol (1995) found that nearly 50% had no members, while Berry (1984) found that about one-third of citizen lobbies were memberless.

The characteristics of a 'Pure' Interpretation of a (Membership-based) Interest Group echo some of the features used by the UN in recognizing Non-Governmental Organizations (NGOs). (As Grant [2002: 3] puts it, a 'hurrah' word compared to the boo word 'interest group'.) NGOs, in UN-speak, need to have aims and purposes in conformity with the spirit, purposes and principles of the UN Charter; a formal organization and a democratically adopted constitution; and require appropriate mechanisms of accountability (UN regulation 1996/31 quoted by Grant, 2002: 2). (Grant points out that in practice sectional and business groups are widely accredited as NGOs. He says that according to Scholte (1999: 171) 65% of 'civic organizations' at Singapore Conference of WTO were business-based.) Accordingly there is a need to avoid too rose-tinted a view of numbers of non-profit organizations. In practice the totals may subsume many organizations that do not fit the common assumptions. Warren (2000: 10) cites van Til's (2000) estimation that '77.5 percent of non-profit expenditures and 64 percent of non-profit employment (in the USA) are within associations that act as much like for-profit organizations in that they pursue economic interests within competitive markets'. Interestingly, Michalowitz (2004) cites Warleigh's study of NGOs active at the EU level which found that most groups that were potential civil society agents (as envisaged by the Commission) were 'wanting' in terms of their internal democratic procedures. Warleigh (2001: 635) argued that the 'internal governance' of many NGOs 'is far too elitist to allow supporters a role in shaping policies, campaigns and strategies, even at one remove. Moreover, and more disconcertingly, it appears clear that most NGO supporters do not actually want to undertake such a role' (quoted in Michalowitz, 2004: 155). In practice, many (normatively superior) NGOs *do not* come close to the pure interpretation of a membership-based interest group.

However, many bodies regarded as groups in important sources in the literature, predominantly in the United States, *lack many of the features* listed above. The consequence of an assumption that interest groups are member-based may lead to a neglect of the influence within the group system of many of these member-free bodies. Thus a more realistic interpretation of the group as found in practice will deviate from the pure interpretation. For example: (i) for some interest groups political activity may not be their primary function; (ii) clearly civil servants, government departments, firms, etc. have interests; (iii) some groups take little trouble to recruit members; (iv) internal democracy may be largely symbolic; (v) a group may be funded by supporters rather than a formal membership, or patronage from governmental or corporate sponsors may be the major source of funding; and (vi) groups may be collective structures of 'organizations of organizations' rather than individuals. In fact, many important groups are collections of institutions – companies, local authorities or other non-individuals (Salisbury, 1984). Even national governments engage in interest groups–*type* activities – the Japanese, UK and many other governments fund lobbying of the US Congress, and the US Government itself lobbies the European Union (see Cammisa, 1995).

Wilson's (1990: 6) *initial* interpretation of interest group reflects the *pure* version (above); he notes that some interest groups 'recruit members with the explicit promise that the organization will pursue certain public policy goals. People who join the League Against Cruel Sports in Britain or Common Cause in the United States are clearly joining together to support an organization which is obviously dedicated to certain relatively well-defined public policy objectives . . . '. However, while his examples match the stereotype, he warns, 'Few organizations commonly regarded as interest groups are like the League or Common Cause'. In line with Wilson, this book assumes that *the organizations that are most significant in particular policy processes tend not to conform to the stereotype that best approximates to an interest group. The paradox is that the most influential organizations are most likely to be far removed from the interest group stereotype*.

The 'pure' interpretation also stresses the importance of delivering opportunities for democratic activity. If these characteristics are absent then the legitimacy of group participation in the governing process is undermined. Group involvement in policy-making is normatively acceptable as long as groups are able to demonstrate 'their' representativeness – beyond formal structures (Grant, 2001: 348).[17]

However, the institutionalization of internal democratic procedures does not unequivocally deliver (internal) democracy. For example, Rothenberg (1992: 160–162) found that formally Common Cause had 'many of the necessary accoutrements to be termed an organizational democracy': members elected the governing board for three year terms; and the organization seeks members' views on a wide variety of issues via a Membership Issue Poll at election times. On closer inspection, there were however a number of issues. For example, the 1981 Common Cause survey showed that 24% of members did not even know that the governing board was elected, and only 20–25% even bothered to vote. Rothenberg's (1992: 162) own survey found that 27% of respondents said that they had never heard of the Membership Issue Poll, thus he (1992: 166) concluded that

> Election results only serve to select from a group of handpicked candidates; the issue polls provide little more than affirmation for any number of policy alternatives that the group might pursue. Like the proverbial drunk under the lamppost, the electoral and polling results jointly provide mainly support, rather than illumination, for the development of group goals.

The (voluntary-member based) image of an interest group set out above is very different from Grant's policy studies version that focuses on activities aimed at *influencing policy outcomes*. The conclusion implied by the policy studies perspective is that an interest group may be defined by *function*: any body that seeks to influence policy is an interest group. *The most important consequence of this approach is that a company can be seen as an interest group.*[18] However, confusion does not simply stem from the assumption that a multitude of organizations will attempt to influence public policy, but in *labelling* each of these actors as interest groups. As argued in more detail elsewhere (Jordan *et al.*, 2004) it is more appropriate (and accurate) to label organizations attempting to influence outcomes generically as *pressure participants*, rather than interest groups. There can be a broad equivalence in functional policy terms between different types of policy influencing bodies without them all being labelled as interest groups.[19]

Within that category a distinction can be made between *policy participants* such as companies and a more restricted conception of *interest groups* (Jordan *et al.*, 2004). The new ('policy participant')[20] term signals that not all bodies seeking to influence policy can be sensibly dumped into the interest group box. It is less confusing to use the term 'pressure participant' for the wider conception (i.e. groups comprising organizations seeking to affect outcomes) and reserve the term 'interest group' for *multi-member, politically oriented bodies* of individuals. If 'interest group' is allowed to take the wider meaning, it causes confusion for students who are directed to the Olson/type literature on the internal life of groups: such issues do not arise for all pressure participants. Our refinement to the language acknowledges the existing heterogeneity and reduces ambiguity through clearer labelling and more importantly captures important empirically and theoretically significant distinctions. Finally, the restricted notion of interest group better fits this book because only collective action style groups have the member interactions that underpin the social capital generating version of groups.

Squaring a circle: The memberless interest group?

The notion that 'interest group-ness' has something to do with *membership and mobilization* is an important thread in the literature. The preferred primary distinction here is between *pressure participants* and *interest groups*. However, caution needs to be exercised when applying the distinction between individual member- and nonmember-based interest groups. As discussed below (in Chapter 4) there are many pseudo 'membership' groups – that is many organizations that superficially resemble member-based bodies, which on closer inspection, turn out to be supporter-based. *Supporters* of these organizations are simply regular financial contributors devoid of any voting or other (internal) democratic rights. For the vast bulk of these 'participants' signing a cheque or a direct debit (automated payment) instruction for the bank is the beginning and end of their involvement. As Wolin (quoted in Shaiko, 1999: 106) observed, 'The new politics has special conceptions of membership, participation, and civic virtue: a member is anyone who is on a computerized mailing list, participation consists of signing a pledge to contribute money; civic virtue is actually writing the check'. These individuals should be referred to as *supporters* and formally distinguished form *members*.

Having acknowledged this distinction, there are several reasons why supporter-based groups are included in this analysis along with member groups. First, these multi-supporter organizations seek collective goods and face the collective 'action' problem of mustering citizen support for political activity (on agreed goals). Secondly, the groups themselves would argue that the support base provides (political) legitimacy – pointing to 100,000 or 1 million supporters can be persuasive in policy-making deliberations. Thirdly, even though these organizations cannot claim to be purely representative of a democratically empowered membership because of the absence of formal *voice*, the *exit* option is a real threat and maintains a link between leaders and followers.

Some view this *democratic form* as superficial. However, many protest business organizations are involved in a fierce competition to attract and retain supporters/members.[21] Loyalty is particularly important to these groups because there is high membership turnover: Significant proportions of 'their' support operate on a revolving-door basis. These groups make membership easy and easy entry may mean easy exit. As Euchner (1996: 124) notes, 'members' need to '. . . be recruited over and over again'.[22] This competition can be seen as ensuring responsiveness and effective representation *of* supporters' interests. If the leadership gets too far out of step with supporters, there may be no followers left to lead. The perspective adopted here echoes Salisbury's (1992) view that interest groups are distinctive because members or supporters can potentially exercise control of leaders through 'exit'. Fourthly, many (large-scale) supporter-based organizations have local chapters and branches that activate a small percentage of supporters. In such numerically large organizations this can amount to large numbers of citizens. For example, Putnam (2000) notes that some 10% of the supporters of the American Association of Retired Persons (AARP) are more actively involved in local chapters. Given that the total supporter base is some 33 million – the AARP mobilizes over three million American citizens.[23]

In short, interest groups, as dealt with in this book, are bodies that attempt to influence policy *and are multi-member or multi-supporter organizations seeking collective ends.* Accepting Salisbury's 'exit' option as a means of forcing leadership responsiveness, the memberless group is an important phenomenon that owes even less to the firm or other non-interest group category and so it is worth subsuming as a subset of interest group. However, in terms of the social capital building potential these bodies appear to have much less to offer. The remainder of this book deals with what happens (or fails to happen) inside supportership/membership groups. The following appendix outlines the source of the original data upon which part of this discussion rests. Two separate surveys are reported.

Appendix 1

The data

Survey of organization leaders

A postal survey of campaigning groups was conducted in late 2001. The sample was drawn from *The Directory of British Associations* published by CBD Research Ltd (1998), which contained 7048 organizations and associations. A sample of all organizations listed, and a subpopulation of *all* the organizations listed as *Campaigning Groups,* were contacted. The latter category was defined as those who identified themselves as conducting 'campaign and pressure group' activities or who were identified by CBD Research Ltd as engaged in such activities based upon the information provided. The sample component of ALL groups was conducted on a ratio of 1:10 (i.e. 416 out of a total of 4160) for groups with less than 1000 members, and 1:3 for those organizations with memberships between 1000 and 9999 (i.e. 401 out of a total of 1204). All remaining larger organizations included in the directory – that is those with memberships in excess of 10,000 (see Table 1.1) – were contacted). The data reported in this book for the broad group population were weighted to reflect sampling proportions (reported as ALL groups).

A total of 426 campaign organizations were surveyed and the response rate was 57% ($n = 241$). The 426 groups identified ranged in size from those with less than one thousand supporters to those with over a million. The smallest organization, the Towpath Action Group reported having 160 members and the largest, the National Pensioners Convention, claimed two million.

Given the importance of size for the protest business perspective, the sample was sub-divided into three categories. First, small-scale groups with less than 1000 members (response $n = 119$ from 195 identified in the Directory); secondly, mid-range organizations whose membership lies between 1000 and 49,999 ($n = 101$ from 134); and, thirdly large-scale groups with memberships in excess of 50,000 ($n = 14$ from 24).[24] (Table 1.1 shows the sampling procedures and response rates.) It is no surprise that the 'n' for the large groups is relatively small.

Table 1.1 Sampling procedures and response rates

Size	No. of groups in CBD directory	Sample (ratio)	No. of questionnaires mailed	No. of questionnaires returned	Response rates (%)
0–999	4160	1:10	416	195	47
1000–9999	1204	1:3	401	222	55
10000–99999	339	1:1	339	174	51
100000–999999	71	1:1	71	38	54
+1 million	9	1:1	9	4	44
Campaigning groups	426	1:1	426	241	57

The empirical reality is that organizations with 'memberships' in excess of 50,000 are not common: the '*n*' is small because the universe is small.

The quantitative data was supplemented by in-depth elite interviews with two environmental/conservation groups, a consumer organization and a medical related group. The groups were of differing membership sizes: The Down's Syndrome Association 13,200 (7500 individuals were 'full members' of the organization (with voting rights) and a further 2500 were associate members (the remaining were based abroad or were schools and clinics); the Campaign to Protect Rural England (CPRE)[25] 40,000; the Royal Society for the Protection of Birds (RSPB) one million; and the Consumers' Association one million.[26]

The nonmember survey: The survey populations and response rates

The nonmembers survey reported in Chapter 5 is drawn from a (*strongly*) pro-environmental subpopulation of UK citizens identified from the initial *Citizen Audit* sample of 20,000 (see Pattie *et al.*, 2004). The Audit allowed the identification of the 'concerned' population who felt strongly about the environment – and whether or not there was associated membership.[27] The Citizen Audit survey received a 50% response rate (circa 10,000) and approximately 21% (2137) exhibited *strong* support for the environment – these respondents were labelled the 'concerned'. However, only 7% of the total (i.e. a third of the 'concerned') were members of an environmental organization. Follow-up postal interviews with members and nonmembers of environmental groups were conducted. Since all 'concerned' were re-contacted (via a postal survey) and only a minority were members; in line with Olson's strictures above, this was primarily a survey of nonmembers – with members as a control group.[28]

Preliminary analysis suggested a distinction between nonmembers who were nonetheless members of other types of group (labelled *environmental nonmembers*) and nonmembers who had joined no groups whatsoever (labelled *pure nonmembers*). It was assumed that the 'habitual' non-joiners are likely to be closest to Olson's free-rider notion. However, the former are the potentially more interesting (for this study). They are concerned and mobilizable (i.e. members of non-environmental groups) – yet they have not joined any environmental organizations. (*So why have environmental nonmembers not joined an environmental group?*) Accordingly, the sample is divided into three subsets:

1. Members of environmental organizations ($n = 359$);
2. Environmental nonmembers who are members of other organizations ($n = 293$); and
3. Pure nonmembers who are *NOT* members of any other groups ($n = 96$).

Only data from the *members* and the *environmental nonmembers* is reported in this book: the *pure nonmembers* are excluded from this analysis.

2

The Collective Action Paradox: What Incentives Induce Participation? Olson Defied?

> Two neighbours may agree to drain a meadow, which they possess in common; because 'tis easy for them to know each other's mind; and each must perceive, that the immediate consequence of his failing in his part, is, the abandoning of the whole project. But 'tis very difficult, and indeed impossible, that a thousand persons shou'd agree in any such action; it being difficult for them to concert so complicated a design, and still more difficult for them to execute it; while each seeks a pretext to free himself of the trouble and expence, and wou'd lay the whole burden on others (David Hume [1739–1740] cited in Hardin, 2003: 3).

Chapter 1 expressed some level of reservation about the usefulness of interest groups as effective participatory instruments. The widespread assumption is that the less citizen involvement (political and social) the greater the pathology; the greater the involvement the healthier the practice – 'more' is definitely 'more attractive'. However, political science discussions of interest group membership in the last 40 years have been dominated by the need to respond to Olson's key proposition (in *The Logic of Collective Action*): 'rational, self-interested individuals will not act to achieve their common or group interests' (1965: 2). In this light 'rational' individuals *free-ride*[1] unless they are coerced into membership or groups offer an exclusive members-only benefit. Olson (1965: 51) said, 'Only a *separate and "selective"* incentive will stimulate a rational individual in a latent group to act in a group-oriented way.'

As noted by Rosenstone and Hansen (1993: 21) there is a 'paradox of participation'. 'If people are rational, the paradox holds, and if they receive only collective benefits, they will not turn out to vote... the result will be the same whether they participate or not.' Applied to groups this means that were Olson correct, groups could only be of limited utility in delivering participation: individuals will not act voluntarily within groups because the costs of doing so will exceed any (individual level) reward. This chapter begins with Olson's very simple observation that participation in groups is likely to be very limited. It then reviews some evidence on this point; and reports a much wider ranging academic debate that centres on why Olson's dominant theory *appears* so unsuccessful in predicting joining levels; and it enters the academic Bermuda Triangle of the nature of rationality. In rehearsing this debate the chapter is in part fairly abstract and arcane, but the Olson material raises an important non-intuitive objection to the commonplace assumption that support for political ends leads inevitably to participation. Instead membership is seen as a response to incentives rather than an automatic instinct. This volume also focuses on the predisposed – *who do not join.*

Olson believed the limitations of his economics-derived approach – which sharply lowered expectations about successful mobilization to secure *collective action* – to be remote. Hardin (1997: 203) highlighted the implications for democracy of such rational choice approaches, 'all of these contributions were essentially negative or destructive. They explained why things were hard or impossible. *In particular, they all undercut certain hopes for democratic theory*' (italics added). Thus the expectation was that participation levels in groups – and hence democratic opportunities – would be seriously curtailed if Olson-type rational choice could not be rebutted.[2] (Chapter 5 sheds some light on this issue: it includes survey evidence contrasting those with strong proenvironmental views who *have* joined relevant organizations and those similarly predisposed who *have* not.)

The *Tragedy of the Commons*

A key element of the political science literature's discussion of rational choice is how can the political system coordinate the preferences of individuals to maximize the net communal benefit? A textbook example (i.e. also a staple of newspapers) is fishing in EU waters. From the point of view of a Scottish fishing boat skipper, if fish stocks are declining the answer might be to fish more intensively and/or to invest in more effective equipment to maintain the level of catch. However, the cumulative consequence of the operation of the personal logic for individuals (with their wish to maximize income, service existing debts, etc.) would put even more pressure on fish stocks. From the individual's standpoint, the ideal would be that while they caught more to maintain income levels, others fished less to reduce the pressure on stocks. In contrast, the optimal (long-term) collective solution would be that everyone cooperated and minimized their fishing to reduce overall catches and allow a recovery that would, in time, allow everyone to increase catches. The political difficulty in arranging such communal action that maximizes consumption and prevents competitive 'lose–lose' actions has been termed the *Tragedy of the Commons* (see work of Garrett Hardin, 1995). The selfish behaviour of those sharing a common facility may so degrade it in pursuit of self-interest that ultimately all users lose – there is nothing left to share.

This tension is implicit in discussions of (say) global warming. Voluntary restraint, in the Olson interpretation, is irrational. Why should an individual incur the costs of pro-environmental behaviour? Olson would argue that the rational individual will not view it as sensible to leave the car at home when making a trip to the supermarket because of the negligible contribution to a solution by this (effectively *symbolic*) act. The inconvenience and cost is perceptible, but the environmental benefits in global and system terms are trivial, tokenistic, not immediately apparent, and enjoyed by all – not simply those bearing the cost. Of course environmentalists would claim that if everyone acted unselfishly then the cumulative impact would be great. Olson would not have disagreed, but he would have argued that for effective *collective* action individuals have either to be coerced or *personally* receive a reward (that exceeds their costs) for contributing to the generation of the collective good. In the absence of coercion or selective rewards, the individual-level logic[3] is to use the car – while encouraging everyone else to leave their vehicle in the driveway.

For the individual to be virtuous while the world proceeds selfishly is like the North Sea skipper single-handedly reducing her/his fish catch in the futile hope that this small personal sacrifice will affect anything. Without the enforcement of some overall rules the uncaught fish will simply enrich the less scrupulous. In the participatory area, the collective action problem appears in the guise of individuals simply not bothering to act – assuming that others will invest the time and effort to secure benefits that can be enjoyed by the *free-rider*.

Traditionally, trades unions and professional associations solved the free-rider problem by coercion: that is via the enforcement of a 'closed shop' that allows only those in membership to work in the specific area. In the fishing example state authority *coerces/obliges* individuals to desist from maximizing their (temporary) advantage: fishing skippers are prohibited from overfishing with the aim of producing long-term viability. However, in much of the group universe, particularly the advocacy, citizen or public interest group areas, coercion is a non-option. These bodies rely on voluntary and altruistic contributions and, according to the Olson thesis, to maximize their recruitment would need to provide a separate and selective incentive to stimulate membership: that is a non-collective reward open only to members. The Olson-style member will not join to secure the collective good.[4] The key for a group then is steering self-interest towards behaviour that might lead to the production of collective goods.[5]

As has been frequently observed, Olson's gloomy conclusions about problems in mobilizing groups appeared to be almost immediately contradicted by an empirical proliferation falsifying the forecast that they were difficult to mobilize. In the 1960s, and subsequently, many *viable* public interest groups emerged in the US and Europe in apparent defiance of Olson's sub-optimal mobilization prediction (see Figures 1.1 and 1.2). For example, Walker (1991: 41) noted that discussants at scholarly meetings at the Mayflower Hotel, Washington, in the 1960s concluded it was almost impossible for certain kinds of political groups to mobilize effectively. But 'As the participants left the elegant and socially isolated enclosure of the hotel, they walked right into massive demonstrations by tens of thousands of Americans who had not heard about the collective action dilemma...'.[6] Moreover, it is not simply a matter of numbers of groups; many public interest groups also have memberships that number in the tens and hundreds of thousands. Both these characteristics of number and scale of membership *seem* to run counter to the Olson argument. Accordingly, if the Olson paradox of participation has been solved, the problem is to revise the theory away from his pessimism to capture the empirical reality (a reality that would be more optimistic about groups).

Rational choice: The collective action dilemma

Rational choice theorists are often accused of ignoring motivations other than self-interest. Their answer, when they bother to answer, is commonly that self-interest *tells the bulk of the story* for the phenomena they study in the market and politics. Increasingly, they even seem to think that it tells the bulk of the story in relationships outside the market and formal politics, that it is the motor even in biological evolution (Hardin, 1995: 14) (italics added).

The rational choice insight gained prominence as a result of Anthony Downs' (1957) simple but powerful proposition that voting is (economically) irrational. He maintained that the costs to participants clearly outweigh any potential pay-off: that is the possibility of an individual's vote being pivotal is infinitesimally small, so the rational person would simply not bother:

> it can be shown to be irrational for individuals to vote at all whenever more than a handful of other voters are involved. This is because the probability that a single vote will affect the outcome is always so small that even large prospective differences in well-being that depend on an election outcome will not outweigh the small costs of actually casting a ballot (Downs, 1957).[7]

Olson's work (1965) is the platform for Rational Choice Theory (RCT) discussions in the group field. His theory was a reaction to the traditional view articulated by Truman (1951) that when a political, social or economic problem impinged significantly on the life of a citizen, they would soon become aware that the difficulty was a shared concern, and would spontaneously combine with others around this common interest. Accordingly in Truman's world, groups can be viewed as the irresistible product of shared concerns and the backward mapping from the pattern of groups reveals the underlying pattern of political preferences in society. Schlozman (1984: 1007) described this approach: 'interest groups emerge more or less automatically in response to environmental changes that render necessary the representation of new political interests'. However, is the mechanism as simple as Truman expected? Or is membership more heavily driven by *supply-side* practices and techniques, and the incentive structures provided by groups (and entrepreneurial skill of leaders)? (see Chapters 3 and 4).

Arguably Olson-type rational choice theory (ORCT) provides the leading explanation on why individuals join (or fail to join) political organizations (particularly groups), but its assumptions have provoked much dissent. However, what is not up for debate is the fact that it is the most notable, influential and enduring model. As Hardin (1995) argued rational choice appears to be a universal tool that fits all political science problems. For Hay (2004: 39) *general* RCT assumes rational (political) behaviour is calculable in any given context: 'If individual conduct can be assumed rational, and an actor's utility function can be specified, then the actor's behaviour is rendered entirely predictable in any given political setting.' This appears to be a bread-and-butter definition of RCT, but as Hay was aware, and as shown below, such a parsimonious definition has important implications. (Hay's general statement of course is NOT coincident with the Olson version.)

Hay (2004: 40) indeed presents rational choice itself as a self-fulfilling prophecy – somewhat ironic given the readiness of Olson-style rational choice theorists to complain about circularity in alternative formulations of *expanded* rational choice (ERCT). Hay (2004: 40) concedes value in rational choice as a hypotheses-generating engine, noting however that this is at 'a price which many rational choice theorists are prepared to concede – namely the implausibility of the very assumptions upon which such a process of deduction is predicated... There is in short, a significant trade off.' He (2004: 41) maintains that the essence of RCT is that individuals can be considered acting *as if* they engage in cost–benefit analysis for each choice and that they will 'rationally' opt for the choice giving the greatest utility. He notes that rational choice writers suggest that they are agnostic about what utility is to be maximized, but in practice most rational choice-inspired game theoretical modelling 'draws on a remarkably narrow set of utility functions which seem to correspond closely to a simple conception of material self-interest...'.[8] Hay is thus pointing to a gap between rational choice (generalized) and the more restricted version used by Olson and followers.

As sketched earlier, Olson argued that mobilization was not a natural process and that involvement would have to be stimulated by selective rewards for those becoming involved. In essence, and at the heart of this chapter, is the Olson assumption that such incentives had to be material and the acceptance of others (ERCT) that the rewards could be psychological or collective. Joining for Olson was an activity pursued by potential recruits following a test of economic rationality – agreement with group goals was *not in itself* a reason to join.[9] Accordingly, selective (material) incentives are pivotal in membership decisions and joining for selective reasons produces the 'positive' externality of resources for lobbying for collective purposes (see below). Olson assumed it was irrational to join in express and direct support of the collective lobbying.

As Berry (1999: 154) notes, Olson's counter-intuitive insight was that successfully organized political groups *probably exist for non-political reasons* – that is lobbying is simply the *by-product*.[10] For example, should a group win a tax change beneficial to its members it is also available (i.e. non-exclusionary) to non-members with characteristics similar to members. Olson said such groups must attract support via the provision of selective incentives or potential members will remain non-mobilized.

However, the typical public interest group has effectively no such incentives to offer. Were this element of the Olson argument unchallenged, the interest group system emerges as potentially biased.

If groups can only overcome membership resistance by offering rewards *conditional on joining* – that is not free-rideable – this implies an issue left unexamined in most discussions of the impact of intra-group political activity. The literature largely takes 'as read' a 'natural' tendency to become mobilized in organizations that represent one's interests or values. (Truman lives on.) If however, as rational choice assumes, the default position is *non*-membership, then the mobilization process requires attention.

The interest group literature has exploded with reactions to Olson's framing of the joining decision. As Mansbridge (1990: 15) points out this rather basic matter of trying to understand voting behaviour and other forms of participation has ignited a classic academic battle that fits the proposition by Kuhn (1970) of the response to an 'anomaly' between theoretical prediction and empirical detail. The dominant Olsonian model seemed to suggest limited participation (and even a rate of voting in the electoral arena that might be criticized in the press as low (say 60%) is *far too high* to fit the rational choice prediction). Similarly for groups ORCT implied that potential members would not join and instead would 'rationally' conclude to conserve their personal resources.

However, many citizens join without selective rewards, and so, arguably, they are 'irrational' in RCT terms. Thus much of the literature focussing on recruitment aims to rescue membership or support from *apparent* irrationality, by extending the list of factors (ERCT) that can be included in the calculus (most importantly, see Opp, 1986). Confusingly, rationality turns out to have competing formulations and in some variants these extensions are seen as compatible with rationality, but in others they are not. The 'rejection of the too-narrow' school has generated a major body of literature that finds the empirical world a 'poor-fit' to Olson's theory, and expands the list of relevant mobilizing factors to generate a better explanation. The broader/revisionist reading of rationality allows that potential members can approach membership decisions in ways other than through *economically* rational analysis – individuals adopt other rationalities and work through other belief systems. They appear to join interest groups and other voluntary associations for a variety of non-economic reasons: psychological factors, a sense of morality, a sense of political efficacy, collective identity, image of self, support for collective goals, etc.

However, because of the power of Olson's argument there remains a real need to give an explicit account for the proliferation of interest groups of all kinds – and the particular expansion of public interest groups (for instance on environmental, ethical or consumer issues) which pursue collective goods. Olson's contribution means that participation has to be explained rather than assumed. Groups for Olson are not likely to be useful democratic forums.

Olson suggested that a group with a limited potential membership might well face an easier organizational task (but see Oliver, 1993: 285): a small 'market' might mean more chance for face-to-face social pressure – and less 'invisible' free-riding. Moreover in a small group the value of a contribution is more easily related to group success. The 'smallness' factor underpins many explanations for the large proportion of business organizations in the group universe. However, it is clearly less powerful in the small business or public interest group sectors that have a potential membership population in the hundreds of thousands. So Olson's proposition that groups with small potential populations might, pro rata, do better in mobilization seems only partially convincing as many groups have prospered with numbers far too large for the face-to-face explanation.

One factor contributing to the confusion that passes as debate is suggested when Green and Shapiro (1994: 81) note that even a very low rate of mobilization for collective action may nonetheless involve significantly large numbers of participants.[11] Thus groups can exist, and indeed appear successful (apparently contra Olson), while failing to mobilize (in line with Olson) more than a minority of potential members. Thus both sides can claim events are in line with predictions.

Green and Shapiro (1994) highlight the ambiguity in the rational term: some observers allow rationality beyond the narrow economic and materially self-interested based version. Such observers do not see participation as irrational when factors other than selective material incentives operate. Such additional factors might well be thoroughly rational (goal-related) but this implies a different sort of rationality from that defined by Olson and his adherents. While Olson (1965) admitted the *possibility* of these wider incentives, he dismissed their empirical relevance (see p. 6, fn 6; p. 61, fn 17; pp. 159–162) (see below for more detail).

In spite of Olson's rejection of 'their' importance, the remainder of this chapter records the range of incentives that may underpin participation in interest groups. It assumes that unless interest groups can be freed from the Olson shadow then they are likely to be flawed tools for democracy as individuals have no incentive to participate, and participation is consequently likely to be minimal.[12]

A repertoire of explanatory factors

A starting point for a discussion of the range of incentives that generate membership is Clark and Wilson's (1961) threefold incentive category – *Material, Solidary* and *Purposive*. This classificatory scheme has served as a basis for most subsequent work and was given an added dimension by Salisbury (1969) – *Expressive* incentives. The list is disaggregated further below, but the main point in this expansion is that many apparently non-selective inducements can be translated into selective benefits by recognizing some psychological benefit to the donor (e.g. self-esteem). The legitimacy of this translation is controversial in the literature. (An important consequence of seeing Olson's list of incentives as incomplete was that the *other types of relevant incentive appear less free-rideable*. One cannot, for example, get an expressive benefit vicariously.)

Selective Material – these incentives are tangible rewards: money, wages, salaries and discounts on services. *This is Olson's main membership driver* and these *exclusive* rewards are open only to those in membership (e.g. preferential insurance or health cover rate).[13] The level of reward might vary within the membership – to encourage individuals to invest personal time in a way they might not if the reward was uniform.

Selective Psychological Rewards – generally it can be argued (contra Olson) that members join because they get some internalized psychological rewards (and commitment theory can be a subset of this). As outlined below, while these rewards (basically a 'feel good' response to joining) are consistent with a *broad* formulation of rationality, Olson would have excluded these from his model. Such an extension to his notion of rationality would embrace a range of factors, that, in the eyes of some, would make Olson's theory non-falsifiable. In the *expanded formulation* most (the reservation is important) membership becomes 'rational' in some sense (see below for a detailed discussion and critique).

Solidary – these are a specific type of intangible psychological reward, and like other such rewards are selective (and *non-free-rideable*) in that they can only be enjoyed within the group. Unlike the category above, this factor sees the reward of joining directly in membership itself and immediately for the benefit of the member. Whereas the other psychological benefit is a reaction to the effects of policy success on others, Wilson (1995: 34) notes that this category includes 'the fun and conviviality of coming together, the sense of group membership or exclusiveness, and such collective status or esteem as the group as a whole may enjoy'.[14]

Specific Solidary – these are available only to those inside the organization (*non-free-rideable*) – but are not available simultaneously to all members (e.g. office-holding positions and status).

Purposive[15] – Wilson (1995: 46) presents these rewards as based on the sense of satisfaction in having contributed to the attainment of a worthwhile cause. Purposive organizations work explicitly for the benefit of some larger public and not chiefly for the benefit of members – except insofar as members derive a sense of satisfaction in helping to secure change. (While this is conventionally seen as an alternative to a selective economic or material incentive, once the selective category is broadened away from the economic-type reward, purposive is in fact selective.) Wilson (1995) highlights that the satisfaction for members of the Committee Against Legalized Murder is not in avoiding being hanged, but the intangible reward of changing policy. Finally, he notes that purposive incentives are complimentary/conjoined with solidary ones: that is those with strong beliefs wish to publicize their convictions and 'receive the esteem of those who think likewise'. The pursuit of purposive incentives may also reflect an exaggerated sense of self-efficacy.

Self-interested Purposive – Wilson (1995) sees the purposive attraction as often not being about the advantage to the membership, but in some cases the beneficiaries of the purposive action can be the members (and potential members) of the group. When conceiving purposive incentives in such a way, the literature assumes that threats and negatives are more effective (purposive) inducements to join than promises of improvement. Hansen (1985: 82) notes that groups go to great lengths to frame membership appeals as insurance against loss rather than a gamble on gain. He explains that political and economic disturbances heighten the attraction of (collective) political benefits and, as such, signify mobilization opportunities for group leaders who can use it to demonstrate the importance of collective defence.

Regret Avoidance – An important motivation was termed 'Minimax Regret' by Ferejohn and Fiorina (1974). Essentially this concedes that the probability of an individual expression of support to be minimal, but it might be rational nonetheless to engage in low-cost actions if the possibility exists that *non*-participation leads to an outcome that would be more strongly regretted. This is of course close to the expressive bumper sticker 'I voted for Gore' in the US in 2000, but it is not only a symbolic gratification. It is saying that low-cost, long-shot investments are worthwhile if the outcome is important. It is to *avoid* the need for a hypothetical, improbably honest (and clumsy) after-the-event Florida bumper sticker 'I did not bother voting for Gore in his contest with Bush as I thought it would make no difference.' In other words, the consequences of some kind of failure are different for the indifferent non-voter from those for a committed voter who did not bother.[16] If losing 'matters', it is better to participate even if there is very little chance of affecting the outcome. The psychological discomfort of losing without participation appears to be greater than that where an effort has been made.

Expressive – Salisbury (1969) identified a discrete incentive that can be distinguished from the purposive. He noted, 'Expressive actions are those where the action involved gives expression to the interests or values of a person or group rather than instrumentally pursuing interests or values... *benefits are derived from the expression itself'* (italics added). This is a personal satisfaction reward separate from attaining a goal. While the purposive dimension can be seen as selective in that the group member will enjoy group success, the expressive is even more straightforwardly a selective type of activity. The reward is in the process of participation itself *not* playing a part in successful policy change. This sort of observation, if accurate, forces an expansion in the notion of 'incentive'.

Commitment Theory (Sabatier, 1992) – bears a strong relationship to the purposive idea and reflects the observation that political activists have more ideologically extreme views than ordinary members. Sabatier (1992: 109) says commitment theory expects to find increasing degrees of commitment to collective benefits as one moves from potential group members to members and then to leaders. Though he (1992: 105) explicitly rejects non-falsifiable assumptions, this idea – appealing though it is – tends to that direction.

Entrepreneur Incentives – The belief here is that the rewards accrue to group architects not members. It is however important for potential members that groups are in existence to give an opportunity for political involvement. Salisbury (1969) largely assumed self-interested behaviour and argued that many groups were formed following the efforts of political entrepreneurs seeking permanent positions in the organization. The initial Salisbury standpoint was that the entrepreneur's reward was economic: that is small business people creating a job for themselves (see Sabatier, 1992: 106). However, it would probably be unusual to find a political entrepreneur who was not also heavily committed to the cause. The personal economic incentive is linked to the pursuit of a collective good. Sabatier cites Berry's (1977) evidence that twice as many groups could apparently be 'explained' by an entrepreneur explanation than Truman's disturbance notion. But he goes on to say, 'Yet most of the examples Berry discussed... hardly fit Salisbury's portrait of a sales-person looking for a staff job. Instead they might be seen as engaging in the organizational effort for policy/ideological reasons'. Entrepreneurs may reflect greater 'commitment' as an incentive to act – not simply be in pursuit of pecuniary self-interest. Many entrepreneurs have exag-gerated purposive attachments and reasonably assume that a group is a better tool to 'lever' their own policy ends than individual action. This goal attainment is a selective, non-material reward (see also Moe, 1980b).

'Pick and mix' explanations

Mundo (1992: 24) notes that different individuals may respond to different incentives – and moreover individuals may respond to *combinations* of incentives:

> in many groups, leaders must differentiate among types of members and supply different benefits accordingly... political activists may require more responsive leadership with respect to group goals, while others may demand more economic benefits – for example, rank-and-file labour union members may want more lucrative collective agreements. Effective leaders recognize these differences and supply benefits to various individuals to retain their membership.

Members' demands, or the allure of specific incentives, may change over time and groups need to respond appropriately (Mundo, 1992: 23). There may also be differences by time: 'members who join an interest group at different times in its history do so for different reasons' (Mundo, 1992: 24). Jordan and Halpin (2004) demonstrated that in the UK the Federation of Small Businesses' membership 'plateaued' while basing its appeal on purposive and expressive action, but grew spectacularly when more selective and material benefits were 'pushed' by a sales force in 1992 (Figure 2.1).

The literature(s) on joining

Strangely, the political science literature concedes and celebrates the importance of Downs (1957) and Olson (1965, 1971), but then generally

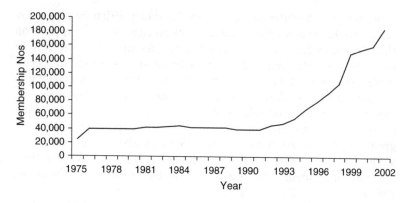

Figure 2.1   Growth in Federation of Small Businesses' membership (direct sales introduced in 1992).
Source: Jordan and Halpin (2004).

stresses why what they predicted should *not* happen, *did* happen. A major contribution to the voting version of the discussion came from Riker and Ordeshook (1968). In trying to retain rational choice (implying low turnout) – while facing up to the fact of voting rates in excess of 50% – they suggested there was a variable (Citizen Duty) that was a utility the voter received through expressing themselves (in support of a particular candidate or in reinforcing the system) – whether or not their preferred candidate won. Instantly, with one leap, voting is not irrational if this extension to rational choice is accepted, but this development is controversial. Barry (1970: 17) said this simply shifts the question to, 'Why do some people have this kind of motivation more strongly than others?' A recurrent issue in the literature is whether 'topping up' the initial version of rationality retains the rational essence?

There are then two streams of explanation as to why members join in numbers greater than Olson implied. One is to build-in as relevant to the rational calculus of joiners additional (non-material) incentives – see next section. Such responses might be seen as weakening the Olson test of rationality? But, secondly, important work more directly contradicts Olson and finds that members *do* join for collective goods. Muller and Opp (1986) using data from Hamburg and New York concluded that protesters acted on the basis of a collective rationality. Knoke (1990: 313) looked at a large sample of groups (of different types) and found different incentives counted in different cases and concluded: 'The empirical literature on organizational incentives is a steady accumulation of findings that refute Olson's emphasis on selective goods as essential for collective action.' Work by Godwin and Mitchell (1982), Cigler and Hansen (1983), Verba *et al.* (1995) and Jordan and Maloney (1997) all suggest that members cede more importance to the satisfaction obtained from supporting campaigning for collective ends than Olson's work suggests. In the US, McFarland (1984: 47) found that 28% of his respondents said they joined Common Cause because they 'Wanted to have a say in Government', while 23% joined because they 'Believed in its aims'. Jordan and Maloney's (1997: 87) surveys of Friends of the Earth (FoE, UK) and Amnesty International British Section (AIBS) found that 32% of FoE and 48% of AIBS members said that they joined these organizations because of a 'general concern for the environment/human rights'. Conover and Gray (1983) indicate that in their sample of 36 right-wing and liberal movement activists, every member gave personal principles or ideology as the primary motivation in joining the organization[17] (cited in Mansbridge, 1990: 311).

But as stressed elsewhere Olson's contribution was to *explain non-participation* – not participation. That members may join for collective benefits (and/or the increased self-esteem of contributing) is not inconsistent with his premise that non-members fail to join because of a lack of selective benefits. The finding in repeated surveys that *members* are in large part motivated by collective gratifications does not shake Olson's central point that *non*-participation is the norm because in most cases those joining can be seen by Olson as the *residual* exceptions to the non-mobilized potential membership. This has to be borne in mind as the studies explaining why a minority of potential members actually participate accumulate. They may do so for collective reasons but for Olson the important aspect is not that they participate, but that they are a minority.

There is support for Hansen's (1985: 94) 'pick and mix' type findings that 'For some people political benefits are sufficient of themselves. Others join both for services and for policy but either alone is sufficient. For still others: political benefits are the crucial quality difference' (see also Moe, 1980a: 607). So some potential members will indeed participate on the basis of a belief in civic duty; others might misunderstand their non-pivotal contribution and join (in effect) in error; and some will join for selective benefits (as Olson suggested) – others to the contrary may reflect 'civic alienation' in that they see no connection between action and outcomes.

This chapter while decidedly leaning towards that part of the literature that sees a need to include a wider array of incentives to account for participation and to include support for collective action *per se* as a factor, also accepts that these incentives *explain minority activity. They do not help understand the bigger phenomenon of non-participation.* Pattie *et al.*'s (2004) *Citizen Audit* survey estimated that circa one-third of the UK population are members of groups (excluding motoring organization membership) – the bigger picture is of non-membership.[18] This idea is set aside temporarily in this part of the chapter, but it is fundamental. Explaining that joiners are not prompted by Olson's belief in selective incentives is not the same as saying that Olson misunderstood non-joiners. In fact, he may have done so, but *evidence based on the beliefs and motivations of joiners is not particularly useful in explaining non-joining.*

The need for 'soft' incentives? The value of ECRT

The expansion of the list of factors that might be considered in assessing rational group membership is consistent with broader trends. Mansbridge's (1990) discussion of the evolution of dissent to rational choice in economics serves, in passing, as a critique of *The Logic of Collective Action.* She (1990: 15) identifies the drift from the (strict) rational choice paradigm and notes the importance of a range of counter-arguments that have accumulated – including Ferejohn and Fiorina's (1974) regret avoidance explanation of 'rational' electoral participation and Riker and Ordeshook's citizen duty proposition. Mansbridge (1990: 17) goes on to summarize the work of Sen,[19] Collard (1978), Hirschman (1986) and other economists who found that self-interest did not fit reality. She noted (1990: 21) that James Buchanan's Nobel Prize in economics may have been for rational choice, but his work emphasized that political participants act both through pecuniary interest *and pursuit of a general interest.* She records work in experimental psychology that found the public trying to act fairly and 'do the right thing' (Dawes and Thaler, 1988). Finally, Mansbridge (1990: 19) concluded that 'we see a mini revolt, in almost all empirical branches of the profession of political science, against the self-interested model of the way a democratic polity actually works'.

While Olson's claims for the value of narrow rational choice may be regarded as 'too great', it may be an over-reaction if self-interest is totally dismissed. As Mansbridge (1990: ix, 20) concludes,

> *Self-interest explains most of human interaction in some contexts, and it plays some role in almost every context*... [However,] the claim that self-interest alone motivates political behavior must be either vacuous,

if self-interest can encompass any motive, or false, if self-interest means behavior that consciously intends only self as the beneficiary (emphasis added).

This interpretation of rationality as encompassing the (still) rational pursuit of non-material incentives is at the heart of the expanded rational choice theory (ERCT) rejoinder to Olson. (Mansbridge refers to 'inclusive' modelers who include factors other than (economic) self-interest under the rational umbrella – requiring only that the decision-maker is consistent and maximizes ends.) Other values such as 'fair shares' or expressive incentives are thought to be needed to explain why some become involved politically.

Chong (1991: 32) succinctly summarizes the major problem with the Olsonian perspective *in relation to public interest groups*:

We would be hard-pressed . . . to account for much public-spirited collective action by tracing it to the material incentives supplied to participants. Even a cursory examination of the reasons behind participation in political causes reveals that selective material incentives are seldom of sufficient value to constitute the primary motivating factor.[20]

Most of the literature is concerned to valiantly bestow a veneer of rationality to the scale of participation that takes place within groups. In ERCT, incentives can be selective, but non-material. Opp (1986: 88) usefully refers to non-material economic factors as *soft incentives*:

Economists . . . concede that there are other kinds of incentives. Olson mentions social and moral inducements; Tullock introduces . . . the entertainment value of participation in revolutionary activities; Breton and Breton refer to the prestige and power which may be the rewards for participating in social movements, and Mitchell mentions . . . self esteem and sociability. These kinds of costs and benefits may be labelled 'soft incentives' because the utilities are not attached to material phenomena.

The empirical revelation of a wider menu of factors than material self-interest allows Petracca (1991: 289) to argue that 'rational choice omits far too much from the complex scheme of political life to be entirely reliable and useful as either explanatory or predictive theory'. However, there is a lack of consensus about how to classify work that re-inserts some of the factors that Petracca, rightly sees as, ignored.

Thus Opp (1999: 172) presents two main versions of rational choice theory: 'Narrow' (which only allows that egoistic preferences are admitted) and 'Wide' (which acknowledges that the assumption of egoistic preferences is important, but sees no a priori reason why 'altruistic preferences are entirely irrelevant'). In this chapter these approximate to the designations Olsonian Rational Choice Theory (ORCT) and Expanded Rational Choice Theory (ERCT) (Table 2.1).

Opp's wide version includes factors such as 'altruism' and 'collective rationality' as part of a rational choice explanation. But how fruitful are such extensions? Whiteley (1995: 215) cites Elster (1983) in arguing that participation based on altruism is 'compatible with rational choice theory'. Whether or not there is consistency of course depends on the definition of RCT. Much confusion emerges here because there is no shared language. Words are repeatedly defined differently and inconsistently.[21]

Thus Leighley (1995) argues that 'various incentives for participation or other concepts central to the rational choice model are often questionable'. Leighley (1995: 193) rejects the Finkel and Opp (1991: 193–194) study that included

> as 'public goods incentives' measures of policy dissatisfaction, feelings of personal influence in achieving the public good, perceptions of the likelihood of group success, collective rationality ('perceptions of the strategic and ethical necessity of the participation of all group members in collective political action'), and moral justification (duty to participate). Even if the parsimony of the models estimates is not challenged, one might take issue with how closely these measures operationalize the concept of a public good, let alone its value, as defined by Olson.

Arguably these are objections to undermining Olson rather than justifications as to why he should not be seen as undermined.

The temptation to expand the list of relevant factors is clear. As Wilson (1995: 160) points out, one aspect of the appeal of organizations such as the United States Chamber of Commerce or the National Association of Manufacturers is 'duty'. Olson chose to ignore such rewards. In his terms such membership is irrational. Is it irrational in a broader sense? A particular form of the expanded incentive idea relates to norms and ideas (see Blyth and Varghese, 1999: 354). If behaviour *is* even partly norm-driven,

Table 2.1 Assumptions of the narrow and wide versions of the theory of rational action

Assumptions of the narrow version (ORCT)	Assumptions of the wide version (ERCT)
Only egoistic preferences are relevant	All kinds of preferences may be explanatory factors
Only tangible constraints are relevant	All kinds of constraints may govern human behaviour
Subjects are fully informed	Subjects may, but need not be, fully informed
Objective constraints are relevant	Perceived as well as objective constraints may be relevant
Only constraints explain behaviour	Constraints and/or preferences may explain behaviour

Source: Adapted from Opp (1999: 174).

then groups can appeal to beliefs about sharing and contributing as well as pocket book preferences.

If public good desires are reformulated by individuals as private wishes, then there is no huge difference between the individual who wants the satisfaction of the $20 CD and the one who wants the satisfaction of the $20 contribution to Amnesty International. But the temptation to 'stretch' rationality in this fashion is widely opposed (see next section). Moore (1995: 427–429) argues that 'social' selective incentives (which includes emotional and psychological goods such as friendship, camaraderie, 'psychic income', 'entertainment value', etc.) are ancillary assumptions. He maintains that

> Olson (1971: 62) was clear on the issue: 'social pressure and social incentives operate only. . . in the groups so small that the members can have face-to-face contact with one another'. Thus, to the extent that rebellion is a large 'N' phenomenon, social incentives are excluded by Olson on theoretical grounds (i.e. they require face-to-face contact, which is not feasible in large 'N' collective action). As a consequence, adding social incentives to the mix is a degenerative solution. . .

However, the ERCT school is essentially translating a social incentive into a standard currency that allows it to be considered along side other (material) incentives. Therefore, if the only incentive offered by a group is some kind of 'feel good' factor and the subscription is $20, then the

ECRT premise is that participation means the feel good is worth in excess of the subscription.

Hirschman (1982: 85–86) makes two important points about the difficulty in calculating for others their 'rational' preferences:

> Indeed the very act of going after the public happiness is often the *next best thing* to actually *having* that happiness . . . Once this essential characteristic of participation in collective action for the public good is understood, the severe limitations of the 'economic' view about such participation, and about the obstacles to it, come immediately into view. The implication of the confusion between striving and attaining is that the neat distinction between costs and benefits of action in the public interest vanishes, since striving, which should be entered on the cost side, turns out to be part of the benefits.

Hirschman (1982) echoes the notion that *participation* to 'secure an outcome' is a distinct and separate reward from '*securing* an outcome' (*the pleasure of participation versus the satisfaction of success*). He is also pointing out that from a narrow rational choice calculus expressive activity is regarded as a 'cost', when, in fact, it could be seen by the participant as a benefit. Civil rights activists in the US turned the cost–benefit calculus on its head: the threat of a prison sentence was traditionally seen as a particularly effective deterrent against political activism. However, many 'authorities' faced activists who directly sought a prison term. As Chong (1991: 86) highlighted, 'When the jail-no-bail tactic was initiated . . . southern authorities were shocked to discover that protesters *chose* prison over an opportunity to pay a small fine.' While Chong has reservations about expressive explanations, he argues that the concept still retains a (restricted) explanatory utility.

Soft dimensions and circularity? Adding realism or wrecking RCT?

This chapter, and particularly this section, reviews a contradictory and complex literature and does so to come to a non-standard conclusion to that debate. The broad simplification that emerges from much of that literature is often to accept Olson's proposition that the academic choice is either elegant simplification or circularity. This chapter is proposing there may be circularity within the Olson account itself – *and* that incentives can be extended without 'flipping' to self-fulfilling analysis. At its core, this section suggests that irrational behaviour can still be recognized even with an expanded menu of incentives, but it would be when individuals ignore *their own* identification of material *or non-material* rewards. This section tries to defend soft incentives from the argument that they undermine the idea of rationality.

The repertoire of incentives set out above was aimed at providing a fuller checklist of factors that may account for participation than the material benefit idea that Olson suggested. But how far can Olson-style rational choice theory (ORCT) be stretched to include a wider variety of incentives without transforming it as an approach? Does adding 'more ingredients' to get a better explanation add realism to the Olson approach or wreck it? The literature repeatedly tells us that the urge to comprehensiveness potentially undermines falsifiability and theoretical parsimony. The legitimacy of this *model stretching* is perhaps the most controversial issue in the field.

As noted earlier Olson conceded the existence of other incentives in the membership decision – but only to undermine their importance. He (1971: 61) accepted that 'In addition to monetary and social incentives [social status and social acceptance], there are also erotic incentives, psychological incentives, moral incentives, and so on.' He argued that the examples analysed in his volume did not require such a 'comprehensive and questionable definition of rationality'. Olson conceded that a charitable organization could be analysed in such terms. The supporter making a modest contribution might do so not because they had a mistaken belief that their contribution would noticeably augment the resources of the charity, but because they got an *individual, non-collective* satisfaction in the form of a feeling of personal moral worth, or because of a desire for respectability or praise. But Olson 'clawed back' his concessions. He (1965: 2) said that generally the exceptions were minor: 'There is paradoxically the logical possibility that groups composed of either altruistic individuals may sometimes act in their common or group interests. But, as later empirical parts of this study will attempt to show, this logical possibility is usually of no practical importance.' Olson (1965: 161) argues that his theory is not very useful for groups characterized by 'a low degree of rationality':

Take for example the occasional band of committed people who continue to work through their organizations for admittedly lost causes. Such a labor of love is not rational, at least from the economic perspective... The existence of groups of individuals that work for 'lost causes' therefore runs counter to the theory offered in this study (*though the insignificance of such groups is of course consistent with the theory*) (italics added; see also fn 93).

Finally, Olson concluded that this approach 'does not seem especially useful... when all action – even charitable action – is defined to be rational, then this theory (or any other theory) becomes correct simply by virtue of its logical consistency, and is no longer capable of empirical refutation'. Is this refutation point legitimate? Has Olson not exaggerated the ERCT position to 'rubbish' it?

In response to the critique that Olson failed to foresee the growth of public interest activity, as we have seen the defence can be offered that his theory was (exclusively) concerned with economic groups. Knoke (1988) – while acknowledging that Olson's text is ambiguous on whether his theory could cover 'all types of lobbies', or if philanthropic, religious or 'lost-cause groups' should be exempted – argued that

> Olson appeared to recognize that motivations in addition to utility-maximization might lead some persons to contribute to collective-action organizations. Rather than subsuming these motives under selective incentives through a *tortured logic* and thereby making his theory 'no longer capable of empirical refutation' [Olson, 1965: 160, fn 91], he preferred to restrict severely the types of collectivities to which his by-product theory applies (Knoke, 1988: 313) (emphasis added).

Olson himself argued:

> At no point in this study... will any such moral force or incentive be used to explain any of the examples of group action that will be studied. There are three reasons for this. First, it is not possible to get empirical proof of the motivation behind any person's action; it is not possible to definitely say whether a given individual acted for moral reasons or for some other reasons in some particular case. A reliance on moral explanations could thus make the theory untestable. Second, no such explanation is needed; since there will be sufficient explanations on other grounds for all group action that will be considered. Third, most organized pressure groups are explicitly working for gains for themselves, not gains for other groups, and in such cases it is hardly plausible to ascribe group action to any moral code. Moral motives or incentives for group action have therefore

been discussed, not to explain any given example of group action, but rather to show that their existence need not contradict the theory offered here, and could if anything tends to support it (Olson, 1971: 61–62).

But those like Mansbridge (1990: 311) who attempt to rescue Olson from criticism of his failure to understand public interest mobilization deliver him into the criticism that his was a rather limited analysis of groups. She said, 'Almost all the analyses that used Olson's work pointed out... that social movements, relying primarily on purposive and solidary incentives, fall into a category of organizations that Olson purposefully omitted from his analysis.' If Olson had nothing to say on public interest groups *his importance shrinks*.

However, it is not the case that Olson clearly restricted his theory from covering public interest groups. As noted (in his fn 91) he said that while for the cases he principally discussed in the book there was no need for 'a comprehensive and questionable' definition of rationality, it might be needed for some non-economic lobbies. Had Olson wanted to confine his remarks to economic-based groups, this was a point he could have clarified in his later edition, or elsewhere, had he strongly felt that his work was being over-interpreted or extended to cover citizen groups. His text qualifies the breadth of his application, but does not unambiguously distance itself from non-economic lobbies. For example Olson (1971: 159) argued that

> Although most of the lobbies in Washington, and all of the strongest lobbies, have some economic objectives, there are also some lobbies with social, political, religious, or philanthropic objectives. Would the theories developed in this book apply to any of these types of lobbies? *Logically, the theory can cover all types of lobbies.* The theory is general in the sense that it is not logically limited to any special case... the theory of large groups, at least, is not even limited to situations where there is self-interested behavior, or where only monetary or material interests are at stake... But it is evident that the theory sheds new light on some essentially social and political organizations, such as veterans' organizations,[22] and that it is not especially useful in studying some other non-economic lobbies. The theory is not at all sufficient where philanthropic lobbies, that is, lobbies that voice concern about some group other than the group that supports the lobby, or religious lobbies, are concerned (italics added).

The more one restricts Olson's scope of relevance, the more his work shrinks in importance.

Had Olson had more explicitly limited himself to be a theorist of a sub-type of group (material), this would have severely undercut his critique of pluralism that looked so strong because it seemed to point to a bias in group mobilization to the detriment of non-economic lobbies. If he really sought to reject the social science assumption of conflict between his rational choice approach and the empirical explosion of public interest groups, he could have made the point very simply. But note his letter disagreeing with the research design of the study of the group Zero Population Growth (ZPG). Olson (1979: 149) argued that 'tens of millions of Americans' believed the population should not grow, but only a 'miniscule minority of 12,000' were members of ZPG. (For Olson, all these non-members are free-riders. See Chapter 5 for a more detailed discussion.) Olson did not say, 'You are overstretching my model to apply it to an altruistic group'; he claimed his model still worked in a non-material field.

The diplomatic fudge is to suggest that 'Olson sketched the Big Picture', and expanding on the basic inventory of incentives adds detail. A better approach might be to investigate cases where Olson does a decent job and cases where he does not. A working expectation should be that Olson works well in some cases and less well in others, but is not universally applicable to the heterogeneous group world.

Olson (1965: 161) argued that where non-rational or irrational (by his usage) behaviour is the basis for a lobby, it would perhaps be better to turn to psychology or social psychology rather than economics for a relevant theory. In a sense post-Olsonians who have wanted to show how groups have been overcoming the 'paradox of participation' have been straying precisely into these fields – changing the focus from Olson's starting point.

It may be crudely (and wrongly) assumed that where a group secures members then Olson is disproved. But Olson anticipated that members would rationally join for selective benefits that exceeded membership costs. However, he also accepted that others would join for other reasons. He did not say that this sort of membership would not exist, but he thought it irrational as it was not economically justifiable. (At this point in the argument it is irrelevant whether the potential member is interested in selective or collective benefits. Even if one is pursuing collective benefits it is irrational to offer support unless that increment of support is crucial and pivotal.) Finally (and importantly), Olson expected that substantial elements who supported the goals of the organization would free-ride because the costs to them exceeded the personal benefits. Much attention is given to points one and three, but Olson accepted point two – that there would be non-rational membership.

The off-the-shelf criticism directed towards those who introduce psychological factors is that they are introducing circularity. Explanation then is seen as self-fulfilling: if material and selective factors do not 'work' then others must 'explain'. But it can be argued that essentially there are as many untestable assumptions central to Olson's thesis as in the work of his critics. First, when non-economically viable membership exists it does not 'disprove' Olson – he simply says/assumes that it is irrational. So what actually disproves Olson? Secondly, when non-membership takes place he sweepingly claims/assumes it as 'free-riding'. *That needs to be tested as an explanation rather than celebrated as a finding* (see Chapter 5).

So part of the Olson explanation of participation is that (some) individuals are *not economically rational* – at least where the contribution is minor or in connection with philanthropic goals. Olson discussed this in a very significant footnote (91). He argued that

> Many theorists simply assume that all individual behavior, what ever the context, is rational in the sense in which the word is used in economic models. Whenever a person acts, it is assumed that he acted rationally to further some 'interest' he had, even if the action was philanthropic, for that means that the individual got more 'utility' (or, better, reached a higher indifference curve) by acting in a philanthropic way than by acting in any other way.

Olson wants to retain a testable model (but see above). In doing so he is reluctant to accept a proposition that all action is explicable by rationality: that is if economic factors are not sufficient then there must be non-economic factors. However, he seems in danger of assuming that non-economic incentives *cannot* be crucial simply because this concession would threaten the testability of his model. Ultimately, the (relaxed) ERCT explanation of participation *does assume* that a soft incentive must exist if a hard one appears inadequate (see Opp's (1999: 179) remarks on tautology). However, soft incentives are exactly what Olson thought should/could not be absorbed into a falsifiable rational choice model.

Many scholars (e.g. Green and Shapiro, 1994; Hirschman, 1986; Marwell and Ames, 1981; Walker, 1991) have argued that the empirical evidence contradicts the Olsonian assumption. But the 'circularity' stick is used to beat those adopting a wide version of rationality. Critics argue (in caricature) that such expanded models say that if there are no selective incentives, then non-selective explanations *must* exist. Chong (1991: 10) is one who identifies that there are problems with expressive benefits as a solution to the collective action problem. First, he says, the expressive concept states that participation has an intrinsic value to individuals. He maintains that this 'only raises the additional question: why do people want to participate?' Secondly, an expressive benefit explanation can be used to justify *any* participatory activity:

> The danger, then, is that we cannot rely on the strength of expressive benefits to explain collective action, or alternatively, their weakness to account for the failure to organize collective action. Therefore what was originally a vexing and difficult collective action problem gets 'solved' in an ad hoc and trivial fashion (Chong, 1991: 10).

Knoke (1990) argues that including non-material benefits is a tortuous logic that renders the concept of rationality as universal and therefore 'useless' (quoted in Walker, 1991: 47) (see also Sabatier, 1992: 105). Walker (1991: 47) argued that

> there is something wholly unsatisfactory about resorting to purposive benefits to make group membership *appear* rational. Like the "sense of citizen duty" motive used by some to explain why people vote, the purposive category is a catchall that verged on tautology. If we work within Olson's structure, the purposive argument goes like this: Why do individuals join a group to advance a collective good? Because they have a purposive desire to see that collective good advanced. Such a circular argument does not take us very far (italic added).

Teske (1997: 66) concluded that 'Whenever collective action appears, and material or solidary incentives do not seem adequate to explain its appearance, one simply has *recourse to vague explanations* based on purposive incentives' (emphasis added). Verba *et al.* (1995: 525) note the unsatisfactory device of the 'invented' explanation – 'Empirical studies of participation in the [expanded] rational choice tradition have typically looked at the benefits accruing to activists and drawn the sometimes tautological inference that, if there is activity, there must be sufficient benefits to justify the effort.' They note the need to go beyond selective benefits to encompass such psychic benefits as the satisfaction attendant to doing one's civic duty. However, Verba *et al.* (1995: 284) note that the theory 'becomes almost unfalsifiable once we enlarge the set of benefits and thus loses its analytical bite'.

In summary, many see the simple Olson approach as the only valid one. However, while a 'parsimonious' model has a social science cachet, it sounds less impressive when re-labelled a basic, preliminary, perfunctory – or even an over-simplified – model. In a literal sense the Olson model is simply not effective in the task of explaining joining. Parsimony refers to the minimum causes necessary to account for the phenomenon: this is exactly what Olson fails to do. This type of defence of Olson *as an explanation of participation* privileges elegance over content. It simply provides an inadequate explanation for the observable fact that many citizens join organizations in pursuit of collective goods with no selective enticement. As a parsimonious model it is both simple to use and simply useless. The point here is to distinguish between Olson as a prophet of non-participation and Olson as a guide to participation. The latter was not his game.

Opp (1999: 188) questions the benefit of the narrow Olsonian version (but the critique is of Olson's understanding of participation):

> because the wide variety of preferences and constraints that may be relevant for human behavior need not be considered... 'simplicity' and 'elegance' are sometimes accepted as criteria for evaluating scientific theories... the major criteria for judging the quality of an empirical theory are truth or empirical corroboration and empirical content (i.e. explanatory power)... the costs of having a simple or elegant explanation will often be that the explanation is wrong. There may thus often be a conflict of goals: simplicity or elegance on the one hand and empirical validity on the other. *In such a situation one will prefer a complicated and empirically valid explanation to a simple and elegant explanation that is wrong* (emphasis added).

It should be emphasized that, like Olson, ERCT observers may find under-mobilization. ERCT does not say that non-rational choice factors make everyone participate. It says if there is non-Olsonian participation (i.e. not induced by selective incentives) then there has to be some other solution. It is not a sensible research strategy to say there is participation not anticipated by Olson, but we cannot factor in non-Olsonian considerations needed to explain the phenomenon. This makes the problem insoluble.

Hay (2004) dismembers the paradox of participation in a less Olson-friendly way. He pointed out the central issue that joining is anti-rational does not come from the general notion of rationality, but from the de facto redefinition by many RC theorists – that the utility function that is pursued *should be* material. In fact, Hay suggests, in following the general theory one cannot make sweeping claims about large classes of action because one would need to aggregate conclusions based on each individual. One cannot reach conclusions on an individual's choices unless one establishes their individual preferences before judging action in pursuit of these preferences. If RCT is simply about 'optimising preferences in a consistent fashion' (Dunleavy, 1991: 3), then the apparent illogic of collective action, and the assertion of irrationality, only appears after behaviour is judged against the assumptions of outside analysts (with economists' assumptions) – rather than judged against the individual's own criteria. In fact the 'working' version of RCT usually *assumes* these preferences.

It is true that one extreme form of ECRT could be that whatever individuals do is thereby consistent with what they wanted: that is *everything* is rational. This argument is not Hay's. He suggests that rationality should be judged against an individual's own criteria. In the Hay (2004) formulation, a person could be irrational in failing to prioritize their own objectives, *but they are permitted to define their own preferences.*

In the eyes of critics of ERCT the main problem is that all kinds of factors *can* be included in the model. Therefore all explanations can be made to accord to broad rational choice theory: it is no longer an evaluation of behaviour to discover if it fits expectation, but a sort of basket of incentives that in aggregate will be 'rational'. Once one judges enough has been thrown in, it is 'rational'. Indeed, even worse by the standards of strict rational choice – the 'explanation' can be made complete by adding non-quantifiable mystery ingredients that are *assumed* to exist because nothing more tangible can be identified. Thus, if there is no obvious self-interest in an action one can 'assume' that there is a non-self-interested motivation.

If an explanation is offered which points to self-sacrifice for the benefit of others, then Opp's (1999) response would either be that (a) while the action is not egoistic, it is self-interested because increasing the welfare of others maximizes personal utility (see Opp, 1999: 173); or (b) a long-run *generalized reciprocity*-type argument that at some future point in time one good deed will be repaid by another. Opp (1999: 173) uses the example of a monk who seeks to maximize his utility, but that might not make him act in his 'own interest' as he might define his utility as helping others. This is rational in a general sense, but not rational as operationalized in many economically rational versions. As Opp (1999:

173) says, 'advocates of the wide version recognize a diversity of humans' preferences . . . '.

If Opp's preference for the wide model is accepted there is the problem of *infinite regress*,[23] but that might be preferred to ORCT which *guarantees inadequacy*. As Opp (1999: 191) highlights,

> From the perspective of a Popperian philosophy it is not useful to restrict the range of applications of a theory if it does not work. The reason is that this decreases the explanatory power of a theory. It is preferable to modify the theory in such a way in that it holds in those 'problematic' situations as well, or to look for an entirely new and better theory.

To sum up, while these arguments have a common-sense ring, ultimately in extreme form they expand rational choice theory into a description of factors thought to account for membership rather than a set of variables that can be tested. Down the Opp route rational choice is an instrument that assembles relevant dimensions that seem to account for membership.[24] In short, Opp's (1999) ERCT theory ('Wide Version') can be summarized as: all behaviour revolves around utility maximization, but what utility is maximized differs in different variants. But one can have an expanded model that is not self-fulfilling. One can fail to maximize expanded rationality, but this would need to be uncovered on a case-by-case way.

Some explanations may be simply labelling *academic ignorance* in a more attractive way rather than reducing it. It *may be*, for example, that Civic Duty is a consideration in explaining voting turnout, but this is something that needs to be tested rather than simply assumed. It need not be the case that any participation not based on economic rationality must, by definition, reflect Civic Duty. However, there is a difference between assuming something like social civic gratification *must* exist because there is no other obvious answer – and the empirical work of Verba *et al.* (1995) which discovered that participants actually advance such reasons.

Another position, however, is that a successful boxing prediction model might state that taller boxers do better: this is simple and may be better than random selection. However, a more accurate approach might be to build in other factors – previous record, weight, age, reach, etc. Simplicity is not necessarily a virtue for successful explanation. One can expand the simple height prediction in many ways short of circularity. Circularity comes when one simply *restates* the outcome as a precondition – for example the boxing champion is the one who defeats his opponent.[25] Expansion should be different from circularity. The chorus of 'unfalsifiable' or 'tautological' need not be persuasive. It is true that the ERCT ambition is to continue adding detail into the model until it provides a rich enough explanation. In the ERCT approach, a mismatch between theory and the problem to be solved does not lead to abandoning the theory, but a trawl for additional factors to build in.

Critics of expanding rational choice perhaps need to acknowledge that the alternative is to accept ORCT has a *very restricted utility*. Interestingly a survey by Hechelman and Whapales (2003) showed that 80% of Public Choice Society members agreed with the proposition that 'Voters vote out of a sense of civic duty'. This is not ERCT academics stretching rational choice – it is rational choice scholars clutching at (expanded) straws to prevent rational choice failing completely in the field of voting.

ORCT theorists such as Hardin (1995: 46) move typically from the general 'you act rationally if you do what you believe serves your interest' to the less explicit 'you act rationally if you make the choices external observers assume are in your interest'. In other words, while rational choice can be seen as the maximization of any desired outcomes, the generality of RCT interpretations quietly substitute an account that requires 'rational' individuals to prioritize a particular (material) function. Hay (2004: 43) powerfully argues, 'The story of rational choice theory is, then, frequently one in which collective goods are sacrificed on the altar of narrowly conceived material self-interest (and, indeed, long-term self-interest is sacrificed for short-term material gain).'

While advocates of ERCT present it as 'intelligent rational choice' of course others dissent. Udehn (1996: 251) says of those who want to keep a narrow and parsimonious notion of rationality that 'Like some religions, it may lead to other worldliness; to a withdrawal from the complexity of the mundane world, into a more simple world of pure abstraction. In this enchanted world of intellectual constructs, many social scientists feel at home, apparently satisfied with activities, such as model-building and story-telling.'[26]

Facing up to the 'the paradox of collective action'

This chapter concludes with two different reactions to 'the paradox of collective action'. The first instinct is to directly contradict Olson's advice and try make the explanation more elaborate and inclusive in the ERCT style. The second is to accept the simple Olson approach. The chapter argues these can be reconciled because two types of Olson prediction are often conflated. His big theme that participation will be suboptimal is qualified, but not totally undermined, by the sort of level of participation actually found. Accordingly, the suggestion here is that there is a need to do a better job than Olson in explaining participation. Expansion is needed and it is simply daft to paint the discipline into a corner that says this means that those citizens engaging with the political system are irrational. *But there remains a sizeable degree of non-participation where Olson may be on stronger ground.* To explain participation there may be a need for 'expansion', but that is a different 'story' from explaining non-participation. Olson may be inadequate in explaining participation, but conceivably (but not necessarily) he could still be right about the motivations of that majority of non-participators.

Accept that Olson's inventory of incentives is too restricted

Arguably, and contra to the Olsonian assumption, the contribution by the supporter/member of resources (i.e. subscriptions) to allow the pursuit of collective goods may still not be a by-product, but central to the decision to join. Individuals *are* prepared to contribute to collective pursuits (see Verba *et al.*, 1995). Individuals may also find personal selective reward in psychological gratification of contribution. This is not irrational in a broader sense of the term. Such non-Olsonian recruitment seems most important precisely in the areas of the organizational map that have seen expansion – public interest groups. So this chapter certainly accepts that selective benefits exist, but they need not (always) be the pivotal factor in membership. Membership may indeed need no material explanation.

As suggested above, ERCT is actually a sort of reconstituting or retrospective description that seeks to *explain* what happened. In a sense ERCT is limitless in the range of factors it can bring to bear. If the menu of factors is insufficient then others can be added until the explanation seems to match the problem. But there can be poor retrospective explanations. In other words, the charge that ERCT is inevitably successful is not always true. It is however based on the reasonable premise that if there is mobilization and Olsonian ingredients do not predict it, then there is an automatic case for assuming that something non-Olsonian is present.

Accept that Olson anticipated low participation

Most interest group scholars accept the Mayflower hotel point from Walker above that there is such an empirical explosion of groups and membership that Olson's thesis is wrong-footed. Clearly participation in groups has taken place on a larger scale than economic rational choice allows. However, in most contexts, explanations about such involvement tell us about a minority. *Olson may be correct to focus on the majority who do not participate?* Hardin (1979, 1995) does not consider that the mobilization of large numbers delivers a 'knock-out' blow to the Olsonian model – if the 'n' is (as is often the case) a low percentage of the potential joiners. Both Hardin and Olson would see the (*low*) numbers joining as a 'residual category' and would claim that Olson successfully predicted the large number of *eligible joiners who remain non-members.*

Chapter 5 discusses the issue of free-riding in groups. This is seen as a serious factor in undermining the success of groups as participatory venues. But Chapter 5 follows the Green and Shapiro (1994: 81) argument that to not-be-in-membership is very different from free-riding. This raises an under-exposed conflation in the notion of free-riding. Hardin and Olson seem to want to claim all sympathetic non-members as free-riders, but is one free-riding: if one has not heard of the group?; or is unconvinced about its effectiveness? Indeed, it was Olson who highlighted that one might not participate if one did not see the value in adding a tiny increment to the group resources. Is a rational non-joiner the same as a selfish free-rider? In trying to get a sense of the scale of free-riding it would not be sufficient to establish the percentage of the non-members among the sympathetic. One needs to establish how many see merit in the group role and *chose* to remain non-members. The crude Olsonian expectation is that free-riding will be the major explanation; the research hunch in Chapter 5, reflecting the previous section, is that all sorts of other factors are involved: for example non-material demand- and supply-side.

Though the support for groups seems to defy the (O)RCT pessimism, Olson believed that the level of actual support should be judged against the scale of potential support. The Olson case actually escapes the Collective Action Paradox charge to the extent that it simply treats participation as an anomaly (minor). Moreover some of the group support found in practice is consistent with Olson and may be material self-interest driven (see Chapter 5). Though for the most part that massive wave of public interest group support from the 1960s onwards seemed remote from the selective benefit incentive. Nevertheless, Olson could credibly argue that the group expansion (of a low percentage of the eligible) did not embarrass his theory to the extent widely assumed. This chapter has extensively reviewed the factors that may lead to participation, *but it must be stressed that Olson was more interested in non-participation.*

The chapter discussed the often perplexing, and usually confusing, debate on rational joining. The topic cannot be avoided in this volume because it is central to the level of optimism that it is realistic to have about groups as participatory venues. If there is some powerful pressure, as Olson suggested, curtailing group participation, then groups would be of limited importance as mass locales of democracy. Empirical evidence of group proliferation suggests that groups have in part been able to 'crack' the Olson ceiling on involvement – partly through the 'supply-side' activities discussed in Chapters 3 and 4. Partly too the public seem willing to embrace more dimensions to rationality than Olson allowed. Groups are therefore successful enough at mobilization to be central to participation. Finally, it is worth noting that the rather underwhelming term 'successful enough' is compatible with seeing groups as centres of democratic involvement because Olson's worldview did not simply imply low participation in groups. It stood as a general restriction on a political world as individuals focus on their private wants because intervention in the mass political sphere is simply too unlikely to yield pivotal impact. Comparing the scale of group involvement with the scale of other political actions is for Olson comparing one sort of unusual and exceptional behaviour with another.

Accepting that Olson has more value in the non-participation story than in the participatory, his concern about the problems of mobilization seem set in a sterile and perhaps unreal world. Rosenstone and Hansen (1993: 23) suggest that a full appreciation of participation needs to accept that individuals are affected by 'family, friends, neighbors, and co-workers, plus politicians, parties, activists, and interest groups'. The next chapter looks at how interest groups frame matters to affect the rational choice by individuals.

3
Making Interests: Creating Members?

Co-authored with Sara Davidson

Over the past few decades conflicting theories have emerged in the social sciences with regard to the bases of public opinion. This chapter discusses the phenomenon of the creation of opinions through examining the case of the environment, but the issue is broad. It questions the commonplace Truman (1951)[1] assumption that group membership relates to some spontaneous expression of opinion, or defence or promotion of some interest. This was of course the assumption that Olson (1965) and others (e.g. Hardin, 1995, 2003) set out to undermine with the *free-rider* observation.

Ironically, the argument advanced below is intended to be as subversive to the major critique of Truman (i.e. Olson) as it is to Truman's 'spontaneous joining' belief. As set out in the previous chapter the rational choice model is usually the centrepiece, either for or against discussions of membership. It assumes that individuals know their interests and seek to advance them in an economically efficient manner. The classic and basic formulation was from Downs (1957: 6):

> A rational man is one who behaves as follows: (1) he can always make a decision when confronted with a range of alternatives; (2) he ranks all the alternatives facing him in order of his preference in such a way that each is either preferred to, indifferent to, or inferior to each other; (3) his preference ranking is transitive; (4) he always chooses from among the possible alternatives that which ranks highest in his preference ordering; and (5) he always makes the same decision each time he is confronted with the same alternatives.

In rejecting Truman's perspective, Olson (1965: 126) argued powerfully that rational individuals will 'not voluntarily make any sacrifices to help their group attain its political (public or collective) objectives'.

The approach pursued here is to disagree *both* with spontaneity and the rationalist core assumption of individually based belief. This suggests that Olson did not recognize the indeterminate nature of public opinion that brings uncertainty into membership decisions. In line with Converse (1964) this chapter rejects the idea that the public secure their views from abstract ideological principles. Arguably, for groups where voluntary membership is the case, there is a need to move from a sort of vending machine image of membership that starts with the values of individuals and sees participation emerging like a nickel in the slot producing a predictable product. Whether an individual holds a particular opinion, and whether that leads to mobilization, is uncertain but for reasons other than free-riding. Drawing on current debates on the bases of public opinion, the chapter attempts to recast 'members' as sites of confusion, rather than as holders of opinions searching for groups to articulate them. It moves away from the assumption of individuals as calculating machines instrumentally seeking minimum cost strategies to examine social construction perspectives. *It stresses the importance of group action in framing issues in a way that crystallize beliefs.*

A focus on the stimulus from exogenous agents – rather than endogenous values or beliefs – is a well-established analytical approach in research on the social bases of public opinion (see Blumer, 1948; Lippmann, 1925). The structure of these attitudes is at the centre of debates. Zaller and Feldman (1992), for example, conclude that instead of one 'true' attitude towards an issue, individuals typically possess 'a series of partially independent and often inconsistent ones'. When answering survey questions most respondents call to mind a *number of attitudes*: question wording and recent events may influence the precise answer. This sort of work undermines the notion that individuals have clear, strong unambiguous opinions – that seems to be at the heart of most group-joining accounts.[2] It is obvious that *some* group membership reflects endogenous interest; but even where there is a material interest at stake the group might be actively trying to *persuade* the potential member about its significance. *Significance might not reveal itself without assistance.* In other areas, such as animal welfare, individuals may hold rather contradictory positions that the group attempts to help them resolve in a particular direction. Gamson and Modigliani (1989: 2) offered the notion of 'interpretative packages – 'On most policy issues, there are competing packages available in this culture.' This chapter suggests that an important role for the group is in marketing a package – adoption of which will lead an individual into a policy preference that makes membership sensible.

As in the work of Zahariadis (2003), this chapter accepts ambiguity in the attitudes of the public and sees this as an opportunity 'for individuals or small groups to manipulate people and processes to achieve the outcome they desire'. Zahariadis (2003: 18) argues:

> Constructivist analysts have attempted to shift the ground from objective evaluations of alternatives to the social construction of meaning... policymaking is conceived as a process of deliberation between competing groups, each crafting a reasonable argument in ways that aim to persuade the other side(s).

The origins of opinion

As noted in Chapter 1 in order to 'explain' membership, one possibility is to see activity as the *purposive* (Clark and Wilson, 1961) advancement of personal opinions. Chapter 5 shows that large numbers of members of environmental organizations, many of which only offer chequebook participation, see their limited involvement as a purposive activity. At issue, however, is the origin of the adoption of the values they wish to further.

Underlying values and attitudes and the postmaterialist thesis

The dominant explanation of environmental attitudes (and hence participation) is probably the *postmaterialist thesis*? From such a perspective, the emergence of modern-day environmentalism is seen as following broader changes in the values of mass publics. In an important sense this is still a vending machine model: new values underpin and lead to new actions. Inglehart (1971, 1977, 1990, 1995, 1997) famously argued that unprecedented levels of economic growth in the post-war era provided younger cohorts with different socialization experiences. They developed fundamentally different value priorities from previous generations,[3] which fostered a gradual shift away from *materialist* values that emphasized economic and physical security, to *postmaterialist* ones revolving around higher-order concerns relating to quality of life and self-actualization. Inglehart (1977: 3–4) further argued that there have been significant changes in the distribution of political skills as a consequence of rising educational attainment. A growing proportion

of citizens have developed the cognitive understanding of (and a sufficient interest in) national and international politics to participate in
decision-making. In short, this has led to a shift from 'elite-directed'
political activities towards new 'elite-challenging' forms of behaviour. In
this view value change and growing political awareness have reinforced
each other and caused a decline in class-based politics that witnessed
the emergence of new postmaterialist political groups around new issues
(e.g. the environment, women's rights, the anti-nuclear cause, etc.).

The postmaterialist thesis has been vigorously challenged with critics
questioning its theoretical tenets, methodological approach and empirical basis.[4] One such challenge of particular relevance in the present
context concerns the *dimensionality* of environmental attitudes. As
Guber (1996) noted, early studies of environmentalism assumed that
various measures of environmental concern, from the perceived serious-
ness of environmental problems, to knowledge of environmental issues
to pro-environmental behaviour tapped the same underlying dimension, namely environmental concern. However, drawing attention to
'moderate bivariate correlations' between such measures, more recent
studies have concluded that environmental concern is in fact multi-
dimensional: *different measures, it is argued, tap very different underlying
constructs.* This hypothesis undermines the postmaterialist thesis, and
indeed any theory which simply associates environmentalism with a
broader paradigmatic shift because multidimensionality implies *a lack
of consistency in attitudes.* In such a perspective 'attitudes towards the
environment are not rooted in abstract philosophical or ideological principles, but are rather crude and disconnected' (de Haven Smith as cited
in Guber, 1996: 648). In the context of this chapter multidimensionality
is important in giving scope for groups to encourage certain elements
that suit their purposes.

Social structural perspectives

A second possible explanation for the emergence of political orientations such as environmentalism centres on socio-demographic changes
in particular class. Several commentators have attributed growing environmental awareness to the rise of the 'new middle class' (see Lowe
and Goyder, 1983). This again is perhaps a fairly mechanical approach
stipulating a direct connection between social structure and individual
activity. Essentially, concern for the environment is regarded as a
'luxury' orientation which the middle class can best afford. As Hannigan
(1999: 26) points out, the 'new middle class' explanation overlaps with

the postmaterialist thesis. However, it places more emphasis on the precise social location of individuals.

Commentators who have used a social structure perspective to discuss environmental concern note that such concern is not spread uniformly among the ranks of the 'new middle class'. Rather it is most prevalent among groups working in the non-market or creative and service sectors of the economy including teachers, social employees and journalists (Hannigan, 1999: 26; Cotgrove, 1982).[5] Whereas market-sector employees show some propensity to support moderate nature conservationist principles, those working in the creative and service sector, exhibit a greater propensity in favour of more radical forms of environmentalism (Cotgrove, 1982; cited in Martell, 1994: 128).

Why should environmentalism be so prevalent among people in the non-market sector? It has been argued that such employment experiences bring these individuals into closer contact with people subject to the direct or indirect effects of environmental degradation (Hannigan, 1999: 26). However drawing on survey data, Cotgrove (1982) argued that people tend to select their occupation in accordance with their existing concerns and values. Viewed in this light the disproportionate environmental concern exhibited by teachers, social employees and journalists may be intensified by their working lives, but it is not a direct product of such experiences. Environmentalism has also been seen as self-interested: that is the non-market sector wants to promote a growth in environmentalism because this would deliver material rewards in the form of jobs (see Hannigan, 1999: 27). Finally, the environment has been described as a positional good which non-market employees use to affirm their social status.

The reflection hypothesis

The *reflection hypothesis* (Hannigan, 1999) asserts a direct relationship between the actual existence of social problems and associated levels of concern. This assumes a high degree of predictability: mobilization will emerge when objective conditions deteriorate. Political views, and hence participation, stem from objective problems in the lives of potential supporters, members and activists. Lowe and Rüdig (1986: 518) claimed that the relative neglect of *objective* environmental conditions in favour of a focus on value change was one of the major shortcomings of the existing literature. Subsequently, successive commentators have pointed to evidence indicating a direct link between the perceptible deterioration of the natural world and recorded levels of public concern (see Beck, 1992,

1996; Brechin and Kempton, 1994; Dunlap, 1991a,b; Jehlicka, 1992; Martell, 1994; Rohrschneider, 1988). For example, Jehlicka (1992, cited in Martell, 1994: 134), suggested that the British are less concerned about global environmental problems like acid rain and river pollution because, compared with other Western European nations, they remain relatively unaffected by such conditions. By contrast where acidification, deforestation, soil erosion, and river pollution are most severe, recorded environmental concern is higher.

While advocates of the reflection hypothesis see environmental degradation as the key causal factor, they disagree over the characteristics causing greatest public concern. Some have emphasized the significance of the proximity or visibility of a problem, arguing that people only become genuinely concerned about the environment when a particular problem threatens to (or) impinge(s) on their daily lives (Inhaber, 1992; Yearley, 1991: 82). The *proximity of concern* is crucial. (Data in Chapter 5 shows that members of environmental organizations perceived environmental degradation as a greater personal threat than potential nonmembers with similar attitudinal predispositions.) Yearley (1991: 82) notes that citizens may not be opposed to nuclear dumping in general, provided of course, the nuclear waste dump is not located too near their homes. (However Rohrschneider (1988) and Jehlicka (1992) argue that general concern for the environment is considerably more pervasive than suggested by this rather dismissive interpretation.)

Social construction

The reflection thesis is consistent with Truman's (1951) *disturbance theory* of group formation – new circumstances generate new shared interests and hence group participation – but it has been criticized on two grounds. First, as Hannigan (1999: 24) notes, it is unable to explain why certain environmental problems have risen to prominence compared to others. Secondly, some regard it as predicated on an uncritical acceptance of the reality of alleged problems (see Bauman, 1991 as cited in Cudworth, 1999: 12; Buttel and Taylor, 1992: 212; Hannigan, 1999; Wynne, 1996: 45). These criticisms have led to the development of a third approach – *social construction*. In essence this perspective sees opinions as structured by third parties, rather than reflecting an external reality. As claimed at the start of this chapter, this is a direct attack on the central interest group assumptions of the rational choice and traditionalist scholars. It supports interpretations that adopt an external, supply-side mobilization and emphasizes the way in which issues *are brought to public attention* by a range of social actors. Discussing the environmental arena Szerszynski's (1991: 3) refers to such actors as *'environmental meaning producing institutions'* (EMPIs) – a label encompassing pressure groups, governing bodies, industry, scientists and the media. Spector and Kitsuse's (1973, 1977) work on the sociology of social problems was a main step in the development of social construction (see Hannigan, 1999; Schoenfeld *et al.*, 1979; Yearley, 1991). Those adopting this perspective argue that social problems *are not rooted in an objective given reality, but are constructed* when personal concerns are transformed into broader collective issues. Specifically they defined social problems as 'the activities of groups making assertions of grievances and claims to organizations, agencies and institutions about some putative conditions' (as cited in Hannigan, 1999: 32).

Accordingly many commentators have stressed the *claims-making* role of environmental pressure groups or new social movements (see Eyerman and Jamison, 1991; Hannigan, 1999: 44; Jamison, 1996; Martell, 1994; Rawcliffe, 1992; Szerszynski, 1991; Yearley, 1991). Yearley describes how UK groups such as Royal Society for the Protection of Birds (RSPB), The Conservation Society and Greenpeace have shaped public perceptions on a range of alleged environmental problems. Such groups, or 'moral entrepreneurs', he claims achieve their aims by attracting the attention of the media, community leaders, religious associations and by lobbying politicians. Buttel and Taylor (1992: 221–222) note that particular types of environmental claim are favoured over others by the international environmental movement. Problems 'positing a global level dynamic and constructed at a global level of analysis' tend to be privileged over more localized concerns.

Buttel and Taylor (1992: 221–222) maintain the thesis has two main strands. First, in line with Olson, they note that because the environment is a collective good, environmental protection is in everyone's interest and hence in no one's in particular. This creates potential collective action problems. Secondly, the environmental agenda comprises a bewildering array of disparate problems in a multitude of arenas. These difficulties, Buttel and Taylor (1992) note, can be overcome by the *packaging* of environmental problems in global (scientific) formulations. Such aggregation enables a multiplicity of problems to be subsumed under a common rubric and to gain apparent scientific legitimacy. Formulations providing 'scientific justification for worldwide alarm or dread are particularly attractive both in authenticating this packaging approach and in creating the urgent political rationale for responses'. The creation of such supranational urgency in turn, Buttel and Taylor (1992) continue, enables the green movement to make authoritative moral and ethical claims that it is imperative for all groups to co-operate to meet the challenge. Such work then sees the bias in the presentation of interpretations of events in the direction of 'worriers'.

For social constructionists, the initial identification of a certain condition or situation as problematic is only the first stage in a lengthy sequence of events, leading to the enactment of solutions. Once established a claim is likely to be subject to moderation or challenge by other interested parties – for example government agencies, industry, the media – that may deny that a problem exists, or present an alternative 'reading' of it. Accordingly, Hannigan (1999: 187) has defined the environment as 'a site for a repertoire of definition and contestatory activities'. Szerszynski similarly discusses conflict among groups. However, he emphasizes that all group share a common goal: to have their definition accepted by the wider public and thus to be the legitimate vanguard of public opinion.

Framing and agenda setting

Increasingly commentators have drawn on the concept of *framing* and *agenda setting* in discussing the dynamics of claims making (Baumgartner and Jones, 1993; Birkland, 1997; Dearing and Rogers, 1996; Jones, 1994; Rochefort and Cobb, 1994). Entman (1996: 79) describes how a frame operates to 'select and highlight one features of reality and obscures others in a way that tells a consistent story about problems, their causes, moral implications and remedies'. Jennings (1999: 8–9) argues that in the area of pain and loss framing usually revolves around individual rights and freedoms: 'the woman's right to have an abortion, the motorcyclist's right not to wear a helmet, the citizen's rights to own guns'. He says:

> Choosing and employing the correct frame is key to a winning position on issues of bodily harm. Abortion is a case in point. Pro-choice forces established and relied on a winning frame based on a woman's right to choose what to do with her own body. In time the pro-life forces also adopted the rights frame, cast now in favor of the foetus (Jennings, 1999: 8–9).

He suggests that this strategy undermined the rights claims of the pro-choice side, for ultimately the foetus's right to life is likely to triumph over the mother's right not to bear the child. He suggested that as the rights frame came under attack, the pro-choice forces began to advance other frames, including those of personal (versus governmental) choice and reproductive freedom defined more generally. Thus in fighting for publicity, the underlying battle is for frames.

More generally, if a given situation can be framed as a crisis, such as the AIDS epidemic, this may act as a significant and immediate trigger for political action. As Euchner (1996: 69) argues,

> Crisis is a powerful motivator because it clears away hesitation and uncertainty, consolidates a variety of motivations for political action, clarifies understanding of common interests, and crystallizes possible strategies for action. Without the urgency of a crisis situation, people avoid confronting social problems... crisis situations give the costs and benefits of political action an urgency that people in the community cannot ignore. People in crisis situations think they can – and must – get involved in politics right away to avert impending disaster.

Euchner (1996: 69) highlights the Three Mile Island accident in 1979 as dramatically shifting 'the "frame" through which people viewed nuclear power from one of scientific progress to one of concern about "runaway" technology and an absence of public accountability'. Birkland (1997) shows the importance of 'focusing events' in agenda setting (see also Jones and Baumgartner (2005); Protess and McComb (1991)).

For social constructionists, the transformation of social problems into issues of public concern is not an automatic process, but is contingent upon a number of factors. Media attention and the connection to pre-existing mass concerns is a crucial feature. (Chapter 4 shows how groups have learned that negativity and fear are more effective.) Hannigan (1995: 61) described how sponsors of competing framings of an environmental problem measure their success primarily 'by gauging how well their preferred meanings and interpretations are doing in various media arena'. Commentators have identified criteria which help explain why certain environmental issues are singled out for media attention, while others slip into relative obscurity.[6] Issues that are novel tend to be deemed more worthy of coverage than those with which the public is readily familiar (Hannigan, 1999: 65; MacNaghten and Urry, 1998: 59). Human interest stories also tend to receive disproportionate attention. Hannigan cites examples such as 'the stubborn but proud homeowner who sits on the roof and refuses to evacuate as the floodwaters rise' and 'the baby who is found alive after three days in the rubble of an earthquake-devastated neighbourhood'. Problems lacking a significantly visual element, for example long-term environmental problems, are often made newsworthy by actors seeking to publicize them, through the staging of 'pseudo events' including protests and demonstration (Brookes *et al.*, 1976: 254; Schoenfeld *et al.*, 1979: 50; Szerszynski, 1991: 15). Finally, commentators have noted a preference among the media for environmental stories that can be presented simplistically in Hollywood blockbuster style – good versus evil (Lowe and Morrison, 1984: 79; Szerszynski, 1991: 14). MacNaghtnen and Urry (1998: 98) describe how Greenpeace tailored its campaign strategies accordingly and

> have become expert in packaging environmental action in simple black and white media sensitive fashion, where Greenpeace activism comes to symbolise heroic action pitted against corporate greed and self-interest.

Similarly, Rucht (2004: 47) argued that organizations such as Greenpeace have professionalized their media activities and have 'learned to frame and stage their actions according to the needs and expectation of the mass media'.

As discussed in Chapter 4, these sorts of stories are deliberately used by groups in their publicity and recruiting material. (In a recruiting leaflet in 2004 Amnesty International (British Section) showed a picture of a (clothing) iron with the vivid strap line 'Now IMAGINE this was your face' – portraying the iron as a weapon of torture.)

Several commentators (see Eyerman and Jamison, 1991: 112; Hannigan, 1999: 47; Szerszynski, 1991: 15–18; Yearley, 1991: 75) have highlighted that successful claims tend to be those which are presented in a way that resonates with existing cultural norms: that is concerns, attitudes or values. Snow (1986, cited in Hannigan, 1999: 47) labelled this process as *'frame alignment'*. Thus Yearley (1991) suggests that animal rights in Britain is likely to succeed as an issue because of the country's existing status as a nation of animal lovers. Hannigan (1999: 47) meanwhile described how the biotechnology industry – when it has been successful – fosters a public image of a benign technology which is beneficial in promoting economic development.[7]

The reflection/realist critique of social constructionism has faced some challenges. As Burningham and Cooper (1999: 303) point out, the main assumption underlying the critique of the model is that it has greater applicability to the strict form of constructionism, not the mild or contextual version utilized in the majority of empirical studies. While most authors are interested primarily in the *nature of claims* made about problems, and not the problems *per se*, this does not deny that environmental conditions have an independent, external existence. As Hannigan (1999: 30) notes, 'it is important to note that environmental risks and problems as socially constructed entities need not undercut legitimate claims about the conditions of the environment thereby denying them as objective reality'. His own use of social construction aims to demonstrate, however, that the rank ordering of problems does not always directly correspond to actual needs.

Even if the realist critique is taken to apply exclusively to a strict construction perspective, its core assumptions perhaps remain problematic. As Burningham and Cooper (1999) maintain strict constructionists are no more in the business of denying the existence of environmental problems than are their contextual counterparts. Rather, their belief is simply that researchers should remain agnostic about the existence of such problems. Even in cases where constructionists do consider issues of ontology, Burningham and Cooper (1999: 308) add, they are not necessarily questioning the existence of reality, but rather inferring that 'what this reality "is", what it means, is socially constructed'.

Thus when faced with contradictory, but equally persuasive, interpretations of a given issue, how should the public evaluate the relative merits of each case? As outlined above, *meaning-producing institutions* select and disseminate specific interpretations with media assistance. In order for these meanings to have the necessary resonance, they must be congruent with existing attitudes, ideas and symbols.[8] Rohrschneider (1993), following Inglehart, argues that the most crucial point to consider in assessing how the public evaluates competing signals from different elite groups is *value predispositions*. He maintained that the recent expansion of postmaterialist values has led citizens to: evaluate environmental groups in a positive light and subsequently to be critical of the governments' handling of ecological issues; attach importance to ecological issues vis-à-vis other issue areas; perceive a need to change society; and make personal efforts to foster ecological awareness. Rohrschneider (1993) argues that the strength of the links between value predispositions, positive group evaluation and political consequences of such evaluation is strongest in Germany and the Netherlands – the countries where the environmental movement has enjoyed the highest visibility and been most active.

Stern *et al.* (1995: 1613) also underlined the importance of values in public evaluations of environmental messages. Rather than simply looking at the way value predispositions attract people to particular definitions of problems, they emphasize the manner in which interested groups consciously frame environmental conditions to appeal to existing commonly held values such as egotism and altruism. This is achieved primarily by 'emphasising or de-emphasising consequences and responsibility'. For example, if an issue is presented as having consequences for employment it focuses attention on the personal implications for directly affected citizens and the altruistic values of those who are not. Stern *et al.* (1995: 1613) note that 'by focusing attention in this way, issue entrepreneurs can use new information about the environment to influence the formation of new attitudes and to mobilise public opinion in support of their positions'.

In addition to appealing to values, environmental groups may be instrumental in *constructing* value predispositions consistent with their own worldview. Through relentless campaigns, group perspectives perhaps permeate the public subconscious to such an extent that the public becomes predisposed to accept these messages as valid, and to be more sceptical and critical of other actors' interpretations. In such circumstances groups would have successfully marketed themselves as the authoritative and trustworthy voice on environmental issues. Citing the work of Hansen, Hannigan (1999: 48) notes how Greenpeace won legitimacy by helping disseminate new scientific developments from researchers to the media; by becoming a 'shorthand signifier' for everything environmental – including environmental caring, green lifestyles, environmentally conscious attitudes; and by producing information that can be used strategically in public arenas.

The manner in which certain environmental problems have been perceived by the public in recent years lends support to a group-led explanation. It is hard to imagine the issue of GM food causing such public disquiet in the UK without: (1) the intervention of groups like Friends of the Earth and Greenpeace which publicized the issue through the media; and (2) the existence of specific background factors, particularly the precedent of the BSE crisis, which appears to have sensitized the public to the issue of food safety. In the US where comparatively little organized campaigning against GMOs has taken place, and where there is less of a history of food scares, the production of genetically modified food stuffs has not produced the same scale of public concern.

Dearing and Rogers (1996: 2, 3) point out that the conflictual nature of an issue helps make it newsworthy,[9] and that many social issues never become concerns: 'Problems require exposure – coverage in the mass media – before they can be considered "public" issues.' They claim that agenda setting is inherently a political process, 'At stake is the relative attention given by the media, the public, and policy-makers to some issues and not to others.' The first example of this process given by Dearing and Rogers (1996) is a brief US television news story on an African famine. They maintain that the *visual power* of the story can secure greater prominence in the news process than might otherwise be the case. The footage might influence millions to give aid, and many to seek a change in governmental policy.

Discussing the redefinition of smoking, Dearing and Rogers (1996: 4) note that 'Successful media advocacy essentially puts a specific problem, framed in a certain way, on the media agenda.' They (1996: 50) conclude that a broad range of research supports the simple conclusion that 'the media agenda sets the public agenda.'[10] Of course the media too pick up cues from groups!

In contradiction to the reflection position, Dearing and Rogers (1996: 43) note that research in agenda setting has found a very weak link between what are termed 'real-world indicators' and media coverage. One reason for this is the existence of what has been termed *artificial* or *pseudo news* when groups generate coverage by 'stunts' or direct action.

For many potential and actual group members the primary source of information available is the group itself. The view on the value of the outputs is likely to be influenced by the version of reality that the group provides. Environmental groups highlight the serious problem for the planet caused by the destruction of the rainforest or the creation of the hole in the ozone layer. These may be both real and serious problems, but it can be seen as a one-sided summary of the technical debate that is skilfully presented by the relevant groups. Newsletters and other communications are a means by which the group can manipulate the evaluation of issues and its role in addressing them.

Marketing membership

As outlined in Chapter 2, Olsonian-type membership emphasized personal material reward as the primary incentive-generating involvement. However, even where individuals are seen as rational maximizers, the sorts of interests they wish to advance may not be as narrow as Olson set out. This notion of an expanded range of benefits subsumes non-material incentives such as 'feeling better about oneself' – an expressive satisfaction in having acted. Far from having simple hierarchies of goals, it may be that individuals have mixed views and the 'constructionist' group and its activities help determine which prevails. In short, it is clear that the *supply-side action* of groups is crucial.

This book proposes that interest group activities can substantially determine the size of the membership: *groups can alter the level of demand for membership*. In previous work (Jordan and Maloney, 1996, 1997, 1998) and in Chapter 4 there is a growing body of empirical evidence to substantiate these claims. Accordingly, group activity combined with the relatively low subscription costs takes the supporting/joining decisions below a 'threshold of (economic) rationality': that is below the 'cost' of exhaustive analysis. The marketing approach to group membership is not necessarily antithetical to the orientation of Olson*. Group size or income is not simply a matter of the aggregation of individual decisions. (Public) Interest groups have adopted the tactics of merchandizing organizations and are simply reflecting a rational choice response to their position. They have evolved into low cost/low demand organizations to increase the likelihood that *rational* individuals will join.

Groups are active in their own account in a way not set out by Olson. They are organized to stimulate applications and not simply to respond to spontaneous joining. Groups find themselves adopting two key marketing strategies: (1) they try to lower the cost and (2) they attempt to increase the potential members' (positive) evaluation of the group 'good'. There are a number of factors which encourage individuals to join: predisposition towards group goals; economic ability; frequency of the consideration of joining; the perception of monetary and time costs; the value of collective goods and collective bads; and perceptions of personal efficacy. These are factors that groups can manipulate.

This marketing approach is most closely associated with *endogenous* groups. Groups where the political issue is something like professional membership may be more suitable for Olsonian analysis. There the individual is likely to value the benefits and may be tempted to do so while free-riding. There is a need to connect the discussion of joining interest groups to the literature of social psychology rather than the economic rationality. A widespread collective interest does not itself generate a group. Johnson (1995: 28) argues, 'Rather, to understand the groups that exist, one must understand that there are organizers and recruiting strategies whose efforts must somehow interact with the attitudinal basis of support in the community.' The stress on marketing in this chapter

---

* See special issue of the European Journal of Marketing, vol. 30, nos. 10/11, 1996.

(and Chapter 4) attempts to explain the large increases in membership for some public interest groups. Groups are in a fierce competitive struggle for supporters/members. They seek to shape public perceptions of issues – and of themselves – in a process akin to a commercial brand war. 'Brands' are successful and enjoy premium pricing because they are trusted.

Professionalized public interest groups are particularly important in the argument about participation because it is such bodies that produce the large numbers of 'members' that appear so impressive in discussions about the decline of party and the creation of alternative modes of participation. But successful large-scale groups tend to be the ones that engage in marketing. Johnson (1995: 15) shows that the direct mail strategy in the US is associated with size. Six out of the seven largest groups in his sample of environmental groups used it.

Group determination of individual preferences

This chapter has challenged the paradigm which focuses on the individual and the range of incentives/disincentives that are relevant to the joining decision. Here individuals are presented as 'steerable' into various behaviours and even to different sides of an argument. Group activity influences the preferences that precede the putting of the membership decision onto the agenda. Moreover, groups actively construct *choice parameters*: that is groups persuade potential members the issue is important and manipulate downwards the perceptions of the costs of supportership/joining. In *Voice and Equality*, Verba *et al.* (1995: 133) note that frequently individuals become active 'because someone asked'. Data presented in Chapter 5 and in Jordan and Maloney (1997 and 1998) demonstrated not just the importance of being asked, but also the skewed nature (*targeting*) of the asking. The most professionalized organizations seek an attainable membership: not simply the predisposed, but those who have the necessary disposable income to fully indulge such predispositions. Thus Verba *et al.*'s (1995) observation is consistent with this stress on persuasion. However, one can take a step backwards when they suggest action arrives 'more or less spontaneously from individuals when they become excited about issues, connect politics to their basic interests, or get involved out of a sense of civic duty'. Such preferences may be traced back to group framing. Verba *et al.* (1995: 392) suggest that issue engagement stems from 'a personal stake' or 'caring deeply' about a particular political issue. This is indeed important. However, before much participation can take place, groups must exist as collective vehicles for citizen engagement. In short, this argument is an extension of a well-articulated perspective on participation: 'a moment's reflection shows that the people initiate little of what we normally call participation . . . Acts of participation are stimulated by elites – if not by the government, then by parties, interest groups, agitators, and organizers' (Nagel, 1987: 3; quoted in Rosenstone and Hansen, 1993). Thus Rosenstone and Hansen's (1993: 5) point that citizens' political involvement is 'not so much because of who they are but because of the political choices and incentives they are offered' is crucial. *Groups contribute to the construction of attitudes that lead to membership.*

In part this may be an answer to the paradox of participation that Olson presented. Insofar as concern is the result of presentation by a group, it is a minor extension to say that activity too can be group determined. Membership, other support of groups (at least some groups, some of the time), is not the result of somehow overcoming Olsonian calculation and free-riding – it reflects the social construction of an interest. It might be argued that it is still logically possible to free-ride a constructed interest, but the nature of some non-material incentives makes free-riding inherently unlikely.

4
The Business of Building Group Membership

organizations are most effective in persuading their members to support the group financially when they match incentive offerings with the members' incentive demands. Incongruence between supply and demand provokes the withdrawal of contributions from members of all kinds of associations (Knoke, 1990: 140).

Membership levels reflect the willingness to expend resources to contact prospective members and the ability to offer them something that they want in return for their dues payment (Johnson, 1998: 38).

We can win here too, but only with your help (Liberty advertisement against ID cards, *Times*, 28 June 2005).

On 1 May 2005 the *Sunday Times* reported that Prince Charles had written to a landowner supporting the construction of wind turbines by Ecotricity. The article said he did so at the instigation of the Soil Association which was concerned that the landowner, who opposed the construction, might withdraw an offer of a large donation to the Soil Association because it also had a deal getting £16 for every Soil Association member who signed up with Ecotricity. Sponsorship deals are common in the group world, but membership (or supporter) income is usually still at the core of group finances. In the same week the Ramblers' Association advertised for support by opposing the development of wind farms. They believed that such developments were unpopular with some pro-environment citizens and were attempting to secure the anti-wind farm niche of the environmental market. Groups have become heavily professionalized in finding (new) money, seeking 'old fashioned' members and in securing other sources of funding. In 2005, the European Union was investigating the 'renting' of charity and group logos by food manufacturers and other bodies to apply to their packaging or advertising. While the groups claim the relationship was simply philanthropic, manufacturers imply endorsement by the group of the healthiness of the food, or approval of the humane or ethical treatment of animals, etc. Groups defended their rights to this *income stream*. Such business-speak is significant (see below).

This chapter extends an interpretation of *interest groups as artefacts*. In line with the premise set out in Chapter 3, membership is seen as being actively *created* rather than passively received by groups (i.e. the Ramblers' tapping anti-wind sentiment). Recruitment methods and the tools of mobilization have altered dramatically in recent years (media technology and direct mail) making it much easier to contact potential members (*customers*). Arguably these changes have transformed the *implications*, and *nature*, of group support.[1] Fukuyama (1995: 311–312) highlights that for Schumpeter (1951) modern capitalism was a process of *creative destruction*; with technological progress, 'markets expand and new forms of organization emerge'. Similarly new technology has been a *creatively destructive* process within the interest group and voluntary association systems. As the tools of mobilization have undergone a dramatic technological transformation we have witnessed the culling of many small-scale groups operating on national level issues, to be replaced by large-scale professionalized *protest business*-type organizations. For example, in the UK, organizations such as Friends of the Earth (FoE), Greenpeace and the Royal Society for the Protection of Birds (RSPB) have, to a certain extent, flourished at the expense of *both* smaller and/or more local environmental groups. The ten-fold increase in membership of the RSPB in the UK between 1971 and 2006 (98,000 in 1971, to 441,000 in 1981 to 85,200 in 1991 to over 1 million by 2006) reflects the adoption, and success, of regular high-profile press advertising and increased sophistication in recruitment rather than an independent pro-bird change in public attitudes. In such large-scale bodies the professionalized business approach affects thought, language and action. From a political science perspective, the business language of these organizations is more appropriate than any discourse of democracy.

As established in Chapter 1 the traditional mental construct of a group was of a locally based unit, member financed and dominated. While such types of organizations have a nostalgic appeal that feeds some of the pro-group social capital-inspired literature of recent years, they are now overshadowed by *protest business*-type-organizations. Mundo (1992) tellingly uses the term *mail order* groups to capture the prevalence of a direct mail recruiting strategy by large high-profile organizations. 'Publics which one may expect to have mobilized via more social network means, have in fact grown in size and stature via direct mail, and television and radio contacting'[2] (Maloney, 1999: 109). Loomis (1983: 173) argued that direct mail and televised appeals were the 'technological foundation of the grass-roots politics of the New Right'. While Guth *et al.*'s (1995: 72) survey of five prominent religious citizen groups in the US confirmed Loomis' argument

> Religious TV and radio, along with direct mail, mobilize conservatives directly for Christian Right causes, and recruit them into specific organizations . . . The role of the clergy as a source of information and mobilization is not altogether obvious . . . ministers and priests are not cited as a source of information by a major in any group . . . interest groups provide a political vehicle not matched by local churches, no matter how successfully they fulfil activists' spiritual needs.

The advent of the Internet has added a new tool to organizations' recruitment and mobilization armoury. It gives groups an additional presence in a widely expanding area and as van de Donk *et al.* (2004: 15) highlight it can be used 'to keep their (physically distant) members informed, [and] to present themselves to outsiders via homepages'.

Thus, Hayes (1986: 134) notes that major modern groups diverge from traditional conceptions – many groups are 'staff organizations' comprised of *checkbook members* 'lacking any face-to-face contacts with other members in a common setting'.[3] The low participation, cash-cow supporter is commonplace. As early as 1977 Berry's survey (1977: 188) found leaders viewing their members as 'supportive rather than participatory'.

Skocpol (2003: 134) summarizes these recent trends:

> All in all, the very model of what counts as effective organization in US politics and civic life has changed very sharply. No longer do most leaders and citizens think of building, or working through, state and nationwide federations that link face-to-face groups into state and national networks. If a new cause arises, entrepreneurs think of opening a national office, raising funds through direct mail and hiring pollsters and media consultants . . . Organizational leaders

have little time to discuss things with groups of members. *Members are a nonlucrative distraction* (italics added).

This is in fact an observation about modern, rather than, simply American groups. As the leader–follower relationship sets the level of internal democracy within groups, these new recruiting strategies and practices have implications for the broader theme of this book. Major contemporary groups are unlikely to conform to the traditional interest-group model where members have policy-making influence and are provided with inter-personal opportunities that might shape their attitudes. The new type groups may offer some annual meeting activities, 'but these gatherings are realistically open to only a small percentage of the group's membership, and then only on a very infrequent basis' (Hayes, 1986: 136). It may simply be the case that only a miniscule proportion might want to *consume* such involvement. For example, Amnesty International, UK, has some 150,000 members and an additional 100,000 financial supporters; however, around 500 members attend the Annual General Meeting (AGM) (www.amnesty.org.uk/content.asp?CategoryID = 10084, accessed 19 September 2006 and interview) and the RSPB's AGM attracts under 1000 members from a total support in excess of one million (interview). The Ramblers' democratic proposition is 'Join our group if you support our policy positions' – not, 'Join us and determine our policies . . . '.

As Walker (1991: 49) noted, 'The process of mobilization cannot be fully understood until we realize that mobilizing efforts often come from the top down, rather than the bottom up.' The argument advance here takes that cue and develops it following Mitchell (1979) who maintained that the outcome of the informal and perhaps implicit, pre-joining cost–benefit analysis done by potential group members is influenced by the activities of the groups.[4] Groups can, for example, keep the initial cost low so that the potential member is rarely being asked for significant sums of money at any one point. Bosso (2003: 409, 410) notes that groups need not grow by expanding their membership but can get 'low start' individuals to 'rise up the pyramid of support'. As Mitchell (1979) points out, the costs of time to the individual in finding out about, and applying for membership of the group, can be greatly reduced by availability of direct mailing applications, leaflet dispensers and so forth. Successful large-scale groups do the 'leg work' for potential members and seek to place the joining decision on citizens' agendas.

Professionalized interest representation requires significant financial resources and therefore usually needs to be underpinned by professionalized fund-raising. One recent advertisement for fund-raising via the Internet by a company called *Votenet* boldly stated that 'Campaigning *is* Fundraising'. But raising income is itself costly. Horton (1990) estimated that 48 cents out of every dollar raised through direct mail goes straight back into funding more fund-raising (quoted in Bosso, 1995: 109). Groups now draw on technical, scientific and legal expertise in promoting their causes, and this expertise usually needs to be funded by applying similar professionalism to recruitment. As Moe (1980b: 39) argued, group managers are in a position

> Analogous to that of the business firm whose products are virtually unknown to the consuming public. In order to sell his products – and thus in order to enlist new group members and retain old ones – he [*sic*] must somehow contact customers, inform them of the benefits he has to offer, and establish the terms of exchange.

The argument that many public interest groups have (particularly since the 1960s) successfully mobilized a *viable* proportion of citizens into membership has two important consequences. It means large numbers have been recruited even though initially their predisposition was latent. And low levels of success in terms of the percentage of predisposed potential members recruited can be significant in absolute numbers. For example, Greenpeace UK had around 221,000 supporters in 2004 but, arguably, there were thousands (if not millions) more among the general population who were at worst not antagonistic towards the group and supportive of environmental protection. Viewed in this way, one might argue the group has recruited only a fraction of its recruitment pool which nonetheless provides sufficient financial support and the appearance of representativeness. *A relatively weak solution to the collective action problem can be sufficient. Groups need only recruit a small proportion of the potential membership to have a viable protest business. A group can be 'big enough' to be policy relevant even though it is well below a feasible size.*

In response to an increasingly professionalized and competitive marketplace groups now try to reduce their reliance on membership contributions by securing income from other sources: for example patronage (government and other institutional support) and the sale of goods and services, etc. Reducing dependence on membership income also reduces the significant costs of servicing members. Bosso (1995: 107) reports a survey of 248 conservation and environmental organizations in 1989 in the US which found that membership dues accounted for only 32% of total revenue, while foundation grants, corporate gifts, federal grants and contracts and state grants and contracts accounted for 24%, a further 19% of revenue came from other individual contributions. His data showed that 60% of FoE (US), 56% of the Izaak Walton League, 42% of the Natural Resources Defense Council and 30% of the Environmental Defense Council funds came from institutional sources. Interestingly, even city-based associations are heavily dependent on non-membership income. Kriesi (2006) reported that in six medium-sized European cities[5] on average only 38% of voluntary associations' income came from membership dues and 10% cent from donations. Some 12% came from government sources and a further 8% from sales of services. Groups thus try to 'solve' the membership problem by increasing other sources of income. (Nevertheless groups also still want to maximize support from individuals: for example Oxfam needs individual volunteers to staff its shops.) Even if membership contributions become a relatively marginal part of a group's income stream it does not mean that it is non-crucial. It can be the difference between solvency and bankruptcy.

Obtaining, then maintaining, membership is key for many (public) interest groups. Cohen (1995: 177, 235) argued that many 'organizations operate on a revolving door model – to compensate for high drop-out, they have to work hard to attract new recruits'. The *illusion* of stability in the group world is usually the net result of balancing large-scale entry and exit. Drop-out rates of between 30 and 40% are seen as healthy by many public interest groups. As Rothenberg (1988: 1129) notes, getting new members 'is fundamental for long-term organizational prosperity'. However, 'signing them up in the first place is only half the battle'. There is also the fact that in many instances the cost of providing incentives at the point of joining exceeds the initial membership fee. Groups need to retain members beyond the first year to recoup the costs of attracting the member in the first place. Partly the renewal decision can be avoided by getting supporters to contribute by direct debit/automated payment. They do not have to act to renew, but to the contrary they have to act to end their support (see Jordan and Maloney, 1997 and Rothenberg, 1988).

While initially organizational efficiency might not seem to be a vital value for groups, of course groups need to be run well to survive. Grant Thompson of the Conservation Foundation in the US observed:

You should never forget . . . that you're in the goodworks business. If you don't pay attention to the business, you won't be doing the good works very much longer (cited in Rawcliffe, 1992: 5).

This often involves them reflecting market organization-like character-istics. Texts exist for running groups as business organizations. Dees, Emerson and Economy edited *Enterprising Nonprofits: a Toolkit for Social Entrepreneurs*. Chapters included 'Understanding and Attracting Your "Customers" ' with passages such as 'Social entrepreneurs don't always use the word *customer*, but the most successful ones focus as intently on their participants as smart businesses focus on their customers' (Dees *et al.*, 2001: 199).

The argument in the *Protest Business* (1997) was based on information from four main organizations. Later, this book reports data on a larger sample of groups and tests the tentative generalizations to build on the Protest Business examples (see Chapters 5 and 6). The central supply-side thesis is that most large examples in the group world 'recruit' rather than 'receive' members: organizations get the membership they seek as opposed to accepting those who spontaneously present themselves. The 'science' of recruitment means that the identification of a particularly distinctive subset of citizens can be very detailed. Shaiko (1999: 184) points out that 'an organization could request a list of 10,000 names with the following characteristics: white, female, married with grown chil-dren out of the home, Gold Card holder, home owner, registered Demo-crat, household income over $100,000, purchases merchandise through catalog mail-ordering, contributes money to political campaigns, wears glasses, reads *Newsweek*, and drive a foreign car'. Such a 'tailored' list, Shaiko says, will cost an organization a great deal more than regular rental rate of $75 per 1000 names, but the response rate is likely to be considerably higher – rising from as little as 1.5–2% to 15–20%. E-mail advertisements offer the services of organizations such as ListLocator and other suppliers of 'names'. Getting names is now a routine operation; it is a basic element in recruitment. In public services reform there has been interest in what has been termed *personalization* – a move away from top–down prescription and acceptance of individual preferences (Lead-better, 2004). Another term in the industry is *demassification*. Godwin (1988a: 13) said, 'Personalization touches recipients. They are far more likely to feel that the person or organization requesting something from them knows how they feel and what they value. Personalization makes people feel important and helps them perceive their contribution as significant.'

This type of group-initiated participation is in fact consistent with a broader understanding of mobilization. Rosenstone and Hansen (1993: 5) argue that while academic attention to the resources, interests and identifications of individuals tells only half the story, strategic mobilization gives a more complete picture. The democratic implications are significant. As Rosenstone and Hansen (1993: 7) note, 'in deciding who to mobilize, political leaders help to determine which people participate': that is those most likely to join and/or those with the deepest pockets.

This supply-side dimension diverges from the basic Olson-type rational choice cost–benefit approach to joining. In the supply-side interpretation the *chance to contribute* can be made rewarding, and contributing in itself is presented as satisfying. In practice, 'members' seem to have an exaggerated sense of their efficacy – they expect their action to influence the delivery of valued goals. Repeatedly, question-naire responses suggest that group members do not accept the free-riding premise that non-membership is marginal to the group (see Chapter 5). As stressed in Chapter 3, *group communications encourage beliefs that view membership as pivotal*. For example, a Greenpeace appeal to its lapsed members said:

> Greenpeace only exists because people like *you* continue to be supporters. Without *you* there is no Greenpeace. And without *your* past support, actions like the ones below may well have been impossible. We can't carry on unless our supporters, people like you, renew their support... Our actions in the future depend on you acting *now... Without you we're sunk. With you we can change the world* (original emphasis).

Invitations to join by modern-style 'new groups' are pitched differently from the 'policy influencing' appeal to membership that may have once been standard. This style is a response to what was described in Chapter 2 as the *free-riding* tendency among potential supporters. Through this lens, membership is not seen as 'natural' or 'inevitable'; groups do not expect (automatic) membership simply because the potential recruit agrees with group goals. An instinct to offer support on its own may not induce potential supporters to join, because they calculate the goal will be attained without their contribution. Groups have to overcome this non-joining inertia.

There are spectacular examples where *technique* appears pivotal. Putnam (2000: 157) compared the membership trends for two US organizations, the Sierra Club and the Izaak Walton League. In 1960, the League had 51,000 members and the Sierra Club only 15,000. The latter adopted direct mail for the next three decades and by 1990 their membership had risen to 560,000 while the League's remained at the same 50,000 level. Wilson (1995: 160) records that the US Chamber of Commerce maintained its political presence and membership in the 1970s despite high annual turnover through a sales staff of 50 – rather than simply passively accepting members. In contrast, Johnson (1998: 58–59) argued that Greenpeace US *lost* members from its peak of 2.35 million to 400,000 in 1997 as a direct result of its decision to reduce investment in direct mail, 'The change produced an almost immediate contraction in membership, which in turn set off cutbacks in staff and recruiting activity.' Johnson (1998: 59) also investigated the membership decline of another large US environmental group in the 1990s. In that case, the explanation was *not* a fall in the appeal of group goals or public concern, but staff reported:

> We had mismanagement in the membership department, it was internal problems... [they] rolled out with a direct mail campaign... without testing it, and it was not too successful, and then they used it again in another campaign... They stopped doing renewal telemarketing and they... cut the last two efforts of the renewal series plus two renewal wraps on the magazines they sent out.

These examples provide strong support for the contention that good marketing can generate membership and poor can undermine it. In fact, for large groups that there is (almost) iron law of active recruitment; groups only get large if they adopt the mechanisms of a pro-active strategy.

The recruitment imperative: The direct mail approach

There are various active recruitment methods open to pro-active professionalized groups – press or TV advertising, direct mail, face-to-face (direct dialogue). In this section we primarily discuss the direct mail approach. As set out in Chapters 2 and 3, the literature on group recruitment strategies has described and analysed three broad approaches by groups to encouraging support:

1. identifying the different incentives provided by membership organizations;
2. examining how groups manipulate the costs of membership and thereby alter the calculus of membership decisions;
3. examining what groups do to stimulate and construct attitudes that are represented by the groups.

Arguably direct mail is relevant in allowing groups to act on each of these dimensions and perhaps its adoption was the most significant technique during the period of group expansion from the 1960s to the 1990s. Indeed Bosso (1995: 113) contended that the use of direct mail by groups 'is ubiquitous and, apparently, essential', and Johnson (1995) showed that *the larger the group, the more likely they were to be dependent on mail recruiting* (see also Berry, 1984; Bosso, 1995; Godwin, 1988a, b; Johnson, 1995, 1998; Jordan and Maloney, 1997, 1998; Putnam, 2000: 156–171). Direct mail (direct marketing) 'spilled over' from business use and Allen (1997: 10) defined it as

> any form of one-to-one communication with potential customers. The ultimate objective of using any of these promotional tools will be to affect a sale but much of the communication will be to keep open a dialogue that is vital in long term relationship building.

However it is possible to exaggerate the business interpretation. Johnson (1998: 45) notes that *some* group leaders, especially those who are volunteers, 'want to view their organization as a spontaneous "bubbling up" of public sentiment and they deride the larger groups whose managers seek to be more professional and businesslike'. One size does not fit all. Not all groups – and certainly not all groups, all the time, for all their members – simply wish passive cash contributors.

The US environmental groups – the Defenders of Wildlife and the National Parks and Conservation Association – began using direct mail in the 1950s (Bosso, 1995: 113). By 1990, Greenpeace, USA, was mailing some 48 million letters a year (Putnam, 2000: 157). Direct mail at least partly explains the rapid growth of groups, including the Sierra Club and the American Association of Retired Persons and organizations such as Common Cause, the National Tax-payers' Union and the Environmental Defense Fund, which were founded upon direct mail and depend almost completely upon it (Godwin, 1992: 309). Johnson (1998: 47) found that the 28 organizations that reported using direct mail had contacted approximately 17.4 million non-members collectively. Such large numbers of citizens were no doubt contacted by more than one organization because many groups are chasing those with similar socio-demographic profiles and lifestyles. This further accentuates the cumulative political involvements of certain types of individuals and the non-involvement of others.

Our survey of British leaders of campaigning groups in Table 4.1 shows that 24% of organizations reported using direct mail and 8%

Table 4.1   How supporters are attracted to campaigning organizations

Individuals contact us directly on their own initiative	92%
Existing supporters encourage friends, relatives or colleagues to become supporters	84%
Supporters are attracted through local groups or branches	43%
Leaflets in organizations/institutions (e.g. libraries/hospitals)	51%
Newspaper advertising/inserts in magazines	33%
National television advertising	1%
Direct mail	24%
e-mail from your organization	11%
Internet: your own website	66%
Paid recruiters	8%
Promotion at events	7%
Other	21%

Note: $n = 229$. See Chapter 1 appendix for details: survey of all campaigning groups.

had paid recruiters ('direct dialogue'). Of the 66 organizations that used direct mail almost all (60) approached 'warm names' (i.e. an individuals whose lifestyle or purchasing habits suggest that they may be predisposed to join, or who have had some contact with the group but was not a supporter). One group said, 'The thing that works best for us are where there has been some kind of contact . . . '. One-third of responding groups bought in lists – as one interviewee put it, 'You can go to London and go shopping for names.' Groups may also swap names with other organizations (e.g. charities or campaigning groups). Amnesty International noted that around 30% of the names they used each year were from lists exchanged with other organizations whose members had an appropriate profile. One-third of the survey respondents identified potential members by targeting possible subgroups to contact. While larger organizations were more heavily represented among those who used direct mail (e.g. over 60% of organizations with a membership between 50,000 and 100,000), nevertheless around 25% of groups with less than 10,000 members also reported using it.

Table 4.1 is also interesting because it highlights the continued relevance of the Truman's proposition that members present themselves to organizations; that social networks are important; and the growing significance of the Internet – for groups of varying size. Although, as van de Donk *et al.* (2004: 15–16) argue, it is the 'large and powerful organizations' (*protest businesses*) that have been quick to exploit the advantages of information and communication technologies (ICTs). 'This process is enhanced by the fact that the big players have the financial means to buy the necessary hardware and to hire the specialists creating websites and running the systems.' These businesses have also recognized that

> these technologies are ... cheaper than distributing letters, papers, brochures, and calls for action by regular mail. Hence we should not be surprised that groups such as Greenpeace International, Friends of the Earth International and the World Wide Fund for Nature are among those who were early adopters of ICTs and continue to use them extensively (van de Donk *et al.*, 2004: 16).

While it is certainly the case that large-scale organizations have quickly sought to exploit the Internet to 'mobilize' supporters to take part in demonstrations, letter writing and e-mail campaign (cyberactivism), the Internet, as Table 5.1 (see below, p. 122) demonstrates, is not yet as vital a recruitment mechanism as direct mail: 21% of the largest category of groups (+50,000 members) identified direct mail as 'the most important' method of attraction and none of these groups cited e-mail or website. (In the other group categories: e.g. *small* (under 1000 members) and *medium* (between 1000 and 50,000 members) it is ranked near the bottom of the most important method of attraction.) Of course over time the significance of the Internet may rise and the importance of direct mail may decline; the Internet has much potential as a mechanism for recruiting support – certainly as a cheap alternative to direct mail. Currently, however, many group members do not have access to the Internet at home or do not use it as part of their membership.[6] Accordingly groups do not rank it as highly as direct mail.

Low cost participation

Ironically in terms of democratic expectations, one aspect of direct mail that encourages recruitment is that it allows a low cost form of political participation. Here 'cost' refers both to cash and time. In other words, the rather 'light' participation is not some sort of poor substitute for 'real' involvement, but it is what citizens want. Democratic theorists judge participation by the degree of personal involvement. *However, much group participation seems to be chosen because it is undemanding in terms of personal effort.* O'Shaughnessy and Peele (1985: 118) noted that direct mail 'offers involvement without wholesale commitment – the gratification of being part of a cause and privy to inside information, which is the gift of political participation, without the effort that usually purchases such reward'. This interpretation of group mobilization explains how viable organizations can be based on low public response rates and *that organizational participation is low because it suits both the group and the (under)mobilized* (see Chapter 6). (Of course activity is itself an incentive for *some* supporters. Thus Greenpeace invites those seeking greater involvement to become 'active supporters', or 'cyberactivists'.)

To the extent that the central Olsonian mobilization problem is that groups will mobilize only a small percentage of eligible support, the advantage of direct mail is that large numbers of those eligible can be contacted. A small percentage response from a large constituency can sustain an effective political presence and secure legitimacy and respectability. Direct mail is cost-effective in low response situations – especially if there is effective segmentation and targeting of the invitations.[7]

So how do (direct mail) groups generate interest and activate involvement (however mimimal)? Geller (1998: 30) describes the elements of a direct mail 'package' as follows:

1. The Outer Envelope
2. The Letter
3. The Brochure
4. The Lift Letter (lifts response rate of contact)
5. The Order Form
6. The Business Reply Card or Envelope.
7. The Catalogue.

Roberts and Berger (1989: 224–237) similarly outline the essentials of the direct mail package. (*The following section closely follows their account.*) The covering letter is seen as the most important ingredient. It aims to convey the message in straightforward language – using short words, clear sentences and paragraphs, and avoids jargon and technical terms. The letter is phrased in personal tones, it is not typeset, is complete with a postscript which emphasizes important benefits or a final call to action and is signed by an individual. Geller (1998: 35) stresses that the letter should be 'humanized' and O'Shaughnessy and Peele (1985: 121) note that it should seek to reinforce viewpoints and motivate involvement. Accordingly, 'it is often nourished *not by cogent argument but by emotion, since the appeal is to the converted*' (italics added). The accompanying brochure should be 4–6 pages in length, tell a complex story or explain costs/benefits at greater length using illustrations, and should be printed in colour. Stone (1997: 272–273)[8] offers a seven-step guide to effective appeal writing:

1. promise a benefit in your headline or first paragraph – your most important benefit
2. immediately enlarge on your most important benefit
3. tell the reader specifically what s/he is going to get
4. back up your statements with proof and endorsements
5. tell the reader what might be lost if action is not taken
6. rephrase your prominent benefits in your closing offer
7. incite action.

O'Shaughnessy and Peele (1985) argue that the Outer Envelope should make an appeal that intrigues the reader: that is it is hard to resist opening. Groups must also make it easy to respond to the invitation: they should use a simple 'response device'. The 'response device' can lower the 'costs' of 'participation', by simplifying the task of joining or donating.

Commonsense suggests that well-produced literature is important and Frazer-Robinson's (1999: 21) research demonstrated that a mailing with a good response device could pull in as much as 25% greater response than a similar mailing with a poor one. A good creative design may achieve a 35% larger response than a poorer one. However, the punch-line to Frazer-Robinson's argument was not to solely commend smart presentation. It was that these were the two *poorest performing* factors in a list of five variables:

Relative importance in increasing response to direct mail

1. Targeting 500%
2. Proposition 200%
3. Timing 100%
4. Creative design 35%
5. Response device 25%

Source: Frazer-Robinson (1999: 21).

Targeting 'the pitch' and timing are in his account key factors. If the invitation to join or contribute coincides with the urge felt by the individual, then direct mail may satisfy this wish to 'do something' at the apposite time. Thus during the build-up to the G8 summit and the Make Poverty History campaign in 2005, many organizations (such as the VSO) sought to exploit the focus on (African) poverty because it was a conducive environment to increase the response rate for particular appeals. The general campaigning heightened concern and particular campaigns allowed the public immediate opportunities to 'be active'.

Targeting and segmenting the audience: Finding the 'probables'

Targeting is the all-important aspect of securing a viable response rate. In his study of Common Cause, Rothenberg (1992: 71) noted how the group contacted 'only those citizens who it believes are most likely to join, to stay in the group, and to contribute more than the minimum dues'. Gosden (1985: 63) succinctly explains why efficient targeting and effective segmentation are crucial:

> some people are good prospects and some people are not prospects at all. To separate them is important. Let's take an example: If you are selling caviar and only one person in ten thousand likes caviar, can afford caviar, and is ready to buy now, there is no reason to advertise to the other 9999.

Groups focus their efforts not on those who need *most* persuading, but on those whose support they are *most* likely to obtain. For example, Rebecca Leuw, Direct Marketing Manager for Shelter said that her job involved 'a lot of numerical work, to segment databases and decide on which types of people to target for particular appeals' (*The Guardian*, 2 June 2003). The number contacted usually has to be large because even a carefully drawn list will be unlikely to produce response levels above 2–3%. In the direct mail campaign the difference between success and failure is very tight. Johnson (1995: 19) explains:

> If a group mails 10,000 pieces at $35 each, at a 1% rate the organization spends $35 dollars to recruit each individual member. The member pays $25 in the first year, so that the group not only loses money on the acquisition but also ends up providing the benefits of the group free during the first year. But the group expects between 30 and 50% of first-year members to renew, and the renewal rate climbs near 100% over the following three years. "So what you are doing is looking at the cumulative value over time of those hundred members".[9]

O'Shaughnessy and Peele (1985: 117) contend that *segmentation* is the 'critical property of direct mail because it identifies the "social differences among people" and the individual characteristics[10] that are more likely to generate a positive responsive' (Godwin, 1988a: 10–17). Direct mail aims to target markets much more precisely than the scattergun of blind random mailing. Indeed, Gosden (1985: 92) argued that direct marketing did not become efficient until segmentation 'entered the field'. Gosden (1985: 83) maintains that focussing on those who subscribe to certain periodicals is a technique used by groups to reach potential supporters spread throughout the country where there are no more precise means to communicate with them directly. Segmentation enables the (cost-effective) personalization of direct mail and all the advantages that brings. Frazer-Robinson (1999: 10) argues that the greater the degree of segmentation the more the organization avoids being seen as a 'junk mail business because you can use the smaller groups of similar people to change your message to suit what you know about them'. Large-scale groups are continually extending and honing their lists to maximize returns on investment, and to identity potential members wherever they may be 'hiding'.

Efficient recruitment depends on an effective contact list. A specialist niche industry creating and managing databases underpins many recruitment operations. At its simplest – and perhaps commonest – this is achieved by using address lists that have proven 'profitable' in related exercises. The assumption is that those who respond to one appeal are disproportionately likely to respond to another with similar aims. Targeting strategies are focussed on the *committed* sharing similar characteristics with current donors. A subpopulation is selected because it resembles the existing membership and is susceptible to an appeal that clones the membership population. This leads to apparent confirmation that this is the best target group – and efforts are likely to be redoubled in that area. Groups will contact those deep-pocketed intuitive givers because they are most likely to sign-up. The 'underrepresented' tend not to appear on mailing lists used by groups, 'because they lack the discretionary income and political interest to subscribe to news magazines or donate to causes that would place them on prospecting list' (Godwin, 1988a: 53).

There are various types of list:

- *Cold names* – These are lists (bought or exchanged) of individuals who have some identifiable (useful) characteristic or set of characteristics, such as being on a subscription list to a relevant magazine.

- *Warm names* – Those who have already responded to the organization. Prior contact will be exploited. (For example, the RSPB follow
  up the 'warm names' left on the visitors' logbook at their bird
  observation reserves as a source of new members.)

Majeska (2001: 203, 139) argues that segmentation makes it appear
that an individual is being selected – rather than a market sector.
Though recipients might not notice they are being influenced (person-
alized), direct mail, based on segmentation, aims to achieve much
better results than undifferentiated 'junk mail'. Direct mail is a *pseudo
personal* communication tailored to 'fit' the targets (the 'personalisation
process'). For example, Maarek (1995) says the suburban dweller may get
a paragraph oriented to commuting problems, while a different (more
appropriate) paragraph on, say, pollution might be inserted for the
urban inhabitant. Godwin (1988a: 13) observed how this ersatz intimacy
'touches recipients' and 'makes people feel important and... perceive
their contributions as significant'. He (1998a: 13–14) cites a mailing
from the President of the Sierra Club to past contributors:

> Your support in the past... [their name], has been crucial to our
> success. I sincerely thank you for your generosity. We can be proud of
> the Sierra Club's accomplishments... Our unparalleled record over
> the past 91 years would not have been possible without your financial
> support. We are counting on you to help us continue.[11]

Not all groups need direct mail: it may be they know with confidence
their actual potential membership. A trades union, for instance, can
determine and communicate with its potential membership. They are
known and can be approached directly. On the other hand a group
attempting to garner support for something like anti-abortion/pro-life
is not likely to have available a 'map' of a well-defined and pre-set
potential constituency. They could try press advertising that targeted
media outlets that might capture the same sort of constituency (in the
anti-abortion area *The Catholic Herald* and other conservative outlets).
Press advertising (and television) is purchased where there are attractive,
well-identified segments of the population where the group thinks it will
recruit well. Direct mail is then different in degree only from press or
TV targeting. The more precisely the desired individuals can be defined
and identified, the more reason to approach them individually.

Direct mail can link particular campaign themes to particularly
receptive audiences. The *Guardian* (14 June 2001) noted, 'Every charity

marketing manager lives in fear of spending thousands, or even millions, on a donor recruitment campaign that doesn't hit the mark. But increasingly charities are finding that highly targeted campaigns carrying a smaller marketing spend can produce attractive returns on investment.' The article described how Muslim Aid ran its 1999 Ramadam campaign, which attracted an award from Royal Mail for its effective use of direct marketing. Judges praised the mailing for demonstrating big impact on a small budget. Muslim Aid used the fasting month as an opportunity to send a copy of its annual report, information about new extensions to gift aid and an Islamic calendar to around 39,000 supporters, each of whom had made at least one donation since 1995. Including postage, the mailing cost Muslim Aid £25,000 (equivalent to around 65p per mailing), but over £600,000 was donated, growing to around £1 million with gift aid. Clearly a spectacular example, but more modest returns would still be good business – the Muslim Aid case illustrates what is achievable. If it were simply a matter of utilizing such techniques all groups would be well resourced, but the skill of application, identification, targeting and segmenting of a realizable support is crucial.

The testing of the message

Direct mail anticipates reactions. Focus groups with existing supporters, surveys of lapsed members, polling of non-members, identifies arguments that will maximize mobilization. It is risky for the group to simply *assume* arguments are effective, thus the initial 'joining' mail shot is *pre-tested*. Organizations do not 'guesstimate' their most attractive propositions. The pre-test ensures satisfactory response rates before incurring the full expenditure required by the large-scale exercise. Groups may in fact mail various versions to see what works best; or to assess to what extent certain omissions impact on response rates (Johnson, 1998: 49). (Godwin (1988a: 3) ascribes the invention of this in a political context to the Eisenhower campaign in 1952, sending a different fundraising letter to 10 groups of 10,000 to discover the relative value of the Korean war as a theme to various constituencies.) Eventually a 'banker' or 'control' is established – the best performer: an average response rate is about 0.35–1.2% for cold lists (with 0.5 considered good) and 1.5–2.0% for warm lists. Not all groups can afford to do experimentation, but these may be the groups that in fact require the information most.

While the Olson snap-shot-type description of the joining process presents the decision as rational or irrational – individuals may come to different conclusions if they are encouraged to reconsider. Repetition of invitation is thus another important direct mail dimension. Experience has shown groups that several contacts are needed to 'squeeze' a response from an identified population. The RSPB representative interviewed said, 'Getting them to join the first time is quite difficult. Research tells us it takes about three exposures to RSPB... to actually get someone to start thinking about joining.' So the group mails targeted individuals three or four times. As Godwin (1988a: 12) points out, direct mail allows for repetition more than face-to-face contact 'without embarrassment'. Prior donors are the best quality contacts. The group responses to non-renewal are similar to those of joining. Groups will try to stress the importance of continued support and multiple contacts may be necessary. Gosden (1985: 67–70) observes that, particularly in fund-raising, repetition can reap rewards: people are 'ready to give to something every six weeks'. There is concern that over-solicitation leads to 'donor fatigue'.[12] But this is too important a revenue stream to be discarded.

Bosso (1995: 116–117) noted this problem of (direct mail) 'over-grazing'. Groups are using the same mailing lists, bought from the same firms, and some individuals receive a 'torrent of mail' that can make them stop donating. Accordingly, some groups have altered their approach. For example, Greenpeace US adopted target marketing: focusing on sending direct mail to the most loyal donors and then adopting door-to-door canvassing as well as telemarketing for other areas (Bosso, 1995: 117). Another group, Conservation International, actually stopped direct mail in 1990 and attempted instead to make its relationship with existing members stronger while simultaneously cultivating funding from other sources such as foundations (Bosso, 1995: 117). Despite such examples test after test 'proves frequency [of contact] helps, not hurts, total programs' (Gosden, 1985: 68).

Massaging the message? The power of the negative

Campaign groups need to publicize their existence and convince predisposed citizens that their membership is pivotal. Accordingly, member appeals increase/exaggerate individuals' political efficacy. However, groups have found that in many instances negative appeals have a greater pulling power than positive ones. Citizens are more inclined to participate to stop a collective bad (threats or fears) than to generate a collective good (Mitchell, 1979). Mitchell (1979: 99) defines public bads as 'entities such as polluted air and water, which have a negative value for individuals and which, once created, are potentially available to everyone in society'. A public bad has a 'disutility' for the individual

(Mitchell, 1979: 112); it is about 'an individual's fear or distaste about litter, polluted air, the extinction of endangered species, the flooding of a valued river valley, the clear-cutting of a scenic wild area, the potential for a nuclear catastrophe'. Godwin (1992: 311) notes how threats build on the basic 'psychological axiom' that people 'will do more to prevent the loss of something they already have than to get something that they might obtain in the future'. The 'here' and 'now' is more tangible and has a greater pull than 'jam tomorrow'. Hansen (1985: 81) argues along similar lines and relates this to Truman's (1951: 26–43) emphasis on the motivational force of socio-economic disturbances. Groups therefore look for crisis or situations they can use to increase support in this way.

Analysing the appeals that environmental groups made, Mitchell (1979: 113–114) argued that bads have attention-catching characteristics: 'visibility, irreversibility, potential catastrophic consequences, and immorality' and will be particularly good for images or photographs on television. Furthermore, bads have 'a very strong no-exit quality to them'. Individuals cannot escape their negative effects, and groups draw on this in their communication material. Godwin (1988a: 24) noted how 'provocative and acrimonious language' (and pictures) run throughout group mailings. They use emotional drama/pictures to attract attention. 'Various wildlife and environmental groups use photographs of the killing of baby seals and the butchering of dogs for food in much the same way as pro-life groups have used photographs of mangled foetuses and bloody operating rooms to attract attention and obtain contributions.' Wilson (1995: 154) argued that the growth of the National Association of Manufacturers in the 1930s 'best illustrates the threat-oriented nature of general business associations . . . '. He pointed to the sharp increase in support when it substituted its emphasis on expanding business opportunities for a militantly anti-trades union posture. He quotes Gable, 'When the common enemy was discovered, the NAM experienced new life.'

The pull of the negative has wider implications. It is likely to influence the nature of the membership and the political opportunities available to the group. Those who Godwin (1992: 319) interviewed 'made it clear' that the reason they chose issues according to visibility was due to the group being dependent on direct marketing. Accordingly, some direct mail–based groups may be less consensual in their policy-making orientation because the members might be activated by conflict. Groups which obtained over 60% of their members, or 40% of their income, through direct mail focused on emotional issues to receive greater media coverage (Godwin, 1992: 318–319). Those based on social networks, while still interested in media coverage, 'choose issues that maximise their expertise and have substantial impact'; their focus is more on what will have an end result (Godwin, 1992: 319). Thus Bosso (1995: 111) noted how Greenpeace USA is often criticized on the grounds that its 'agenda is shaped powerfully by whatever new eco-crisis it can exploit in the millions of pieces of mail it sends out annually'. This 'raises the concern that groups may focus less on what is really important than on what appeals most to their contributors' (Bosso, 1995: 115). Komatsu and Misaki (2001: 119) argued that such intellectual inertia is partly prompted by financial dependence on emotional campaigns:

> 'Save the Whales' campaigns have been the most effective tool for their revenue. Once misguided by the anti whaling propaganda, the gullible public has donated generously to these NGOs... So, these NGOs end up producing ostentatious campaigns for 'Save the Whales'. The more they misguide the public, the more money flows into their coffers (cited in Kawashima, 2004: 9).[13]

Peter Wilkinson, founder of the 'Save the Whales Campaign' (and former chair of Greenpeace UK), conceded:

> The problem is, of course, that the conservation group cannot turn around now and say, 'We sanction whaling', because they've made such an issue out of saying to their supporters, 'We will stop every whale being killed'... Now to say that 'we accept a limited amount of whaling' is not tenable (quoted in Kawashima, 2004).

Cynics would argue that whaling has generated a significant anti-whaling 'industry' and ironically without whaling there would be no need for anti-whaling groups. Kawashima (2004: 10) quotes Ray Gambell, the former Secretary of the International Whaling Commission:

> One of the extraordinary things about the whaling issue is that... There are more than one hundred NGOs accredited as observers to the IWC meeting. Most of them have to raise funds from the public. If there was no whaling... what would all these NGOs do? They would be out of a job.

However, given the professionalized nature of many of these bodies in all likelihood they would seek alternative 'business opportunities' in the animal welfare field.

There are other externalities of emphasizing collective bads. It may increase political alienation. Godwin's (1988a: 33) content analysis of mailings found that opponents are portrayed as 'enemies' who want to destroy the values that the recipient of the mail are assumed to hold dear. 'Propaganda techniques pervade direct mailings, tapping emotions designed to generate an immediate response, not to help think through a complex issue.' Groups seek to demonize opposition.

Kawashima[14] (2004: 3) notes:

> direct mail is not a panacea but a powerful medicine that has a strong side effect. In order to maintain present supporters as well as attracting potential supporters, environmental organizations which rely heavily on direct mail are, to a large extent, destined to target noticeable issues that are visibly appealing and simple – in other words, the issues that are media-genic... Issues that are important for (the) ecosystem but not 'media-friendly'... are often neglected... If dramatic issues are not found at hand... media-genic issues have to be created, or mediocre issues have to be overstated or dramatized.

However, many campaigning organizations are increasingly drawn into collaborative relations with business and Government. Bosso (1988: 17) saw the tendency to compromise as reflecting the maturation of the environmental lobby: that the chemical industry also no longer dismissed environmentalists as 'hopeless modern Luddittes' as environmental values were recognized as 'mainstream'. He thought that the environmental side abandoned simplistic 'devil' theories of corporate intentions and actions and admitted more readily that 'economic imperatives' had to enter into solutions. Moreover, there has been, Bosso (1988: 17) notes, a professionalization of lobbying techniques and strategies on the environmental side:

> Environmental groups are no longer run by volunteers longer in zeal than Washington experience, but instead by paid professionals who both know the policy-making game and are prepared to stick with it over the long-haul... The contemporary relations between environmental and corporate lobbies now resemble less a holy war – where 'good' is pitted against 'evil' – than the dynamics found in any lobbying situation.

Bosso (1988) argued that while environmentalists had long assumed that transparent political processes were superior, they found that public forums encourage 'grandstanding' and deals that required compromises were perhaps easier to conclude in private. Such a 'balanced' treatment of issues may increase policy influence at the cost of member mobilization. Back stairs lobbying is not as effective in recruiting terms as demonstrative symbolic action. Arguably the *Make Poverty History* campaign in 2005 contributed more to issue definition and awareness than policy action.

Finally, collective bads also have implications for Olson's by-product theory. As Mitchell (1979: 121) argues,

> Olson's denial of the motivating role of these goods and bads in his by-product theory is incorrect. In a situation where individuals have a high disutility for public bads that they are unable to escape, where they have imperfect information, and where the cost of contributing to a lobby is low, the act of contributing is consonant with a rational strategy of seeking to minimize the maximum regret.

Face-to-face recruiting

Direct mail may have reached saturation point. Within the past decade face-to-face[15] direct dialogue contact has become prevalent. This new industry already has a professional (self-regulatory) body – The Public Fundraising Regulatory Association (PFRA) – with over 60 members. The PFRA describes its focus as being on direct contact with donors through face-to-face fund-raising on high streets and door-to-door canvassing, and generating *pledges through direct debit or banker's order* (automated payments). While many of the clients are charities rather than membership groups, the line is very blurred as many organizations on both sides are essentially seeking a stable set of contributors rather than 'members'. In 2002 on-street agents persuaded 700,000 individuals to commit via standing order to generate some £240 million over five years (*Times*, 21 December 2004). A donation might cost the recipient group £50 from the on-street firm and so donors are only 'profitable' if they let their commitment run for several years. These operations to secure direct debits are only possible because this avoids restrictions on soliciting for cash donations – but in any case a direct debit is much more valuable to a group than a one-off payment. When large numbers of supporters are claimed for British charities and campaigning bodies (as well as direct mail), the basis of 'membership' may well be the response to *solicita-*

tion by street recruiters rather than a decision by a potential member to actively seek out the organization.

Whereas Direct Mail targeted the audience (segmentation), the face-to-face recruiters have a more blanket approach, but they are at least subconsciously selective in their contacts. Young people may relate better to other young people – or a different technique can be used with the elderly in exploiting the age gap. Organizations such as GIFT advertise for 'full-time Street Fundraisers' (£8.17–£13.82 per hour). An advertising slogan in December 2004 was, 'Outside at 2 degrees Centigrade You'll never feel warmer.' The implication is that the staff will feel good about themselves as well as earning money. Another company, DialogueDirect, says on its website that it is one of the UK's leading face-to-face (or direct dialoguing) fund-raising agencies. (The nature of the business may well be better captured by the term 'Direct Debit' than 'Direct Dialogue'.) In 2002 it said that

> We work in partnership with charities and not-for-profit organizations. This method of fundraising starts with the idea that charities and NPOs need to build a valuable long-term relationship with their supporters and that committed support is best gained initially by directly engaging individuals in a personal face-to-face dialogue. We pioneered this method of fundraising in Europe in partnership with Greenpeace in the mid-1990s. DialogueDirect launched in the UK in 2000 with a successful test campaign for Greenpeace. Since then we have represented more than 15 social, environmental, and medical charities and non-profit organizations. These include Greenpeace, Barnardo's, WaterAid, Medecins Sans Frontieres, Mencap, Scope and more recently, Amnesty International.

Web-based material from DirectDialogue, in 2004, said:

> DialogueDirect pioneered the concept of face-to-face fundraising in Europe, in close partnership with Greenpeace who continue to be one of our major partner organizations.

> *Cathy Anderson* of Greenpeace said, 'DialogueDirect allows Greenpeace to reach new groups of people that have not been attracted by conventional marketing. Because of the success of face-to-face recruitment we have over 60,000 new supporters, all giving regular, reliable financial support to Greenpeace.'

Stephen Last, of the Soil Association, said, 'We embarked on our first face-to-face recruitment campaign last year when we used Dialogue-Direct to recruit 1,000 supporters. I have been consistently impressed with the quality of service, and we are using them again this year to recruit a further 2000 supporters.'

Michael Naidu, Direct Marketing Officer for MENCAP, said, 'In partnership with DialogueDirect, Mencap aims to offer better services and support to people with a learning disability, by recruiting well-informed and loyal regular givers.'

Finally DialogueDirect's website also says:

> Our face-to-face fundraisers or 'Dialoguers' as we call them, work in public and private sites, raising money for our not for profit (NPO) and charity partners. Their role is to inform potential donors about the aims of our charitable partners' latest campaigns and encourage them to offer their support through regular monthly financial contributions... They work for one NPO/charity at any one time, enabling an in-depth understanding of the organization that they are representing... This is your chance to make your own contribution to something worthwhile. You travel in teams throughout the UK, having fun, forging new friendships, working hard and making a difference.

Though this technique is motivated by fund-raising rather than membership creation, the main point is this is not aimed at one-off 'charity tin' sort of contributions. The average donor will continue to give for five years. Face-to-face fund-raising it is not only financially effective, but it changes the demographics of giving – being particularly effective in motivating the young. In 2002, 350,000 members of the public set up direct debits through such contacts. By 2003 the PFRA was claiming 690,000 donors in the previous year. The *Guardian* described how for the housing charity Centrepoint face-to-face donor recruitment resulted in 3000 new supporters of whom 85% were under 35. Greenpeace registered 25,000 supporters through a street campaign in 2001 and half were in their 20s and 30s (*Observer*, 8 March 2002). The PFRA (*Charity Times News*, 16 June 2003) cited a Henley Management Centre study estimating the average lifetime value of each new donor as £350. The recruiting company may get six months or even a year of the income as their fee. Therefore for the NPO (non-profit organization) the longer the relationship with the donor the better, as the percentage of the recruitment cost will diminish over time.

An article by Anushka Asthana (*Guardian*, 8 March 2003) described how 'You may have seen the sort on your local High Street. Strategically stationed to ensure attempts at evasion are fruitless, they are usually young, bright-faced and impeccably polite. They wear bibs. They carry clipboards. They smile a lot. Many describe them as the most annoying people in Britain.' She described being trained as a 'chugger' (charity mugger). Asthana says the pay is a flat rate with no commission, but crucially – targets have to be met – these may be seven new donors per day (*Guardian*, 20 June 2002). Asthana said:

> We were taught how to approach the public: ask people if they have a minute for the cause, introduce yourself, tell them the problems facing the charity, the proposed solutions and then be upfront in asking for money . . . It's not an easy job: although it may be for a good cause, chuggers are trained to be as tough as any other salesperson vying to relieve shoppers of their hard-earned cash.

The *Guardian* (8 March 2003) recorded that Shelter's on-street methods brings in 15% of its income – and has been important in raising awareness. The report continued, 'Shelter is very misunderstood', says Liz Monks, deputy director of fund-raising. 'We are not only about helping people on the street but also helping people to stay in housing. Face-to-face people are trained before they go out so they can tell people about us.' As argued in the *Guardian* (20 June 2002) however, 'When the face-to-face fundraising method was first tested in the UK, its success surprised almost everyone. But despite the initial boom, when people reportedly queued up in the streets with open wallets, the now rather bloated face-to-face profession is being threatened by both fierce opposition and diminishing returns.' There does seem to be some significant consumer resistance; the novelty has worn off. The BBC news website reported on 14 September 2006 that local councils in the UK have begun setting up cold calling exclusion zones partly in response to chuggers moving from city centre high streets to potential members' homes (http://news.bbc.co.uk/1/hi/magazine/5341696.stm, accessed 19 September 2006). The report by Mireille Thornton in the *Guardian* (20 June 2002) based on her experience as an employee admitted:

> Naturally, charities are largely in favour of developing an innovative technique that has brought welcome results, including younger

donor profiles and an increase in regular giving. But talk of market saturation holds some truth, and is backed up by my experience in London. Although the company I worked for was clearly facing financial decline, and falling numbers of donors, it was not acceptable to mention the possibility of a public largely fed up with street fundraisers.

The DirectDialogue group uses 'roaming teams' to move to different locations every week, with a view to preventing over-exposure. Typically on-street recruiters wear vests that state the name of the client rather than the employer. This may aid recruitment as the public are suspicious of intermediaries, but DirectDialogue says it gives the added bonus of a regular public presence that raises the profile of the charity, and fosters a public perception of the charity as dynamic, active, campaigning and committed.

The implication of supply-side success for participation

For some organizations direct dialogue has proven to be very successful. Amnesty International, when interviewed in September 2000, had just begun using direct dialogue and hoped to recruit 16,500 new members. FoE cited it as 'one of [their] most effective ways of recruiting supporters' and 'the most cost effective way'. Greenpeace noted that while it has been a 'massive success', they believed that it was quickly reaching 'saturation point' and they were looking for the next 'big' thing. FoE recognized that there was a danger of direct debit recruits being less 'sticky'. 'We lose them more than any other kind of supporter. It tends to be much more a gut reaction and they think "oh yeah I'll do that" and then they have a rethink and think, "oh no".' FoE thought that the initial success of Direct Dialogue was in picking up people already predisposed. 'Oh great, Friends of the Earth, we've been meaning to join you for a long time.' This backlog may be cleared.

The decision by groups to use a particular recruiting strategy is not neutral in terms of overall participation. Strategies determine *who* is mobilized – and the demands of the mobilized members may be different from the self-generating. Recruitment can influence the qualities in terms of values, resources, and willingness to act, of the support. Godwin and Mitchell (1984: 829) proposed that the method of mobilization used by groups 'may create changes in the patterns of political participation and influence in Western democracies'. This is discussed in the concluding chapter.

5
Understanding Joining – And Not Joining

Following the discussion of the growing professionalization in groups, this chapter presents two new sorts of evidence from surveys. First, it documents responses from group managers giving a top–down *insider* perspective on joining. Secondly, it reports on a survey of (environmental) non-members. This work matches group members with non-members (who have joined other types of group, but not environmental bodies) with similarly strong pro-environmental views. Olson's views are usually discussed (inappropriately) in terms of surveys of members – i.e. those who Olson thought were exceptional in that they were acting in contradiction to his prediction of free-riding. This population of non-members thus offers a better chance to explore the extent to which free-riding *is* a fatal flaw for group-based participation.

Accordingly, the aim here is to make a remarkably simple but neglected point. The discussion of membership is usually subject to the bias – evident in the first part of this chapter; the focus is on joiners and their reasons for joining. Though everyone concedes that the mobilized element of the population is a minority, there is very little attention paid to the non-mobilized. Instead they are simply left out of account. Why some people participate perhaps says remarkably little about why others do not? The second part of this chapter follows Olson and sees the majority (often an overwhelming majority) as the interesting proportion and finds they have reasons for *not* joining. They are neither free-riding nor absent-minded in their non-membership: non-joining needs its own explanation.

The breadth, depth and consequence of the professionalization process

Initially this chapter documents the changing pro-managerial style in many campaigning groups. The *Protest Business* interpretation (Jordan

113

and Maloney, 1997) differed from the New Social Movement perspective that portrays modern campaigning in a participatory light. The *Protest Business* generalization that essentially saw rather *passive* individuals financially supporting *active* organizations was based on a limited number of large-scale examples and this chapter looks at the perceptions of managers more widely to see if the simple characterization has broader validity.

While there may be a sentimental preference for group activity that admires collecting tins and teas served in village halls, the alternative caricature that instead sees 'members' mobilized, recruited and organized by business-like groups has been underscored in other work. Skocpol (2003: 127) in a chapter significantly entitled 'From Membership to Management' wrote:

> By now Americans are no longer such avid joiners, although they may be organizing more civic endeavours than ever before. Professionally run advocacy groups and non profit institutions now dominate civil society . . . Understanding civic America's recent transition from membership activities to professionally managed institutions and advocacy groups is vital if we are to reflect wisely on prospects for our democracy.

Bosso (2005: 84–85) gives a classic description of the Wilderness Society stagnating while being activist-led and then rebounding when outside management was brought in:

> In one month Turnage fired all but one of the society's staff members and began to reshape the traditionally nonhierachical advocacy group into a more structured and professional organization . . . By the time he resigned in 1985, Turnage had tripled the society's membership and doubled its budget.

Bosso (2005: 85) notes, 'the political landscape is littered with the detritus of groups that failed to make that critical transition from protest vehicle to professional advocacy organization'. He (2005: 91) relates the growth in environmental membership in the 1980s to a new generation of leaders that were better known for their 'management expertise', than 'environmental activism'. Murphy and Bendell (1997: 58) observed that the depth of the penetration of professionals in large groups is such that 'in the near future environmental groups may have people in top management with no fundamental ideological commitment to environmental issues. These people may have more in common with company directors than... the people whose environments they are meant to be protecting'. In support of the Murphy and Bendell (1997) argument, Bosso (2005: 91) highlights that 'in 1984 and 1985 alone, new presidents or executive directors were installed at the Sierra Club, National Audubon Society, Wilderness Society, Friends of the Earth, Environmental Defense, Environmental Action, Greenpeace USA, World Wildlife Fund, the League of Conservation Voters, in several instances following major organizational shakeups'.[1] He cites the example of Rodger Schlickeisen who joined Defenders of Wildlife in 1991. 'Within five years, using direct mail, Schlickeisen doubled Defenders' member base – and its revenue – even as membership levelled off in other organizations.'

Rawcliffe (1998: 97) notes the recruitment of 'neutral professionals' on the fund-raising, media and organizational side. He quotes Szerszynski (1995: 33), 'in all the large NGOs, it is the campaigners who at times have seemed like the guardians of the flame of environmentalism, while around them have sprung up departments of specialists, who often have no particular reason to work for an NGO rather than for any other company'. Rawcliffe (1998: 97) also cites Baroness Young talking about her appointment at the Royal Society for the Protection of Birds (RSPB), 'they were quite nervous of me because I didn't have a conservation background... at the end of the day I got the job because the organization was expanding so much that they needed a Chief Executive, with a strong management background'. Law in her study of the modern RSPB noted how it

> has become less sentimental and more professional in its choice of staff. It now employs membership development professionals, some of whom have been drawn from the commercial world... The society's own market analysis confirms fewer and fewer of the million plus members are recruited on the basis of the organization's campaigning profile.

A Down's Syndrome Association staff member interviewed said, in short, 'The voluntary sector really had to get its act together and become more business thinking.' She described her prior career, 'I had no experience with Down's syndrome or any learning disability... it was fund-raising methods and techniques. It's almost regardless of what the issue is in a way... professional people are attracted into it (the voluntary sector) now, it's not just about "being worthy".' While an RSPB staff member stated that 'my job is to identify the names of people who could be approached and asked to become members; so it is a first sort of trawl. We have a target of names to bring into the organization and we then work on them to encourage them.'

The measure of success for the job is the level of skill: having a commitment as well is common, albeit not essential. An RSPB interviewee claimed that recruiting was 'just a job'. However, he expanded, 'It is helpful if you have an affinity and some sort of understanding... you can do your job better if you have some sort of affinity for what you're trying to sell.' A similar perspective was advanced in the Down's Syndrome Association case:

> the reason I am here is there are people with Down's Syndrome and families who need information and support. And I'm here because I help raise the money that pays for that... I've learnt more about the issue since working here. Generally speaking however, it seems more important to know the return on investment from recruiting strategies than policy detail.

The professionalization of the recruitment process described in the previous chapter demonstrated that organizations get the membership they seek. Law (2000: 284) highlighted that the RSPB's 'database could distinguish between different potential and actual markets. It can sort paid up members from non-members, separate frequent donors from occasional donors and even record the names and addresses of RSPB website browsers.' Like other large organizations, the Society does not treat members as a homogenous undifferentiated mass, but segment it in diverse ways and tailors the RSPB *product* to variegated markets. As an RSPB interviewee noted, if someone joins 'thinking we are all about gardens and robins, then the first communication they get from us is an appeal (to save a rare bird) they may well be a bit confused... so the idea is that in the first year of membership we will need to be pretty careful sending them information that meets their expectations of membership'.[2] The RSPB's ambition is thus to micro-manage this dance between expectations and incentives even further.

This chapter seeks to refine, and test, supply-side explanations of group membership: the core premise is that (interest) groups are not neutral conduits for spontaneous political activity, but crucially stimulate participation. As indicated by the quote from Skocpol and others above this perspective is now well established. As Crenson and Ginsberg (2002: 182) argue, 'ordinary citizens usually lack the financial wherewithal, the organizational skills, and the political knowledge to make more than fleeting appearances on the political stage. They generally require assistance from groups in possession of these resources . . . '. Thus groups do a great deal more than simply aggregate pre-existing voiceless concerns. For example, Rosenblum (1998) maintains that 'association precedes voice': voice is stimulated and manipulated by groups. Group supportership/membership is not an autonomous indicator of public concerns. As presented in Chapter 3, focus group are *manufacturers* of concerns and interests and stimulate support through professionalized recruitment and marketing strategies.[3] In line with the arguments here, and in Chapter 4, Bosso (2003: 402) argues that the determinants of group size may be on the group side as much as the potential member:

> the wide disparities in revenue growth (among environmental groups) can have organizational roots – leaders, strategic plans, fundraising techniques, and so on – as much as they can result from shifts in patterns of support owing to changing donor perceptions about organizational effectiveness.[4]

Law's (2000: 286) description of the operation of the RSPB concludes with an essentially apolitical explanation of membership: 'My research has established that most of the current million members of the RSPB are attracted to the organization by the selective materials it offers, are recruited through direct mail and other modern marketing techniques, and confine their political participation to the regular writing of subscription cheques.'

Where there is a political dimension to membership, the political aspect can be 'contracted out' by members to the professionalized group as described by Richardson (1995) and Maloney (1999). This fits in with Evans' (1995) description of the British constitutional reform group, Charter 88. The organization reviewed various scenarios with *Option C* being 'the constitutional equivalent to ecological groups . . . This would take a team of about ten people in the first instance, and could be self-financing with between 15,000 and 25,000 regular supporters' (Barnett and King, 1989: 1). Discussing this option Bernard Crick commented, 'Do we have to be democratic? Let's not get like the National Council for Civil Liberties . . . We should set up a supporters' association, if we go for OPTION C *we will avoid the impasse of membership*' (Evans, 1995: 99). Evans (1995: 99) reported further Charter 88 discussion: 'Kevin Boyle – this is the 1980s, people don't want action. We are about membership. *They want passive participation i.e. Greenpeace style, to support the centre.* The centre itself should be generating the activity' (emphasis added).

Lowe *et al.*'s (2001) study of the Council (Campaign) for the Protection of Rural England (CPRE) finds basic confirmation of the Jordan and Maloney (1997) picture of a top–down organization. Lowe *et al.* (2001: 93) say, 'There is an inner policy making "core" surrounded by a "mass" of inactive members.' They noted that the CPRE, in line with most environmental groups, had strengthened its HQ staff and 'professionalised a whole range of its activities'.

There is thus a broadly held belief that large-scale groups exist, and flourish, through professional recruiting and with a diminished role for members. Groups in this perspective are *brands in competition*. In caricature, members have sub-contracted their political activity to professionalized group staff. Rawcliffe (1998: 103) summarizes this as the Weber-Michels' 'law' that sees bureaucratization as the inexorable fate of social movements. In this view goal transformation leads to a 'conservatization' of the organization. Change is characterized by increased functional specialization and professionalization. He argues that in many of the British groups in the 1990s, staff have increasingly felt that the management of the groups have become preoccupied with organizational goals and have lost sight of broader campaigning objectives. Murphy and Bendell (1997: 230) in discussing the tendency for environmental groups to engage in partnership with companies and Governments observe that 'Experience thus far shows that conflict between environmental groups and business or government attracts media attention and stimulates new membership.' They go on, 'Mark Gilden of the UK's leading direct marketing provider for environmental groups notes that, "In 1995, WWF-UK's direct mailing to potential new members came hot on the heels of the Brent Spar confrontation between Greenpeace and Shell. WWF obtained the highest number of new members from a mailing in 8 years" . . . '.

While groups like Greenpeace are now seeking a positive public policy role in contributing to more environmentally friendly policies (so-called *solutions campaigning*), there may be tension between this style of influencing political outcomes and recruitment of support. Murphy and Bendell (1997: 196) discuss the Environmental Defense Fund (EDF) partnership with McDonalds on waste management strategy. Even to sit at the table with McDonalds was a threat to the support from part of the EDF constituency. Fred Krupp, Executive Director of the EDF, noted, 'Most of our members are people with deep suspicions about corporations' behaviour toward the environment; they give to environmental groups as a way to have a watchdog over the corporations; so it is very risky to take an organization like EDF and work with corporations.'

So organizations are dragged in competing directions – what raises the required resources might not secure the intended influence. As noted in Chapter 4, Bosso (1988: 17) characterized this as part of a maturing process of the environmental lobby where the chemical industry no longer considered environmentalists to be 'hopeless modern Luddittes' and environmental organizations stopped presenting the interface with industry as simply a *holy war* of 'good' versus 'evil'. However, these changes may come at a membership price. Exerting effective influence over policy outcomes might count for less with potential members than (say) Greenpeace dogging the trail of ships bringing nuclear waste back to Britain. Potential members may be more likely to join a group engaged in ineffective symbolism than insider influence. An insider strategy may have a policy pay-off, but it is not necessarily what motivates members. A major premise in the literature is that groups who depend on a membership that receives no selective material rewards must stick close to the protest mode. In effect, they are selling protest.

Survey 1: Professional opinion

The issue of group viability is of particular interest in an era of a perception of a decline in political and civic activity (Putnam, 1993, 1995a, 2000) – and of course the decline of party thesis (see Chapter 1). Campaigning organizations, like others, need resources (political and financial) – accordingly most groups try to secure them by attracting and sustaining support through memberships and/or regular donations. This chapter reports on a postal survey in which campaign group staff comment on their perception of the nature of the support for their organizations and the political impact of such groups. The data are based on a (representative) sample of all national associations listed as campaigning groups in the (CBD) *Directory of British Associations* (and they are compared with a control survey of all types of group).

Loosening preconceptions

The simple intent of surveying campaign groups proved hard to operationalize. The category 'campaign' proved difficult to pin down. Interest-group studies have to be wary about assuming rigid categories such as 'campaigning group': there is little internal homogeneity in the 'box'. The existence of 'membership' in groups also turns out to be other than simple black and white/in or not. Moreover motivations underpinning membership are many and they need not be discrete: individuals may, as suggested earlier, be influenced by a 'pick and mix' bag of factors.

So the research itself raised queries with its starting point. The central assumption that there is a coherent entity that can be labelled campaigning groups which seeks collective goods while offering few (if any) material incentives needs to be questioned. There are serious boundary issues. Certainly the incentives offered by campaigning groups can be as selective and material as for non-campaigning organizations (see below and Chapter 2).

While studies of groups tend to adopt the useful fiction that groups have 'members', in practice the issue is far less clear-cut. In practice there is often not subscription-controlled entry to secure a policy-making right within an organization. For some organizations the constituency is really of *supporters*: that is there are subscription-paying supporters rather than rights-holding members – and even where there are formal participatory powers it is often atrophied. Even groups that have members are often reluctant to terminate membership and the total might be inflated by 'members' who are not engaged (actively or financially) in a current financial relationship with the group. However, bigger numbers indicate popularity, relevance and credibility to current and potential members, and to other organizations (e.g. business and government) that the group may be seeking to influence. Groups allow subscriptions to lapse for different lengths of time before removing individuals from subscriber lists. This results in some group *members* not paying a subscription, but continuing to receive goods and services.

The practice of counting differs by organization. Some have family memberships counting as 'one', others multiply by 2.8 to gain an individual figure. Some label those who make purchases as 'members'. The general point here is to underline that in the interest group area figures can be 'softer' than in the electoral area where the numbers in terms of voting are much more reliable (though party membership totals are similarly 'grey'). FoE had a support (rather than membership) of 90,000 (in 2000) but this figure was a composite of 60,000 committed givers, 12,000 cash members and 12,000–14,000 one-off donors. Greenpeace gave a figure of 179,000, but this included members/supporters/donors (subscription or donation in last 18 months) according to criteria set by Greenpeace International.

The survey background

The survey paid particular attention to membership size to explore the possibility that there might be a difference between larger and smaller membership bodies in terms of passive or active involvement. The questionnaire explicitly stated that 'Throughout this survey the term "supporter" is used to mean all types of regular supporters: including members, activists and regular donors.' This chapter uses 'membership' as a simplification for the clumsy reality that within some organizations so-called 'members' are more strictly to be regarded as supporters. Some such rubric is needed to tap into organizations such as Greenpeace or FoE who lack what might be referred to as 'old fashioned' individual members with formal intra-organizational rights, but have a far more direct political dimension than many 'membership-based' organizations. If the questionnaire simply asked for *members*, such high-profile cases would have been excluded. Important campaigning examples may well not have stereotypical arrangements of formal membership within an organization.

This point is not always clear *even within groups*. For example, the printed recruiting literature and the information on the Web for Greenpeace refer both to supporting and becoming a member. The Web information loosely refers to '*Joining* Greenpeace' and more accurately to 'people who *support* us'. A newspaper insert (March 2002) asked for money to '*support* Greenpeace'; it claimed 2.5 million individual *supporters* internationally, but elsewhere the document stated that 'Just by *becoming a member* you can be part of the world's largest campaigning organization.' It is significant that Greenpeace does not have a membership services section, but a Public and Supporter Services Department.[5]

In some cases survey respondents took the question even more literally than expected and gave us unanticipated responses; the three organizations in our sample that reported having over a million *supporters* (i.e. *members and regular donors*) were Earl Haig Fund,[6] National Pensioners' Convention[7] and NSPCC.[8] None of these were membership organizations with the sort of 'tidy' membership in excess of one million as the RSPB (which we interviewed intensively as opposed to surveying). The very small campaigning (group) population (14), with reported support in excess of 50,000, cumulatively reported a *minimum* total supportership/membership of 4.25 million. (Calculated from the minimum level of each category in our survey. This is likely to be a substantial under-estimate of the actual total support.)

What group leaders think matters in the recruitment process

Why (and *how*) people join is a question that is of importance for group leaders in so far as it helps them determine successful strategies for gaining and retaining members. (The *political significance* of high membership and the financial resources that flow from such density is the same *regardless* of why members actually support the organization.) Group leaders reported in interview and the survey that members 'joined' via a variety of means: self-mobilization, encouragement through social networks and organizational recruitment (marketing) activities (e.g. leaflets in public buildings and magazines, newspaper

Table 5.1 'Most important' method of attracting support: Campaigning groups by size vs ALL groups[9]

	−1000 Members (%) *n* = 95	1000–49,999 Members (%) *n* = 91	+50,000 Members (%) *n* = 14	ALL Groups (%) *n* = 605
Individuals contact us directly on their own initiative	30	24	–	25
Existing supporters encourage friends, relatives or colleagues to become supporters	28	31	36	38
Supporters are attracted through local groups or branches	4	8	–	5
Leaflets at institutions (e.g. libraries/hospitals)/ newspaper advertising/inserts in magazines	6	10	7	5
Direct mail	7	8	21	4
Email from your organization/ organizations' website	5	8	–	6
Paid recruiters	–	–	14	4
Other	14	10	20	10
More than one mentioned	5	2	–	3

advertisements and the now obligatory website). However, when group leaders were asked to indicate *the most important* method of attraction, self-starting and social networks were ranked highest (Table 5.1). Truman (1951) was partly right! However, while the impact of marketing mechanisms may appear marginal in comparison for small and medium groups – their effects can be the difference between viability and liquidation, especially for medium-sized organizations. Hence this is why these groups invest income and staff resources in the recruiting process. It is also worth emphasizing, with regard to self-starting, that there is an obvious, but crucial caveat: *before one can join an organization one must have heard of it.* The investments in marketing and advertising places (and 'pushes') the joining decision up the agenda of many potential supporters. However, for the large groups, it is a particularly important method of attraction and in this respect pushes these bodies closer to the protest business ideal-type.

Table 5.1 shows that under 10% of small and medium, and 21% of large campaigning groups identified direct mail as *the* most important method of attracting members. As expected direct mail is particularly important for large campaigning groups – vis-à-vis smaller campaigning and non-campaigning groups (see Chapter 4 for a more detailed discussion).

Why members join?: Group leaders' perspectives

Many modern groups are engaged in intra-sectoral competition for support. Of those groups sampled who believed that there were serious competitor organizations in their area – over 60% of small and medium and almost 90% of large and 71% of all groups said that they try to actively distinguish their organization from competitors.[10] Most said that they emphasized their specific niche expertise or (market) position.

In line with the standard response to the Olson paradox, large numbers of campaigning groups also offer members a range of benefits that can be presented as *selective*. The selective benefits provided take tangible and non-tangible forms: that is *material*, *solidary* and *purposive*. Generally in the discussion of the motivation for joining, groups look to factors other than *active* participation as an incentive; it is no longer thought there is a high demand from members for a role in contributing to policy-making. However, group leaders do not have *carte blanche* in the development of policy. They are constrained to the extent that they need to pursue policies that will attract/retain support and cannot easily change policy as their 'customer base' has preconceived notions or expectations. Wilson (1995) suggests that the consistency required between action and posture might actually be stronger in campaigning groups than in others. He (1995: 35) observes that in ideal type groups, 'Persons motivated chiefly by money incentives will display greater indifference to purposes than persons motivated by purposive incentives, the latter group will often care passionately about goals.' Wilson (1995: 37–38) further argued that if the membership is materially based then the leadership might have more freedom in altering public policy stances as the membership will see policy as marginal: 'Executives in organizations of any size offering members highly valued individual benefits will experience few constraints with respect to stated purposes but sharp ones with respect to the maintenance of the value of benefits.' Indeed, logically, there is a pressure for the political dimension to atrophy completely or for the policy freedom to be the incentive for the group organizer. Wilson (1995: xi) concludes with a powerful simplification, 'ideological incentives, especially if threat oriented, tend to constrain and radicalize the leaders of an association, whereas selective incentives, especially material ones, tend to bestow discretionary authority on such leaders'.

A commonplace assumption might be that membership in the campaigning sector would be motivated by spontaneity and the pursuit of other-regarding interests as opposed to a self-interested quest for selective incentives. Such organizations would be seen as far removed from Olsonian selfishness. But when leaders were asked to indicate the primary purpose of their organization, as Table 5.2 illustrates, there is more self-interested – as opposed to other-regarding – behaviour in the

Table 5.2   Primary purpose of group: Campaigning groups by size vs ALL groups

	−1000 Members (%) $n = 117$	1000–49,999 Members (%) $n = 98$	+50,000 Members (%) $n = 14$	ALL Groups (%) $n = 681$
Primarily to benefit members	13	9	29	58
Primarily to benefit non-members and/or promote a particular cause	45	45	57	15
Both equally	42	46	14	27

sector than might initially have been assumed. As expected from the categorizations used only 13% of small, 9% of medium and 29% of large campaigning groups (and while 58% of ALL groups) said their organization existed primarily to benefit members. The number of small- and medium-sized campaign groups that indicated that their organizations benefit both members and non-members was substantial.

Large campaigning groups (+50,000) were both more member-incentive driven *and* more non-incentive-driven than their other campaigning counterparts.[11] (Once again the details above demonstrate the difficulty of drawing accurate generalizations about even a relatively small category such as a 'campaigning groups'.) The small and medium categories demonstrate another constraint on oversimplification. Over two-fifths of both categories gave equal weight to *self-interested* and *other-regarding* responses. This 'foot in both camps' quality undermines the clear expectation of large campaigning groups all being of the Amnesty International public interest type: empirical examples routinely cross the basic (academic) boundaries. However, what is clear is that in the sample of ALL groups attention to member benefits appears vital. In fact, relatively few of ALL groups (15%) exist solely for the benefit of others or to promote a cause – though such responses are around 50% in the campaign categories. So while there may be more member reward orientation than one might anticipate within campaigning groups, it is still much less than the interest group universe as a whole.

So what incentives draw and retain support? Motivations underpinning membership are many and they need not be discrete: individuals may respond to a mixed bag. Incentives offered by campaigning groups can be as selective and material as non-campaigning groups.

In 2003 the RSPB in Scotland was offering an informative welcome pack with details of how to make the most of your membership:

FREE Bird feeder with birdseed.
FREE birds identification guide.
The award-winning *Birds* magazine four times a year.
Quarterly *Scottish Newsletter*.
FREE entry to over 60 RSPB sites in Scotland (150 throughout the UK).
AND if you pay by (automated) Direct Debit 15 months membership
    for the cost of 12.

The 'sales pitch' said membership would help tackle the decline in bird populations (i.e. purposive), but even that was overlain by selective expressive benefits. 'In addition you'll get the greatest membership benefit of all – the knowledge that you're helping to conserve our native wild birds.' This is a fairly private 'feel good' factor. Groups have to evolve different patterns of attraction. One size does not fit more than a few.

Table 5.3 catalogues the variety of incentives groups offer. Of course what some members see as an incentive others may perceive as a cost: for example voluntary work and the opportunity to be involved in campaigning activities might in themselves be a reward for some members – and not the 'cost' assumed in an Olsonian economic rational choice perspective.

Table 5.3 Benefits offered to members/supporters: Campaigning groups by size vs ALL groups

	−1000 Members (%) Min. $n = 84$	1000–49,999 Members (%) Min. $n = 74$	+50,000 Members (%) Min. $n = 13$	ALL Groups (%) Min. $n = 536$
Free benefits (e.g. organizational newsletter/ magazine, video, gift)	82	90	86	90
Opportunity to purchase discounted goods or services of 'benefit' to the member (e.g. services with other organizations such as car insurance)	30	46	64	50
Opportunity to purchase goods or services that benefit the organization (e.g. organizational credit card)	7	34	86	24
Events and personal contacts (e.g. group meetings, conferences, social outings; support; and training)	84	85	93	96

Support on individual members' problems (e.g. information/ advice helpline, representation on individual cases)	65	70	64	71
Support on a specific group problems (e.g. information/advice helpline, representation on individual cases)	54	63	64	64
Campaigning activities (e.g. voluntary work, involvement in national campaigning)	80	90	93	52
Rights within your organization (e.g. attendance at your AGM, vote in election of leaders, influence on decision-making)	91	87	69	95

Once again the data demonstrates the importance of selective incentives in organizations of all sizes and types – over four-fifths of groups in all four categories offer free benefits. The incentive most frequently offered for all four categories is events/professional and social contact (helpline type support on individual problems is also offered by over three-fifths of all groups and help to groups of people offered by over half of all four categories).

Naturally, campaigning activities are ranked highly by the campaign groups and are less common for ALL groups. But the other dimensions where variations can be identified are less predictable. For example, the main difference about the propensity to offer goods for sale is not campaigning versus ALL, but the frequency within the campaigning category. Clearly it is the relatively sophisticated larger organizations that offer goods. Finally, many organizations offer internal democratic rights – but at 69% it is the largest campaigning groups that are least likely to resemble the traditional bottom–up model.

Respondents were also asked what they believed were the most powerful incentives in helping to attract and retain members. Arguably *the results are the most revealing in this volume* (Table 5.4). Supporting the idea advanced above about the need to 'loosen preconceptions', campaigning groups are not at some polar opposite to other groups (i.e. ALL) in terms of membership incentives. There is a broad tapestry of explanations, with organizations offering 'lots of little hooks' to catch members (and keep them on the 'line'). Nevertheless, while promoting a more general 'good' may be the raison d'être of many campaigning groups, in mobilizing and retaining members campaign group staff (in all three size groups) identified *selective benefits as the most important*

Table 5.4 The 'most important' benefit for attracting and retaining support

	−1000 Members (%) Min. $n=83$	1000–49,999 Members (%) Min. $n=79$	+50,000 Members (%) Min. $n=11$	ALL Groups (%) $n=533$
Free benefits (e.g. organizational newsletter/ magazine, video, gift)	29	35	36	32
Opportunity to purchase discounted goods or services of 'benefit' to the member (e.g. services with other organizations such as car insurance)	–	1	9	2
Events and personal contacts (e.g. group meetings, conferences, social outings; support; and training)	27	24	9	39
Support on individual members' problems (e.g. information/advice helpline, representation on individual cases)	17	14	–	11

Support on a specific group problems (e.g. information/advice helpline, representation on individual cases)	5	3	9	4
Campaigning activities (e.g. voluntary work, involvement in national campaigning)	12	15	36	4
Rights within your organization (e.g. attendance at your AGM, vote in election of leaders, influence on decision-making)	7	3	–	5
More than one mentioned	4	5	–	2

single weapon. Circa one-third of all campaign organizations and ALL groups indicated that the free *tangible/material* benefits were the *most effective* in helping to recruit and retain members. This is more than double that for active campaigning in small and medium groups, but identical to the level for campaigning in the large organizations. Indeed other important responses are also selective: support on 'individual' problems – 17% small and 14% medium groups; and 27% of small and 24% of medium groups identified solidary benefits as most important (i.e. 'events and personal contacts'). This data is slightly surprising given the 'public good' nature of much of the campaigning activity in this sector.

There is a noticeable difference between the campaign sector and the group universe in the area of social and professional contacts. Almost two-fifths of ALL groups claimed that this was the most powerful incentive. The constituency of the large campaigning mail order groups are, almost by definition, not as susceptible to the social dimension.

The evidence shows that groups are searching for a stable membership and income and to do so may well stress selective incentives. But other incentives also work. Qualifying the *Protest Business* argument that a lack of activity is precisely the attraction for cash-cow members, there is nonetheless a large 'market'[12] in the clientele of the large campaigning groups for campaigning activities. However, as indicated earlier in the same category 45% (36% plus 9%) suggested that free benefits and purchase opportunities were important factors.

Therefore some groups simply attract support while offering no selective benefits – other than the selective benefit of the opportunity to give expression to values. So there is fragmentary evidence to join the mountain that says that some members at least join to indicate their personal support for collective ends. This is the sort of 'free-rideable' activity that Olson thought rational individuals would eschew.

On the other hand, a RSPB staff member pointed out that the attraction of free incentives was perhaps under-recorded in research because of the social (un)acceptability of some responses:

> We've been very strong on offering lots of benefits to members, lots of freebies... *what people say and what people do very often don't add up*... no-one really likes to say well I joined because I got a free bird table because it doesn't sound very good.

Organizational leaders were also asked *why* they thought their group was supported (Table 5.5). There was one area of notable differences vis-à-vis organizational size – only 6% of small groups identified the simple Olson economic/material dimension – 'to obtain discounted services' as important. However, 13% of medium and 29% of large groups saw this as important. So rather counterintuitively large campaigning groups are in part popular because they offer selective material benefits.

Over 50% of respondents in all campaigning group categories said that supporters wanted 'information, advice, support and representation' *for themselves*. Again this is somewhat counterintuitive. The three percentages were slightly higher than in the ALL category. There was also (more expected) evidence of support for others; representativeness of the organization; and chequebook participation. In the three campaigning subcategories 51, 66 and 64% of group respondents endorsed the *contracting out* idea that members 'pay the organization' to assist a cause that they support (cf. 20% for ALL groups).

Groups were asked to identify 'the most important reason' for support of their organization (see the second part of Table 5.5): the chequebook and representation options were strong across all groups. The pure Olsonian option of discounted services was not particularly popular, but 'information, advice, support and representation in dealing with their own personal problems' was ranked high by small and medium

Table 5.5 Reasons for organizational support: Campaigning groups by size vs ALL groups

	−1000 Members (%)	1000–49,999 Members (%)	+50,000 Members (%)	ALL Groups (%)
Reasons for support	*n* = 99	*n* = 101	*n* = 14	*n* = 666
To campaign on behalf of others	40	46	50	10
To obtain discounted services	6	13	29	14
They want to help your cause but do not have the time, so they pay your organization to do it for them	51	66	64	20
To obtain information, advice, support and representation in dealing with their own personal problems	50	52	50	47
Because your organization generally represents and protects people like them	56	55	71	57
Other	15	17	29	21
The most important reason for support	*n* = 99	*n* = 92	*n* = 14	*n* = 619
To campaign on behalf of others	14	15	–	3
To obtain discounted services	3	2	7	3
They want to help your cause but do not have the time, so they pay your organization to do it for them	16	24	28	7
To obtain information, advice, support and representation in dealing with their own personal problems	21	21	–	22
Because your organization generally represents and protects people like them	21	19	21	30
Other	20	19	43	33
More than one mentioned	4	1	–	2

groups. However, in other respects, selective incentives are downgraded. Only a handful believed that obtaining discounted services was the main reason for support.

But a campaigning group membership is not always the same as an altruistic investment. The representative of a consumer group interviewed said that

> People subscribe for selfish interest. They do not subscribe, from the evidence I've seen since I've been here, for the good of the consumer, or the greater good. They're not interested at all in our lobbying activity, they're not interested in the charitable side. Most people don't view us as a charity at all . . . there's no altruism at all.

Law's (2000: 283) study of the RSPB also noted the power of selective incentives: 'the modern RSPB is tailoring tangible goods and services to satisfy *this politically quiescent consumption oriented market*' (emphasis added). In other words, for *some* members in *some* groups Olson is correct, but not all membership in a conventional category like 'campaigning groups' is like that. Classificatory tools do not fit well with the problems. Moreover, within groups the nature of support/membership is based on multiple combinations of incentives that are effective for different people.

Group organizers were also asked two rather difficult trade-off questions regarding the balance between 'delivering services to members' and 'acting politically'. Undoubtedly there is some artificiality in getting respondents to express a priority where there is likely to be an underlying ambivalence, rather than a pre-considered preference. Nevertheless, Table 5.6 shows that reducing core campaigning would be the more damaging option for smaller groups, but reducing member services would hurt the big groups more. Large campaigning groups were as member service–sensitive as ALL groups.

If the general academic literature believes that the bulk of members of campaigning groups are essentially motivated by altruism and 'other-regarding' activities, then once again industry professionals appear to dissent. Though the question was no doubt difficult to answer, the results conform to expectations in that ALL groups are less concerned about the effects of a reduction in campaigning activities. However, more unexpected is the extent to which organizers of large campaigning groups are concerned at the impact of reducing member services.

In general it can be suggested that group leaders identify selective incentives as more important than much of the empirically based liter-

Table 5.6 Greater loss of support: Campaigning groups by size vs ALL groups

	−1,000 Members (%) $n = 74$	1,000–49,999 Members (%) $n = 89$	+50,000 Members (%) $n = 13$	ALL groups (%) $n = 512$
Reduction in member service resources	32	35	54	53
Reduction in campaigning resources	41	38	31	19
Both would impact equally	27	27	15	29

ature has stressed, and certainly a great deal more than research on members/supporters reasons for joining (or not joining) groups.

Finally, campaign groups leaders (non-campaign groups not reported) were asked an open-ended question on the maintenance of membership: 'In your view, what are the important issues in maintaining a healthy membership in voluntary organizations?' Many respondents mentioned issues such as *responsiveness* ('being responsive to membership needs', 'consultation with members', 'listening to members and making sure they know what you are doing on their behalf'); maintaining *visibility* ('visibility', 'keeping the organization in the public eye', 'controversy'); and involving members ('involving membership in determining the organization's policy and strategy'). However, the greatest proportion of responses could be categorized under two headings: *communication* and *information*, and *incentives*. Communication and information was mentioned by the largest proportion of those answering the question: 'communicating with members', 'keeping members informed', 'regular newsletters' and 'up to date information'. Responses that mentioned the provision of incentives added further evidence of the importance of membership benefits and included: 'deliver more to members than they contribute', 'provide services members want', 'value for money – provide real benefits' and 'constant membership benefits'. Two more detailed comments echoed the views of the campaign group leaders interviewed on the importance of incentives and the level of self-interested motivations:

Giving members value for money. They want to feel they receive something for their money. Would not just support the objectives of the organization – sadly!

Membership organizations requiring payment of subscriptions usually flourish if they satisfy members' self-interest. A minority participate/are interested in campaigns. In many respects this criticism also applies to all voluntary organizations.

In support of these findings, Grant (2005: 368) quotes the (then) Chief Executive of the CPRE, Kate Parminter, suggesting that the successful conservation groups in terms of recruitment were organizations that offered selective incentives such as the National Trust and the RSPB. She stated that 'In a time-poor society, there was less interest in organizations like Friends of the Earth or the CPRE that encouraged active participation in civil society...'.

Survey 2: Self-interest and non-participation: The non-member perspective[13]

This section examines in a complementary fashion the reasons for *non-participation* in groups. The starting point is that political science has a well-entrenched explanation for low political involvement – Olson's (1965) free-rider proposition. The chapter accepts the influence of Olson in the discipline, but through survey data investigates whether non-participation is a self-interested strategy, as he suggests, or whether it reflects broader differences in resources and orientations to political action. It proposes that free-riding (conscious and calculated) is a specific type of 'tactical' non-membership and examines non-participation in relevant groups by the *concerned unmobilized* (i.e. non-members of organizations with policy preferences congruent with group members). While Olson implies that free-riding is logical for almost all potential members, the argument (supported by the data presented below) suggests that non-participation is not simply a 'left over' from those not mobilized, but is itself based on specific factors.

Olson saw non-participation as 'natural', not pathological. His thesis was a reaction to, and rejection of, the traditional Truman-type (1951) argument that when a political, social or economic problem impinged significantly on the life of a citizen, they instinctively act collectively on the basis of that shared interest. Olson's counterargument was that: *mobilization* was not a natural or *spontaneous* process. In short, he proposed that large numbers of sympathetic and predisposed citizens *free-ride* groups whose ends they share. Accordingly, prospective members – of a group seeking collective goods – will assess the organization's capacity to secure such goods. If the group is perceived as likely to be successful, then why 'pay' (i.e. contribute to group costs) when the benefits will be available without contribution? And if the group will not succeed, why waste support? As established in earlier chapters famously Olson (1971: 2) proposed:

> If members of a large group rationally seek to maximize their personal welfare, they will *not* act to advance their common or group objectives unless there is **coercion** to force them to do so, or some **separate incentive** distinct from the achievement of the common or group interest, is offered to the members of the group individually . . . (bold emphasis added).

Rational participators, for Olson, are special cases, either forced to do so (e.g. compulsory membership as in union 'closed shops') or attracted by (excludable) incentives only available to those in membership.

As is well documented, just as Olson's volume was appearing, his identification of a mobilization problem was apparently being contradicted. There was an explosion of the types of organizations Olson claimed were the hardest to mobilize – that is membership-based groups seeking public goods that had no obvious selective material inducements on offer. Not only did the number of groups emerging suggest that Olson had over-emphasized the difficulties of mobilization, but many surveys found that members joined to secure collective ends *per se* (Sabatier, 1992: 107). However, Hardin (2003) and others do not accept that group proliferation, and even large membership numbers, deliver the 'knock-out' blow to Olson's thesis – given that the '*n*' mobilized might still be a relatively low percentage of *potential* joiners. The powerful rejection of these (member-centred) critiques essentially says surveys demonstrating that members join for collective ends do not 'disprove' Olson's thesis. *Surveys of joiners tell us little about those who do not join.*

Thus almost all the challenges to Olson's prediction of under-participation have in practice advanced evidence drawn from the wrong population – by focussing on joiners. (This observation underpinned the identification of relevant non-members of groups as the key target in this survey. The core data in this section compares non-members with strong pro-environmental attitudes with environmental group members.) Responding to Tillock and Morrison (1979), Olson (1979:

149) made the point that generalizations about the inactive should not be based on activist studies:

> The problem that it is too late to deal with is the fact that you have an 'experiment' with no control group! Out of the tens of millions of Americans who believe the population should not grow ... you focus on the miniscule minority of 12,000 who *do* belong to ZPG (Zero Population Growth). The relevant group is the group of millions that wants ZPG, not the handful who have proven themselves to be wildly unrepresentative by joining ZPG ... your sample excludes all the members of the group who make nondeviant choices.

In his letter (above), Olson assumes that there are tens of millions of free-riders on the ZPG group because large numbers back zero population growth (the cause), but few are organizational members. Thus Olson accepted that (trivial) numbers of members would join (in addition to those seeking selective benefits), but argued that the number joining for collective goods would be dwarfed by those failing to participate. These he assumed to be free-riding. The test set out in this section only assumes that those with a *strong* concern (but who do not join) are *potentially* 'free-riders'.

Olson (1982: 34–35) specifically cited the environment as an example of sub-optimal mobilization due to the lack of material incentives:

> almost everyone is interested in a wholesome environment, and poll results suggest that in the United States. There are tens of millions of citizens who think more ought to be done to protect the environment[14] ... Despite this, and despite subsidized postal rates for non profit organizations and reductions in the cost of direct mail solicitation due to computers, relatively few people pay dues each year to environmental organizations ... There are surely more than 50 million Americans who value a wholesome environment, but in a typical year probably fewer than one in a hundred pays dues to any organization whose main activity is lobbying for a better environment.

It does not necessarily follow that those who share the concern about the environment with members of environmental groups also agree with the goals of the environmental organizations. However, as indicated by the above quotation, this assumption *is* made by Olson and his cohort. Indeed, they make the even looser assumption that those who *in some general* way support a cause, and do not join, are free-riding.

The empirical evidence in this section is drawn from the environmental area. This sector was selected for several reasons – apart from Olson (1982) himself identifying it as an appropriate field. First, generally environmental groups seek collective goods that are non-exclusionary with benefits accruing to members and non-members alike. Secondly, typically (but not always), environmental groups do not offer (significant) material selective incentives (or coerce people). Thirdly, there are a large and diverse number of well-organized groups that one can join – catering for 'general' to 'niche-driven' concerns. (Ignorance of opportunities can hardly be a factor in non-joining.) Fourthly, many (large-scale) environmental organizations have high-brand recognition, are professionalized recruiting machines, and membership/supportership is relatively easy and comparatively cheap. These factors all reduce entry barriers.

This chapter assumes that environmentally concerned non-joiners have *not* declined membership because they are unaware of the joining options. For Olson free-riding is possible even if one is ignorant of the membership opportunities. Instead here free-riding is delineated as a deliberate, calculated political strategy and hence needs to be based on the information that there are groups to free-ride. At its widest (and most simplistic) free-riding is simply a synonym for non-participation: those not in membership obtain non-excludable benefits and are therefore free-riders. However, this chapter perceives free-riding as an explanation for some, but almost certainly not all, non-participation: it reflects a *choice* not to participate. Free-riding as simply an umbrella for all non-joining is rejected and is seen as a specific type of *conscious non-membership*. Accordingly, a free-rider is someone who

- is concerned (i.e. values the group goal)
- is aware of the group[15]
- believes group activity will produce desirable outcomes
- considers the group(s) to be efficient
- and still chooses not to join.

The essence of free-riding adopted here is that it is a *rational choice* to preserve one's own resources rather than contribute to a common pool – even when supporting the collective cause. This definitional revision alone swiftly reduces the power of Olson's thesis. In fact, this *strategy-based* definition in reality is a better fit to Olson's argument than the operationalization he himself used that assumed free-riding was synonomous with all non-membership. Accordingly, this chapter seeks to explain why (*strongly concerned*) non-participants may still rationally – and without free-riding – choose not to join any relevant organization. *So why are many strongly concerned citizens not mobilized in line with their attitudes?*[16]

Olson and alternatives: A comparative assessment of the factors contributing to the non-joining decision

The empirical evidence summarized below in below Table 5.7 examines why two-thirds of the environmentally concerned (i.e. citizens holding strong pro-environmental beliefs) are not members of any environmental organization[17] (see Chapter 1 for details of the non-member survey and the response rates). It focuses specifically on alternatives to the Olson premise that non-members are free-riders. First (to rule out one factor), it examines the depth of environmental *commitment*. A basic explanation for group participation by a minority of concerned respondents could be that non-participants' beliefs are shallower – hence it might be anticipated that they would be less likely to engage in pro-environmental behaviour. To minimize this issue the data focuses only on those (members and non-members) exhibiting similarly strong pro-environmental views/behaviour. Accordingly, a series of 'trade-off' questions were asked on 'environmental attitudes'; the propensity to report a willingness to make 'material sacrifices' in support of environmental protection; and 'environmental action' (recycling, buying organic food and using public transport).

Secondly, it examines the *resources* respondents possess (e.g. income, educational attainment and occupation). Resources of course are a standard, but crucial, variable in accounting for political participation. Thirdly, previous research has highlighted the importance of supply-side recruiting methods in contributing to *distorted* participation. The data looked at the possibility of *skewed participation* as a result of *skewed recruitment*. Is being asked to join a crucial factor? Finally, it addresses the rating of group *efficacy* by potential members – that is respondents' views on the effectiveness of environmental organizations and the effectiveness of different types of political involvement. Not supporting a group because one thinks the effort is wasted is not the same as free-riding. It follows Sabatier's hunch (1992: 125) that free-riding may be important, 'but let's be careful about following Olson in *assuming* it to be *the* reason'. Such caution is well advised.

The multivariate design permits comparison of different factors which potentially account for non-joining. In combination (model 6) these discriminate powerfully between joiners and non-joiners. (All the variables are constructed using additive indices, based on a binary logistic regression and all variables/indices have been standardized.)

In Table 5.7 both sets of respondents (environmental group members and pro-environmentalists who are not environmental group members – *but are members of other group types*) are in the strong commitment category which naïve pluralism suggested produced (spontaneous) membership. Thus attitudes (as correctly anticipated in the research design) are not a differentiating dimension. However, there are large differences regarding other commitment measures. While members are more likely to act environmentally (e.g. recycle on a regular basis or buy organic food) in Model 1 (Commitment) than are environmental non-members, this difference evaporates in Model 6 (All-inclusive). However, the significant differences in the preparedness of members and environmental non-members to make material sacrifices in defence of the environment remains strong in both models. Members are reflecting their values which may be similar in terms of environmental commitment, but differ from non-members in that they are more willing to pay higher (hypothecation) taxes or donate part of their income (material sacrifice) to fund environmental improvements. Table 5.7 also demonstrates the significance of resource differences (income) and recruitment emerges as a strong factor: being asked to join can be important. As demonstrated, in Chapters 2 and 4, it can be expected that those with higher incomes are asked more frequently (i.e. 12% of environmental non-members with household incomes below £20,000 said that they had been asked to join an environmental organization – but refused! The figure for those earning in excess of £20,000 was almost double: 23%.) Thus a self-reinforcing process of *segmented mobilization* witnesses groups recruiting on the basis of their existing membership profiles and (for groups) reflects an efficient use of organizational resources (see Jordan and Maloney, 1997: 154–155). That the supply-side is crucial has significant democratic implications. Large numbers of participation studies have highlighted that those who stand to gain most from participation tend to be those who are least involved. This study confirms other work suggesting that non-involvement also results from a lack of asking. Many groups, rationally and understandably, seek to minimize 'their' costs and increase the likelihood that the citizen will respond positively. They ask those who can afford to join and who have shown willingness in the past. These organizations are in the business of protest and campaigning, not the enhancement of democracy.

Table 5.7 Explaining membership, standardized coefficients (Environmental group members vs Pro-environmental non-members)[18]

	Commitment Model 1	Resources Model 2	Recruitment Model 3	Efficacy Model 4	Free-ride Model 5	All Model 6
% correctly classified	63.6	67.9	57.8	67.0	54.5	73.9
R^2 Nagelkerke	.12	.20	.07	.18	.01	.38
Commitment						
Pro-environmental attitudes	.01					.05
Material sacrifice	.54***					.39***
Environmental action	.28***					.06
Resources						
Income		.45***				.35*
University degree		.33***				.30*
Gender: male		–.15				.02
Professionals		.41***				.31**
Recruitment						
Been asked to join			.49***			.39**
Efficacy						
Organizational efficacy				.57***		.66***
Efficacy of participation				.60***		.54***
Material self-interest					–.19*	–.15
Constant	.22	.27	.20	.11	.18	.09
Number of cases in analyses	607	588	652	540	629	468

*$p < 0.05$, **$p < 0.01$, ***$p < 0.001$

Members were asked if they would be *more or less likely to continue to support an environmental organization* 'if it reduced the resources used for core activities (e.g. campaigning, conservation, etc.) to increase the amount of benefits/services available to members'. Non-members were asked if they *would be more or less likely to join* under the same circumstances. Table 5.7 demonstrates the weakness of the Olsonian free-riding assumption that members and potential members are selective benefit-driven. While the non-members were more likely to endorse the material self-interest propositions, the overall impact of this variable is close to nil.

In the final column of Table 5.7 (model 6), the most powerful variables concern the evaluation of organizational effectiveness and the efficacy of various modes of participation. In short (and unsurprisingly), members join environmental organizations because they believe they are effective in goal attainment. Non-members do not perceive environmental groups or political involvement to be as efficacious as members. In short, the multivariate analysis clearly demonstrates that there are other non-Olsonian *rational* reasons for not joining. Non-members are less convinced of the simple efficacy of the action – not much irrationality there – nor is it Olson-type free-riding.

In summary, the data above strikingly demonstrates that the non-mobilized act consistently within a *broad* view of rationality. They may have strong pro-environmental concerns – but report themselves as less able to invest in support (i.e. poorer), less willing to make sacrifices, have fewer of the well-known demographic qualities that lead to invitations to join groups and above all rate the efficacy of the organizations less generously and are less attracted by chequebook participation. While free-riding is seen as peculiarly important in the interest group literature (compared with its marginalization in voting studies), the findings here do not sustain the elegant proposition that low participators are simply being economically rational. With remarkable certainty Olsonian-style free-riding can be discounted as the major reason for low participation. Non-joiners are not making such self-interested calculations. The participatory 'instincts' may be different for the non-mobilized: they are declining to participate not because they want others to do it for them, but because they are sceptical of the effects of political action.

Conclusion

As demonstrated above, there is such diversity within the sector that the utility of the umbrella term 'campaigning group' could be questioned. Charter 88, the RSPB, health and childrens' charities, pro-hunting and anti-war groups are strange bedfellows. The internal practices within organizations are also heterogeneous and further challenge coherence. However, it is as much a virtue of empirical research as a defect that such problems are identified. The empirical world (inevitably) turns out to be fuzzy, messy and, at times, chaotic.

The data presented above also provides some support for the proposition that many groups both provide opportunities for the involvement of the minority that see this as important and, much more significantly, allow chequebook participation for the overwhelming bulk of the supportership/membership that seek minimal involvement. If members desire the reward of participation, or the vicarious reward of contracting out participation, groups deliver whatever is demanded (see Chapter 6 for a more detailed discussion).

This chapter found campaign group leaders remarkably forthright about the language and tactics of using *selective*, and often *material, incentives* as a key tool in the recruitment of supporters and members. Survey evidence of members (such as the one reported here) that point to members being essentially motivated by altruism and 'other-regarding' activities have been qualified by those most *in-the-know*: the industry professionals. Experienced practitioners hold a divergent view.

Membership then is often, at least in part, derived from self-interest (especially in the expanded notion outlined in Chapter 2). This was recognized by Putnam (1993) and Tocqueville who concluded that joiners are not altruistic saints. Tocqueville argues that 'Private interests, which always plays the greatest part in political passions, is more skilfully concealed beneath the veil of public interest; sometimes it even passes unobserved by those whom it prompts and stirs to action' (quoted in Elster, 1993: 155). Putnam perceives social capital as 'simultaneously a private good and a public good' (Putnam and Goss, 2002: 7). He (1993: 88) further argued that citizens pursue what Tocqueville (1966) termed '"self interest properly understood", that is, self interest defined in the context of broader public needs, self-interest that is "enlightened" rather than "myopic", self interest that is alive to the interests of others'. Thus many group members seek selective (tangible and non-tangible) benefits *and/or* collective benefits.

Such self-interest need not be seen as such a dangerous pathology. Were all citizens motivated solely by the regard for others, then it is likely that their appetite for involvement would quickly evaporate (see Maloney, 2007). The fact, that in many instances, citizens are incentivized to become engaged through self-regarding behaviour contributes to democracy. On the basis of complementary (empirical) evidence, Lansley (1996: 222) concluded that 'many public-regarding associations also offer particular benefits to their members, to a point where they may be seen as a specialized subgroup of the organization's clientele'. There is a need not to be misty-eyed about why people join organizations, why they remain members. (Or indeed how they generate and access social capital – see Chapter 6.) It is clear that citizens do seek to advance collective ends and/or to promote and defend causes – some of which do not deliver a direct (selective/material) payback. However, this is only one part of the membership equation – the self-interest factor also engenders much citizen action. Thus, irrespective of how citizens are motivated to participate – their (continual) involvement *makes democracy work*. Even if narrowly self-interested or selfish *behaviour* is seen as pathological, Rosenblum (1998: 48) argues that it should not be a major cause of concern because groups limit it and act as a democratic safety value. Organizations provide 'relatively benign outlets for . . . narrow self-interest behaviour' (see Maloney, 2007).

There may be a tension between the thrust of the two main parts of this chapter. On the one hand the professionals were interpreted as suggesting that selective benefits *counted* in recruitment. On the other hand Table 5.7 says there is little claimed difference between members and non-members in terms of their likelihood of joining if selective benefits were reduced. This does appear to suggest the members were not as benefit-conscious as Olson would have expected. Group organizers could be wrong or members could be self-deluding? But need there be conflict? The difference between members and non-members is certainly not that the members are more attracted to the benefits on offer (which might be the exaggerated interpretation of the professionals), but that is not to say that group 'triggering' cannot be important in helping the strongly attracted into membership.

There may also be tension between the supply-side propositions in Chapter 4 and that in Table 5.7. The previous chapter argued for the importance of the techniques of recruitment and this chapter stresses the characteristics of the sub-population who join. Again some resolution is possible. It may be that the 'joining effect' of the group efforts does not act randomly on the eligible potential members. It is those with the sort of features identified in Chapter 5 that are more likely to be mobilized. Table 5.7 is saying that it is the 'committed', with an ability and a willingness to afford the subscription, with high sense of personal efficacy and a belief in the efficacy of the group and participation that are prone to join. Other than in demographic terms, these are features that groups can shape (as argued in Chapter 3). The willing joiners have been persuaded of the efficacy of participation.

6

The Social Capital and Democratic Potential of Campaigning Organizations

As established in Chapter 1 there is a widespread concern about a decline in political and civic activity (Putnam, 1993, 1995a, b, 2000). However, this volume has been indirectly commenting on a broadly held view that group activity has ameliorated the adverse consequences of party decline. For example, Farrell and Webb (2000: 123) note that 'Fewer individuals now take on political roles as loyal party members, perhaps preferring to participate via non-partisan single-issue groups.' Lawson (1988) argues that major party decline correlates to a failure of linkage between the parties and the political process, and that the replacement representative vehicles (groups) have been successful because they offer a more responsive and direct form of 'particularized' linkage. Mair (2005) reviews a growing indifference to political matters and an erosion of party support. Authors have highlighted the significant reductions in party membership and the corresponding dramatic rise in both group numbers – and numbers in groups (see Chapter 1 for group numbers). For example, between 1950 and the mid-1990s 'Aggregate Party Enrolment' declined in many advanced democracies from: 1.3 million to 600,000 in France; 3.7 million to 1.9 million in Italy; and 3.4 million to 800,000 in the UK (Scarrow, 2000: 89). The Eurobarometer reported only 3% of EU citizens as holding a party membership – the figure for France, Italy and the UK was 2%.[1] As noted in Chapter 1, in the UK, the last 50 years has witnessed Labour Party membership fall from 1 million to 280,000 and the Conservatives from 3 million to 318,000 (Butler and Kavanagh, 1992; Ware, 1996; Webb, 1994; *The Guardian* 28 January, 2002).[2]

While the evidence of greater group mobilization is compelling, this chapter investigates to what extent a citizen in search of a political role is better engaged with the political system via group – as opposed to party – membership. Why do people participate in a variety of political (and social) organizations? The data below reports the reasons that campaigning group organizers and leaders believe underpin involvement in their organizations. It examines the opportunities for citizen involvement offered (e.g. internal democratic structures and processes). As in Chapter 5 the sample of ALL national associations listed in the Directory of British Associations (CBD) is compared to a census of campaigning bodies. In short, the focal interest is what are the social capital- and democracy-building potentials of campaign groups?

As noted earlier previous work on campaigning groups (Jordan and Maloney, 1997) focused on large examples – this chapter extends the scope to examine the importance of group *size* (as measured by supportership/memberships) in affecting participation opportunities. It is of course no surprise that there is a correlation between membership size and organizational resources: mobilizing large numbers of supporters generates economic muscle. *Large-scale* campaigning groups (FoE and Amnesty International British Section) were found to exhibit *Protest Business* qualities whereby the major role of members was as financial patrons of professionalized pressure and lobbying. Such groups were elite dominated; they traded a financial contribution for action on behalf of, rather than by, individuals. Certainly *exit* rather than *voice* is the limitation on leaders in most large groups. Hirschman (1970: 21), writing about organizations generally, noted that

> the exit option is widely held to be uniquely powerful: by inflicting revenue losses on delinquent management, exit is expected to induce that 'wonderful concentration of the mind' akin to the one Samuel Johnson attributed to the prospect of being hanged.

The large-scale groups studied previously offered what Barber (1984) would label *thin democracy*. This confirmed the Cigler and Loomis (1995: 396) reference to *astroturf* as opposed to *grass roots* participation, and at best internal decision-making in large groups could be termed *anticipatory* rather than *participatory* (Jordan and Maloney, 1997).

However, while the protest business notion was based on a few better-known large-scale beasts, it has been extrapolated as a generalization for the whole campaigning sector in a way not originally intended or specified. This chapter seeks to map a wider terrain to discover if the business features are associated with the campaigning sector generally. What participatory opportunities are available in campaign groups? What is the membership take-up rate of any opportunities? What, if any, impact does group size have on an organization's participatory potential? The scale factor may limit the face-to-face interaction that is perceived as especially relevant to the democracy- and social capital-building potentials of large chequebook groups. Do large-scale campaigning groups only offer ersatz participation? Do the small-scale organizations come closest to the participatory democracy ideal? Or, conversely, do they largely suffer from the same democratic 'pathology' exhibited by larger protest business-type organizations – limited (or no) member involvement?

Protest business-type involvement

The protest business approach has been confirmed by complementary research in the UK and the US. For example, Bosso (2003: 408) suggested, 'In the main, these mature advocacy organizations closely fit the notion of a "protest business"...' Evans' (1995) description of the British constitutional reform group, Charter 88, is also consistent with the model. He uses the neat formula coined in connection with Greenpeace/FoE – *We act* – *they support* – to describe the relationship between leaders and followers. Evans (1995: 100) argued that a 'division of labour between the Charter's elite political activists and the exiguously participating signatories was deemed crucial for a pragmatic, efficient organization. This perpetuated the paradoxical line that participatory democratic principles were incompatible with institutional efficiency.' The organizers believed that the movement could survive through an indefinite growth of signatures that would be self-financing and mobilized through mail advertisements and direct mail shots. Evans (1995: 98) quotes the Executive Director, 'the initial thought was that *we must not be a membership type organization* and get bogged down in a whole series of service arrangements' (emphasis added).

While regarding the protest business model as pessimistic, Lowe *et al.*'s (2001: 8–9) study of the Council (Campaign) for the Protection of Rural England (CPRE) noted that 'In the course of repositioning itself as an *environmental*, rather than a countryside group, CPRE professionalized its organizational structure. The number of full-time staff at the head office increased from 10 in 1980 to 49 in 1999. A succession of professional campaigners with media experience were recruited to "front up" the group and its major campaigns.' They (2001: 93) concluded:

The process of professionalization has extended down through the regional tier and into the branches. At the branch level where we would expect public participation to be most pronounced there is invariably a local elite dominating the participatory process. In important respects, then CPRE conforms to the protest business model outlined by Jordan and Maloney (1997): there is an inner policy making 'core' surrounded by a mass of inactive members.

However, Lowe *et al.* (2001) warn that the protest business characterization should not be carried too far. It is precisely because of similar concerns that this chapter assesses the approaches general relevance by looking across the whole campaign sector rather than generalizing from a handful of prominent examples.

What counts as participation?

The Citizen Audit carried out in 2000 by Pattie *et al.* (2004) was a population survey aimed at illuminating who participates in politics and why, the forms of participation and the democratic impact. Table 6.1 appears to provide a striking confirmation of the 'groups as participatory solutions' interpretation. The total percentage of memberships (in 25 categories and counting multiple memberships) is 93% with circa 40% of the UK population being members of at least one group.[3] Seyd *et al.* (2001) estimated that almost 19 million adults 'pay a membership subscription'. However, there are two significant caveats to the notion that this represents substantial political participation. First, almost one-third of their respondents (29%) indicated that they were members of motoring organizations. The nature of these memberships need to be questioned. Essentially these organizations have moved completely to a service industry basis and the retention of the language of mutuality is misleading. Accordingly, when Pattie *et al.* (2004) excluded these memberships from their analysis they estimated that almost one-third of the UK population are members of one group.[4] Secondly, it has to be stressed that even beyond the motoring 'memberships' many of the other links reported in the 93% are also likely to lack much direct (if any) political content. It is of course not surprising that non-political organizations are the most popular (sports, outdoor activity groups, hobby clubs, etc.). However, Pattie *et al.*'s (2004) data is suggestive of groups as the democratic successors to parties because citizens are also members of professional, environmental, human and animal rights groups. Of course, the proportion of the population in membership of the more overtly political groups is low (in 12 of the 23 categories it was 2% or below). Nevertheless, as Pattie *et al.* (2004) highlight, a membership level of 1% translates to over 440,000 members.[5] The cumulative effect of individually low rates can be great.

The second and third columns of Table 6.1 illustrate that those willing to *financially support* organizations are a much larger pool than formal members: 62% of respondents said they had donated money to an organization and 75% said they were prepared to do so.[7] For some organizations donation is overwhelmingly more prevalent than formal membership. What percentage of the population participates in the fields of Animal[8] or Human Rights – the 1% claiming membership or the 25 or 11% (respectively) making a donation? Seyd *et al.* (2001: 7) maintain that 'If donating money is considered to be a kind of surrogate participation, then it is thriving in contemporary Britain.' It is also worth

Table 6.1 Membership and participation in organizations[6]

Type of organization	Member (%)	Participated in activities organized by the group (%)	Donated money (%)
Motoring	29	1	0
Trade union	9	1	0
Sports	8	6	1
Gymnasia	6	1	0
Residential/Neighbourhood	6	7	0
Professional	5	1	1
Social	5	2	0
Conservation	4	2	6
Hobbies	3	3	0
Religious/Church	3	4	3
Cultural/Music	2	4	1
Ex-service	2	1	23
Animal Rights	1	1	25
Business/Employers	1	1	0
Consumer	1	2	0
Disabled	1	1	32
Environmental	1	1	5
Human Rights	1	1	11
Medical patients	1	2	37
Old/Retired	1	2	19
Parent/Teachers	1	4	1
Women	1	1	0
Youth	1	2	3
Peace	0	0	2
Social welfare	0	1	15

Source: Abridged from Seyd *et al.* (2001).

emphasizing that, in her work on the RSPB, Law (2000: 283) noted that 'Though today's ordinary members may not be politically active, they are vital to the welfare of the group... because *they are paying for the political activism of others*' (emphasis added).

The chequebook participation notion implies that group members/ supporters are *primarily* cash cows. The additional information from the Citizen Audit is that there appears to be a bigger herd that are not in any loose sense of the word 'members' at all. *This makes definition difficult: what counts as participation?* It is difficult to handle these issues empirically, but it is a merit of the empirical approach that it raises those problems that are not necessarily recognized otherwise. Such issues of interpreting behaviour are highlighted by the challenge of gathering data. Seyd *et al.* (2001) accepted donation as a form of participation. However, when there are only donations as opposed to membership, or where there are great gaps between membership and donation levels, then conclusions about the level of participation are fuzzy. The empirical picture may be confused, however this reflects real world ambiguity.

Organizational activities and variation by topic of concern

An important theme of this chapter is the extent of diversity among the set of campaigning organizations. This is evident in the range of size, organizational activities (demonstrated below), but also in the variegated nature of organizational concerns. Most groups were involved across more than one area (Table 6.2). The areas of concern of the largest proportion of campaigning groups (i.e. those with memberships below 50,000) were environment, education and health. The largest groups had a heavier focus on pensioner/elderly and charity/welfare issues than their smaller counterparts. However, the key finding on the campaign sector is the heterogeneity of organizational concerns which undermines any ambition for simple categorization. As before data are also reported for the wider category of 'ALL' national bodies reported in the *Directory of British Associations*. This allows a contrast between the characteristics of the campaigning sector and the wider group population.

When organizations were asked to indicate *their most important* activity, campaigning/lobbying and representation were predictably highlighted by all three categories of campaigning respondents and were not ranked so highly amongst the ALL population (Table 6.3). This merely confirms the sample selection. While many of these campaigning organizations are engaged in a range of activities, the largest number

Table 6.2 Areas of campaigning groups involvement: Campaigning groups by size vs ALL groups

Area	−1000 Members (%) n = 119	1000–49,999 Members (%) n = 100	+50,000 Members (%) n = 14	ALL groups (%) n = 687
Health	26	33	14	21
Humanitarian Aid/Human Rights	11	15	14	4
Arts/Sports/Leisure	13	13	21	24
Business/Professional/ Employment	13	6	21	31
Environment	28	46	29	19
Animal Welfare/Rights	5	11	–	5
Pensioners/Elderly	11	8	36	3
Children and Youth	19	18	14	11
Women	14	11	7	5
Disabled	12	9	14	7
Minority Rights	13	10	7	1
Charity/Welfare	11	17	29	9
Education	29	40	14	34
Housing	7	7	7	3
Heritage	3	5	7	3
Religious	–	–	–	1
Community	1	2	7	–
Other	36	26	21	24

saw engagement with the political process as their most important function. The 'core business' of the overwhelming number of campaign groups is policy rather than service orientation (but small organizations conspicuously emphasized services to supporters). However, within the universe as a whole (i.e. ALL) services to members were by far the most important organizational activity. Nevertheless, it is important to note that only one-third of small groups and one-half of medium and large campaigning group categories identified campaigning/lobbying as the most important activity.

When organizations were asked to identify their *main* activities (as opposed to the forced choice of *the most important*) most groups were active in many areas. Most importantly, however, the significance of volunteering and mobilizing grew – notably among medium and large groups. Table 6.4 shows that while 26% of small groups noted mobilizing members as a 'main' activity, the figures for medium and

Table 6.3 Most important organizational activity: Campaigning groups by size vs ALL groups

Most important activity	−1000 Members (%) n=94	1000–49,999 Members (%) n=91	+50,000 Members (%) n=14	ALL groups (%) n=613
Campaign/Lobbying	36	52	50	8
Representation	10	4	7	15
Providing services to supporters	22	10	14	38
Providing services to non-supporters	6	8	14	4
Promoting volunteering	−	1	−	1
Mobilizing members	1	−	−	2
Fund-raising	1	2	7	2
Education	7	13	−	12
Other*	9	5	7	16
More than one mentioned	4	4	−	1

* Other includes research, media campaigns, etc.

Table 6.4 Main organizational activities: Campaigning groups by size vs ALL groups

	−1000 Members (%) n=118	1000–49,999 Members (%) n=101	+50,000 Members (%) n=14	ALL groups (%) n=686
Campaign/Lobbying	70	77	86	37
Representation	41	48	57	46
Mobilizing members	26	37	29	18
Media campaigns	29	40	71	16
Research	36	48	50	34
Services/support to supporters	53	51	50	65
Services/support to clients not supporters	31	35	29	19
Fund-raising	15	40	43	11
Promoting volunteering	5	22	43	7
Recruiting supporters	20	32	57	19
Education	43	65	29	50
Other	10	11	7	12

large organizations were 37 and 29% respectively. Some 30% of small and just over 20% of medium size campaigning groups did not see campaigning/lobbying as one of their main activities. (This is despite their classification in the CBD Directory of British Associations as campaigning groups.)

Finally, while volunteering and mobilizing members are important activities in terms of the democratic contribution of groups (especially in the social capital-building perspective), they were not seen by organizational leaders as being of *greatest importance* to their groups. Promoting volunteering had far more support from medium (22%) and large organizations (43%) (5% of small organizations). Even if one were inclined to discount the figure for the large size category (because of the low '*n*'), the fact is that the difference seems to increase across the categories from low to high. This result resonates with Maloney and Roßteutscher's (2005) findings on voluntary welfare organizations in Britain and Germany. Large groups – who are likely to employ larger numbers of staff – appear more efficient at engendering volunteering than medium- or small-size organizations. Thus, it appears that professionalism does not necessarily 'drive out volunteerism' and that smaller organizations – where the likelihood of greater face-to-face interaction is valourized under the Tocquevillian/Putnam model – are not necessarily the vanguard of volunteering.

Campaigning activities: The political focus

Unsurprisingly given the focus of the research, almost all the groups in the campaigning sample attempted to influence public policy-making (Table 6.5).[9] But this activity is not confined to Campaigning Groups – even in the ALL category 63% met with Ministers, 71% met with civil servants, 82% responded to consultation documents. Strategies utilized by campaigning groups to influence policy-making are diverse. There are, however, some large differences between groups of varying size. For example, around 60% of groups with fewer than 1000 members identified meetings with government ministers as an important strategy – the corresponding figure for the largest groups was 100%. Petitions were more than twice as likely to be used by the largest groups and these groups were also much more likely to engage with electoral politics. In general, the larger the organization the more likely they are to engage in a broader range of policy-influencing activities.

In comparing campaigning groups and the broader population, for some activities the ALL category is within the range of the three

Table 6.5   Lobbying strategies: Campaigning groups by size vs ALL groups

	−1000 Members (%) Min. $n=107$	1000–49,999 Members (%) Min. $n=94$	+50,000 Members (%) $n=14$	ALL groups (%) Min. $n=492$
Litigation	8	16	21	6
Meetings with government ministers	58	80	100	63
Conferences/Seminars	68	62	64	68
Electoral politics	7	15	36	6
Demonstrations	10	27	21	5
Petitions	21	42	50	13
Letter/e-mail campaigns	38	60	50	29
Meetings with Civil Servants	60	71	86	71
Public education	56	68	36	43
Research	54	62	64	43
Technical assistance to Government	27	35	29	44
Respond to consultation documents	84	79	93	82
Release information to the media	75	82	86	64
Other	7	2	7	5

campaigning sections (meeting with Ministers, meeting with civil servants, responding to consultation documents, seminars and public education). In other cases, however, the ALL category is outside the campaigning range (litigation, electoral politics, demonstrations, petitions, letter/email campaigns, using media – *lower* – and technical assistance to Government – *higher*). In a sense these differences predictably reflect preconceptions about the differences between campaigning and non-campaigning groups, and hence the real surprise might be in the areas of overlap (above) where differences in the strategies of campaigning and other groups are eroded. In fact some of the differences appear to be more based on group size than organizational type.

Table 6.6 shows that the array of strategies that groups use to influence public policy-making are matched by the arenas in which they focus their efforts. All tiers of government (including Europe) and both elected members and non-elected officials are approached by groups keen to influence policy outcomes. Within the campaigning samples: more than 78% focused their campaigning/lobbying efforts on

Table 6.6 Lobbying targets: Campaigning groups by size vs ALL groups

Targets of Lobbying	−1000 Members (%) n = 102	1000–49,999 Members (%) n = 93	+50,000 Members (%) n = 14	ALL groups (%) n = 480
Government Ministers	78	89	93	69
Backbench Government MPs/MSPs	65	72	86	48
Opposition MPs/MSPs	54	57	57	34
MEPs	24	42	36	24
Civil Servants	61	52	50	69
Local Government Councillors	34	41	36	22
Local Government Officers	30	41	29	28
Other	17	17	7	13

Most important	−1000 Members (%) n = 79	1000–49,999 Members (%) n = 70	+50,000 Members (%) n = 13	ALL groups (%) n = 374
Government Ministers	41	34	69	37
Backbench Government MPs/MSPs	8	17	8	7
Opposition MPs/MSPs	1	1	–	–
MEPs	–	1	–	1
Civil Servants	22	16	15	33
Local Government Councillors	8	1	–	2
Local Government Officers	4	9	–	3
Other	10	10	–	9
More than one mentioned	5	7	8	6
All are equally important	3	3	–	3

Government Ministers; over 60% devote time and resources to lobbying backbench MPs/MSPs; 50% to civil servants; and circa one-third targeted Local Government Councillors and Officials and MEPs. Comparing the campaigning groups with ALL shows that for the three categories of campaigning groups approaching Government Ministers, Government Backbenchers and Opposition MPs/MSPs councillors is higher than for the ALL respondents. However, in terms of contacting civil servants and council officers the ALL category reports the highest scores. This is a rather unexpectedly clear signal that campaigning groups are more connected to the 'political' than the administrative worlds. This is confirmed in the lower half of the table when a third of the ALL category select civil servants as 'their' most important target – as might be expected from the notion of 'insider politics'.

In terms of the *most important strategy*, the pattern of involvement between small and medium size campaigning organizations is broadly similar. However, the very limited number of large campaigning organizations reveals a different – and somewhat surprising – result. It is not unexpected that they focus on government ministers (69%), rather than governing party backbench MPs (6%) and civil servants (15%). But the rank order is a little surprising. However, many of these (campaigning) groups are likely to be engaged in 'outsider-style' politics. The strategy drives them towards pressurizing elected politicians rather than being inside the policy tent. They are also more likely to pursue other outsider (profile-raising) strategies such as contacting the media (as shown in Table 6.5) to affect policy outcomes and possibly also as a mechanism to recruit and maintain members (see Chapter 4).

Members as a resource

Members are a necessary resource for most groups in the financial sense (i.e. membership dues, donations, purchasing goods and services, etc.) – circa 90% of campaign groups and over 80% of ALL groups said that membership/supportership subscriptions and donations were crucial to the organization. This was confirmed in face-to-face interviews. A Greenpeace staff respondent – a group almost wholly dependent on supporter income (90%) – stated that 'They (supporters) are absolutely vital to the organization because we don't take any government money or company money, there is no corporate fund-raising. Our supporters are completely the reason we exist. The income they provide is the life-blood of the organization.'

However, group leaders see members' contribution as extending beyond simply financial support. Table 6.7 shows that groups believe that members are important in influencing government policy, identifying problems, providing suggestions about policy and strategies, and doing voluntary work. Large campaign groups are enthusiastic about the contribution of members across all these areas – rather qualifying the cash-cow interpretation of mail order membership. Indeed large campaigning groups give *the highest* rating in terms of using members as a means to influence government policy-making.

Table 6.7 Importance of supporters to the organization: Campaigning groups by size vs ALL groups

	−1000 Members (%) Min. n = 87	1000–49,999 Members (%) Min. n = 92	+50,000 Members (%) Min. n = 12	ALL groups (%) Min. n = 312
	Important	Important	Important	Important
Providing evidence of support from affected or concerned citizens	58	70	67	68
Helping to influence government policy-making (e.g. contacting their MPs/MSPs)	75	80	93	79
Identifying problems for your organization to act on (e.g. a local environmental problem)	78	74	85	88
Working voluntarily on behalf of the organization	73	80	93	92
Running local groups or branches	43	71	79	86
Providing a source of income for the organization – through fees/subscriptions	88	89	93	95
Providing a source of income for the organization – through fund-raising	22	53	62	57
Providing ideas about your organization's policies or campaigning strategies	84	77	86	90

Individually members can act on behalf of the group goals and collectively they can be represented to government as a proxy for the scale of public concern. Organizations see 'big numbers' (of members/supporters) as an important part of the policy-influencing armoury. As an RSPB interviewee highlighted, 'Having a million members is a great lobbying and persuasive tool to dangle in front of the government...that's why we put a lot of emphasis on keeping the million.'[10]

The active membership core

As argued in Chapter 5, large-scale campaign groups are dominated by professionals, but importantly many groups pursue a dual mobilization strategy whereby they seek to develop *both* passive and active members. FoE receive approximately 95% of their income from members and supporters, thus recruitment and maintenance is crucial for campaign funding and organizational survival. However, *they also recognize that without an active membership the ability to effectively campaign is limited.* A Greenpeace representative said, 'We can go to government and business and ask them to do something and they might sit down and say that's really lovely and do bugger all about it...It's only when...information really lands in the hands of citizens and ordinary people that it becomes politically possible to do [something].'

Evans' work on Charter 88 was cited above to confirm the *We Act – They Support* tendency, but he also notes that over time – and for ideological reasons – Charter 88 also developed a national and regional dimension. While the CPRE study by Lowe *et al.* (2001: 93) was cited as (generally) supporting a Protest Business interpretation of professionalized centralization, it also went on to qualify that 'the "protest business" characterization cannot be carried too far: in a multitude of local areas, volunteers are tracking policy as it comes down through the tiers of government and are having a significant impact on the implementation of policy. The "core" consists of an extensive network of local activists...Moreover, CPRE's own central policies are drawn in ways that are sensitive to the views of members.' So Lowe *et al.* (2001: 96) credibly propose that while some members are passive, 'very particular types of activists...wish to get more and more involved in policy'. Our interviews with a CPRE staff member shows that the organization positively encourages active involvement. However, the group is also partly driven to protest business-type behaviour by the reluctance of the many members to become activists. The CPRE representative said that they tread very carefully in trying to activate supporters because *many seek passive membership*:

We think we'd lose them if we did that (press for more active membership) because they're people who want to give money and they don't

want to do anymore than that... My remit has been to develop a
supporter base as opposed to a member base. It's much easier to
recruit people who just want to pay money than recruit individuals
into an organization where they potentially see it as a time-related
activity which they don't have time to do basically... So the whole
task (of recruiting people) has to be geared around saying 'oh don't
worry, we're not expecting you to come to meetings and things, we
just want your support'.

Groups provide advice to members and supporters on how to
be *effective* or *persuasive* if they wish to get active. In the US
the Sierra Club's website has information on how to 'become
an instant activist'. This includes: copying and pasting pre-written
customized messages that can be forwarded to elected politicians;
tips on how to write a powerful letter and how to convey
one's opinions persuasively in meetings with elected officials; and
how to 'raise hell at public hearings and community meetings'
(http://www.sierraclub.org/takeaction/toolkit/activist_tips.asp, accessed
20 September 2006). Thus a protest business interpretation that sees a
fully professionalized core simply cashing the member cheques and then
acting broadly on their behalf can be overdrawn. For various reasons,
the group strategy is likely to welcome *some* kind of member involvement, but on the other hand the idea that many groups operate on a
bottom–up democratic agenda is unlikely. As the main reform document of Charter 88 pointed out, local activity can reinforce national
lobbying:

> A Home Office official told us he had taken a straw poll of MPs at the
> height of the Freedom of Information Campaign. None had received
> a letter from their constituents... He and they concluded that 'the
> people don't care about constitutional issues'... (U)nless national
> demands are reinforced from below, they will be ignored (*Prospects
> and Plans*, 1990: 15, cited in Evans, 1995: 108).

Groups also seek to involve members in local groups and chapters.
Table 6.8 provides data on the range and depth of local involvement. It
is not particularly surprising that large groups were more likely to have
local branches: 79% as opposed to 36% (small) and 69% (medium) and
45% of ALL groups. But it is relevant that almost four-fifths of these
groups offer such avenues for involvement. These findings combined
with that highlighted in Table 6.5 on the promotion of volunteering

Table 6.8 Local organizational dimension: Campaigning groups by size vs ALL groups

	−1000 Members (%) n = 111	1000–49,999 Members (%) n = 97	+50,000 Members (%) n = 14	ALL groups (%) n = 661
Organization has local group/chapter	36	69	79	45

Percentage of supporters involved in local group/chapter	−1000 Members (%) n = 30	1000–49,999 Members (%) n = 54	+50,000 Members (%) n = 11	ALL Members (%) n = 368
0–19	40	54	46	38
20–39	13	19	36	22
40–59	23	9	–	9
60–79	10	9	–	8
80–100	13	9	18	24

and Table 6.7 on the role and contribution of supporters across a range of areas suggest that many large groups are contributing more to citizen's engagement and involvement than might be assumed (e.g. Putnam, 2000). Large organizations may have redeeming participatory features. In the UK organizations such as FoE, Amnesty International, Greenpeace, the CPRE and the RSPB have networks of local branches and chapters. The Sierra Club has over 700,000 members and state and local chapters. As Foley and Edwards (1996: 43–44) highlight, these chapters 'routinely sponsor community-service projects like urban clean-ups and "environmentally aware" outdoor activities'. The RSPB has 11,900 volunteers delivering some 700,000 hours of assistance which the group claims is worth over £3.7 million and is the equivalent of around 360 additional members of staff (RSPB, 2004: 3). As Foley and Edwards (1996: 48–49) argue, 'decidedly political associations may well play the role attributed to civil associations in the civil society, and may play them better... social movement organizations, grassroots interest groups, and grassroots political associations of all sorts are far more likely to generate Putnam's activated citizenry than the choral societies, birdwatching clubs, and bowling leagues he is so fond of citing.'

It is clear that for large-scale organizations most members' contributions are financial and these supporters are content to embrace a politically marginal role and contract-out their participation. On balance it is clear that organizations seek out passive supporters to provide regular contributions, and members who wish a more active role may find limited opportunities. However, it is too simplistic to suggest that groups want *only* passive cash-cow members, rather than activists. More accurately it should be seen that groups are prepared to accept membership on that basis, and may welcome more active involvement. However, they may not always be keen to roll out the red carpet for a *policy-making* membership (see below).

There are many (varied) reasons why large-scale groups seek to limit membership involvement. Lansley (1996: 222–223) identified the following six factors. First, *size* creates logistical problems. It is impracticable (and impossible) to involve large numbers of members in a group's work. By necessity groups are drawn to staff-run/dominated structures. Secondly, *the degree or complexity* or the depth of professionalization. The division of labour in large-scale groups will be predicated on specialization. Thirdly, Lansley says, Michels' (1915) 'iron law' also operates in these groups. As they have evolved into large organizations ('who says organization, says oligarchy') *differentiation* and *specialization* have seen some players recognized as carrying out key tasks and duties and gaining power and control. Fourthly, the *organizational structure* – that is the degree of centralization or decentralization – is important. Groups that have a regional structure comprising local branches and chapters have greater room for member involvement – although in many cases this does not lead to a policy-making role in the organization. Fifthly, the *ideological commitment* of members is relevant. If members actively seek out groups or join because of a strong commitment to the cause then there may be greater pressure on the leadership to either pay close attention to their concerns or to offer internal democracy. If the ideological commitment of members is weak, or if the group has used sophisticated marketing techniques to recruit members, then members may make little demands on the organization. Sixthly, legal restrictions or organizational constitutions may limit the degree of membership involvement.

In addition to those factors noted by Lansley (1996), there are several other reasons why organizations seek no-strings-attached financial support rather than an active democratically imbued membership. Servicing a membership can be a drain on organizational resources – members are more expensive than supporters or donors. Moreover being a supporter – as opposed to a member-based organization circumvents the problems of internal democracy and policy interference. In addition the *Protest Business* concept implied supporters are content to 'contract out' their political involvement (see Maloney, 1999). Survey evidence demonstrates that members share this view. In our own surveys in the early 1990s of AIBS or FoE, very few members saw their membership as a means of being 'active in political issues': circa 70% of FoE and Amnesty members said it is largely or wholly irrelevant in their decision to join (Jordan and Maloney, 1997). This view was also echoed in group leader interviews. In 2000 an RSPB representative stated that

> When we ask them that question (Why did you join?) invariably the answer comes back to support nature conservation. And most want to support nature conservation financially through their subscriptions and through appeals. So I think they really see us as the organization that acts on their behalf to ensure that wild birds in the places that they live are looked after and protected. So we're sort of acting as a *de facto* for an individual relationship ... if they could do it themselves they would but because they can't, they trust us to get on with it ...

Finally, the growth of patronage has undercut the need for active members. Cigler and Nownes (1995: 82–84) found that 50% of the public interest groups they surveyed received 50% of their funds from patronage. The figure for membership fees was 36%. Organizations heavily reliant on patronage may not require a grassroots membership. Thus for some group members have become a luxury because they can exert influence without them. They use litigation and have developed expertise that has a currency in the policy-making process. As Crenson and Ginsberg (2002: 147) argue, 'The new politics of policymaking attempts to open itself "to all those who have ideas and expertise rather than to those who assert interest and preferences". Those admission requirements exclude the great mass of ordinary citizens.'

In his work on fostering neighbourhood democracy, Chaskin (2003) also highlighted the importance of expertise within groups. He pointed to the changing nature of the relationship between groups and policy-makers as being partly driven by the professionalization of public agencies. Chaskin (2003: 179) quoted a director of a well-established community-based organization:

> You go downtown and talk to city council or a legislator or someone, of course you speak for the neighborhood. You don't want to do it, but sometimes you have to do it because that's what people expect you to do ... In the old days, we could get a few busloads of people to come down scream at the city council and that seemed to work,

do what we wanted it to. But largely, the agencies have grown up. We know how to tweak public policy, we know how to get enough to make sure that we run and we know how to game the system. We've learned a lot in the last 25 years. We don't have to bring out the buses anymore and that bothers me to no end.

In this respect it appears that the groups have responded to the changing policy-making context. Affecting outcomes appears to require less membership muscle and more policy expertise and professionalism.

Internal democracy

It is difficult for well-socialized academics to abandon judging the democratic contribution of groups by the standards of the traditional voluntary associations – that policy is made by members and implemented by accountable officers – the Lilliputian democracy notion. There is a powerful expectation that groups that contribute to democracy should themselves have attributes of internal democracy. But in fact the evidence appears to be that the nature of the democratic choice is in the support itself, rather than trying to influence policy within the group. Put bluntly, the Schumpeterian democratic choice is between groups. If you do not like the group, do not join it.

In assessing the extent to which groups offer meaningful opportunities for involvement it is important to establish: (i) if members have the ability to participate in the group; (ii) what form such participation takes; and (iii) (crucially) the intra-organizational participation rate. (What Berry *et al.* (1993: 55–56) refer to as the *breadth* and *depth* parameters of participation. *Breadth* refers to the extent that the opportunity to participate is offered to all members of a community. *Depth* relates to the extent to which those who seek to participate have the opportunity to do so.) In short, how closely do campaigning organizations approximate to Barber's 'strong democracy' model? – 'a self-governing community of citizens who are united less by homogeneous interests than by civic education and who are made capable of common purpose and mutual action by virtue of their civic attitudes and participatory institutions rather than their altruism or their good nature' (Barber, 1984: 117).

What level of involvement is there in the sector generally? It might reasonably be anticipated that active participation is a minority activity and that size would be an important factor: that is smaller organizations would be expected to involve a higher proportion of members than the larger counterparts. However, somewhat surprisingly, size appears

Table 6.9 Level of active members: Campaigning groups by size vs ALL groups

	−1000 Members (%) $n = 107$	1000–49,999 Members (%) $n = 99$	+50,000 Members (%) $n = 13$	ALL groups (%) $n = 623$
0–5%	46	34	46	32
6–10%	23	29	23	26
11–30%	19	20	23	20
31–50%	8	7	−	10
+51%	5	9	8	13

Table 6.10 Intra electoral turnout[12] (for groups with voting opportunities)

	−1000 Members (%) $n = 62$	1000–49,999 Members (%) $n = 57$	+50,000 Members (%) $n = 6$	ALL groups (%) $n = 506$
1–10%	29	70	100	42
11–20%	27	7	−	18
21–30%	18	7	−	10
31–50%	10	10	−	11
+50%	17	6	−	18

to have little impact. Table 6.9 shows that circa 70% of small and large groups and roughly 60% of medium size and ALL groups indicate that less than 10% of supporters/members are active participants.[11] At the other end of the spectrum the pattern between the groups is broadly similar, although groups in general (i.e. ALL) appear to enjoy slightly greater levels of active involvement.

Table 6.10 shows the turnout at internal elections. Approximately half of the organizations in all three campaigning categories and almost three-quarters of ALL groups have elections. Turnout is especially low for the medium and large groups. The figures for the small and ALL groups appear more 'healthy' than may have been anticipated. The larger groups do conform more to protest business characterization. Of course the 1–10% classification may be a too wide. If all these medium and large groups were mobilizing 8 or 9% then this would translate into large numbers; however, if it is nearer the 1% end it would not be so impressive in terms of participatory activity.

The overwhelming majority of campaign groups – regardless of size – had decision-making venues that members could attend. Small- and

Table 6.11 Participation in decision-making forums: Campaigning groups by size vs ALL groups

	−1000 Members (%) n = 63	1000–49,999 Members (%) n = 58	+50,000 Members (%) n = 6	ALL groups (%) n = 578
0.5–19%	41	72	100	58
20–39%	38	14	–	21
40–59%	6	9	–	8
60–79%	10	3	–	9
80–100%	5	2	–	5

medium-sized groups were slightly more likely to have such opportunities than their larger counterparts – 86%; 83% compared to 71% (Table 6.11). While the existence of such mechanisms is important, the participation take-up rate is more crucial. These are highest among smaller organizations and fall as membership size increases. However, the contribution of large organizations, in absolute terms, is important as these bodies mobilize larger number of citizens. While take-up rates may be relatively low for the tastes of *participatory idealists*, are expectations of higher levels of citizen involvement realistic?

The large-scale organizations included in our qualitative interviews tended towards autocratic leadership. In the mid-1990s an FoE staff member bluntly stated that 'Members have to decide to back us or not. We make policy and if they don't like it they can join some other group' (Jordan and Maloney, 1997: 188). Subsequent interviews in late 2000 echoed such views. A CPRE representative said that

> they (members) don't make policy, the policy is made within the organization, but they are the sort of watchdog to make sure that what we're doing is sound... We're a particular organization that believes in a particular set of values, 'Come along and join us if you agree with us'. It's not a case of tampering with our message or changing our message to suit potential supporters. We believe in a particular cause and its 'come and join us' on that basis.

Evans (1995) concluded that the leadership of Charter 88 realized that the internal decision-making structure of the organization was more oligarchical than the liberal democratic concerns of the organization implied. He quoted a Charter 88 document, 'this has been inevitable given that resources have not been available to contest elections... Charter 88 remains an issue group and not membership responsive' (Evans, 1995: 99). The former office supervisor explained:

> Well the problem is that if we set up huge democratic structures inside, then we develop a political party mechanism and all our energy will be lost on servicing committees and mailing our members. It is not and hopefully never will be a membership organization, we are a movement (Evans, 1995: 100)

While internal democracy is atrophied in many organizations, if groups lack effective mass policy-making influence through traditional means, most groups try to anticipate positions that would cost support. In the large public interest groups under consideration there is little by way of political control: many organizations deliberately avoid democratic structures. The market research used by groups means that their policy direction is steered to some extent by supporter/member attitudes. The group policy tends to be that which will maximize support. There are anticipated reactions: leaders know that members' ultimate recourse of action is exit. In fact, Dahl (1961) sees the relationship between leaders and citizens in a pluralistic democracy as reciprocal: 'leaders influence the decisions of constituents, but the decisions of leaders are also determined in part by what they think are, will be, or have been the preferences of their constituents'. These organizations operate on a minimalist democratic basis, treading carefully to avoid members taking the *exit* decision – particularly where they have no *voice*.

The role of such 'anticipated reactions' can be powerful in maintaining a link between the leadership elite and membership 'supporters'. There are many examples of organizations adopting certain positions after canvassing membership views. Rothenberg (1992: 10) observed that Common Cause gave top priority to electoral finance at the behest of its membership, via polls of members' interests. He (1992: 27) noted the leadership selects its policy areas carefully to maintain membership loyalty: 'The staff employs polls and other less formal mechanisms to gather data on constituents' preferences... The National Wildlife Federation in the US did not join with other environmental organizations in lobbying for the removal of James Watt as Secretary of the Interior until it received the result of a poll of its members who took a position against Watt.'

Given the importance afforded to members by organizational leaders it is unsurprising that leaders seek to establish why people support

Table 6.12 Methods used to gauge opinions on why individuals support or fail to support the organization

	Potential supporters (%)	Existing supporters (%)	Lapsed supporters (%)
−1000 Members			
Informal feedback (e.g. talk to supporters at meetings) $n = 88$	59	90	27
Direct contact (e.g. phone campaign, email) $n = 45$	40	69	51
Focus groups $n = 13$	38	62	8
Survey/polls $n = 36$	25	92	25
1000–49,999 Members			
Informal feedback (e.g. talk to supporters at meetings) $n = 83$	61	92	25
Direct contact (e.g. phone campaign, email) $n = 40$	50	70	43
Focus groups $n = 22$	41	73	18
Survey/polls $n = 42$	31	81	41
+50,000 Members			
Informal feedback (e.g. talk to supporters at meetings) $n = 12$	75	100	50
Direct contact (e.g. phone campaign, email) $n = 12$	42	83	25
Focus groups $n = 5$	80	80	20
Survey/polls $n = 8$	38	75	13
ALL groups			
Informal feedback (e.g. talk to supporters at meetings) $n = 535$	55	90	36
Direct contact (e.g. phone campaign, email) $n = 338$	55	74	53
Focus groups $n = 523$	33	87	17
Survey/polls $n = 382$	22	92	20

their organization (or not). As Table 6.12 shows almost all groups irrespective of size reported using informal feedback mechanisms to gauge members/supporters opinions and a majority also claimed to utilize this avenue for contacting potential members.

Across the range of supporter categories focus groups and surveys/polls are used more by organizations with large memberships. Several of those interviewed indicated that their organizations had canvassed members' views on certain issues and some had used commercial polling organizations to gather the views of potential members and the general public at large. The Consumer Association said that 'We get feedback from our members particularly through our internet site ... That's become a great forum for debate within our membership talking to themselves and also talking to us and saying what they'd like us to campaign on.' The RSPB buy questions in omnibus surveys by MORI and others and check 'their' profile annually by asking which conservation organization comes to mind among the public. This research is also crucial for recruitment and maintenance. Thus, they might do 'remedial' advertising if they are too far from the top answer. They do competitive testing of different recruitment packages to find optimum performers and they will check on first-year members to discover their 'experience' of membership particularly because 'they're the ones that are difficult to retain'.

Groups in the democratic process: The leadership perspective

The final open question in the survey elicited campaign group leaders' views on the contribution of voluntary associations to the health of British democracy: 'In your view, how important a contribution to the health of democracy in Britain do voluntary organizations like yours make?' Over 50% of respondents answered the question and unsurprisingly they almost all argued that voluntary organizations make an important *positive* contribution. A handful of responses were mimimalistic – 'nil', 'vital', 'essential', 'huge contribution' – but most provided fuller statements. This contribution was identified in a number of different ways. First, groups were seen as offering a critical function, 'They challenge well established, much better funded interests such as business' and 'to provide a counterbalance to corporate lobbying and influence'. (Not all saw that counterbalance as having been achieved. One respondent said they were 'not impressed with the "health of democracy in Britain" ... Big Business rules – not OK!') Secondly, groups were seen as playing an informative role, acting as 'a "conduit" for a two-way flow of information and experiences between direct services and policy makers', or 'can provide useful information'. Thirdly, an agenda-setting function was noted, 'raising awareness of vital issues' and to 'provide the ideas and pressure which governments will respond to'. Fourthly, groups were seen as more effective representative and linkage entities:

Whilst people are increasingly disinclined to sign up to an entire party ideology by joining a political party, they can still show their strength of feeling on particular issues, and thereby still participate in the political process... [and] I think they're crucial because a lot of MPs won't represent every issue their constituents want to raise.

Fifthly, groups were characterized as a hallmark of a democratic system: 'Very significant. Its part of an accountable society', 'There would not be any democracy – it is the capacity to organise change and the tolerance of the state to allow it and the occasional success', 'Quite a lot – otherwise we would lose the ability of free speech', and 'I believe that any organization which tries to assist members of the public to have their voices heard contribute to democracy...' Finally, they were defended as vehicles for participation, 'voluntary organizations are one of the principal mechanisms by which people participate in making a democracy' and 'they enable active democratic participation "voting with feet, hands and head"'.

Conclusion

A major theme of this chapter is to provide some basis for generalization that encompasses the entire campaigning group sector, and not simply a few notable brand leaders. The chapter also focused on the *breadth* and *depth* of participatory opportunities offered by campaigning groups. What emerged was that participation is far more of a 'mixed bag' than may have been (reasonably) assumed. The large-scale component of the campaigning group sector shares many of the characteristics of 'protest businesses'. Many supporters/members of these organizations willingly and deliberately 'contract out' their participation to the paid professionals. Furthermore, as the elite interviews demonstrated these groups seek to lead *supporters*, as opposed to being democratically accountable to a vibrant participatory *membership*. However, this is only half the story. Large groups also offer opportunities for active involvement through participation in local groups and branches, decision-making forums and volunteering. Accordingly, these groups should be characterized as pursuing a *dual strategy* – valuing both the active and the inactive. The vast bulk of members are useful for professionalized organizations as: evidence of significant numerical support from concerned or interested citizens; and a crucial income stream. Groups also seek to engender and encourage activity from a fraction of the membership. These activists and volunteers may be, as Lowe *et al.* (2002: 96) argue, largely *self-selecting*, but they fulfil some important organizational roles and reflect the reality that a minority of supporters and members seek active involvement. On balance, while large chequebook groups may contribute more to the generation of social capital than Putnam (2000) perhaps assumed, it would be too great a leap to conclude that the campaigning sector fulfils a role as a major participatory vehicle offering the majority of members the ability to participate. Such participation that occurs is more on *behalf of* groups than making policy *in* groups. Viewing campaigning groups as superior 'linkage vehicles' appears prematurely optimistic.

Finally, the contradictory evidence from group leaders regarding the importance of the contribution they consider members and supporters make and the apparent self-interested behaviour of members accompanied by the low levels of participation, is, arguably, symptomatic of the attempt by campaigning group leaders to affirm the importance of their organizations beyond the issues around which they have developed. The aim is probably to point towards a wider contributory role in democracy. However, the role of groups in a democracy is probably to increase the level of contestation over policy, rather than as locales for participation.

7
Reinforcing Polyarchy: What Groups Do for Democracy?

The *dangers* of chequebook participation

Much discussion of the role of groups has a caricature feel. On the one hand, there is celebration of the democratic merits of old-fashioned, cosy (bottom–up) organizations where, in theory at least, there is policy-making initiative at the local level and meaningful accountability of leaders to members. This is seen as 'good', as is the *comparatively* structureless participation of turning out on big demonstrations such as Make Poverty History in the UK in 2005. On the other hand, there is the less 'respectable' Not in My Back Yard (NIMBY) participation that is seen as self-interested, or involvement that is 'thin' – simply monetary – that is chequebook participation. Both the latter are poorly regarded compared with 'real' participation.

As noted in Chapter 4, Godwin and Mitchell (1984: 829) suggested the changes in the method of mobilization used by groups 'may create changes in the patterns of political participation and influence in Western democracies'. In fact, as might be expected, there are contradictions in protest businesses' roles as vehicles of political participation. The implication of most of the sources cited in this first section is that in general 'participants' in modern large groups contribute only passively and the 'contracted' organization (Richardson, 1995; Maloney, 1999) acts vicariously in politics *for* subscribers. Two major participation studies – Verba *et al.* (1995) (US) and Pattie *et al.* (2004) (UK) – found that chequebook participation was the most popular form of political involvement: money is a more common contribution than time. As Verba *et al.* (1995: 68) commented, '[f]or many people, political activity consists of giving money and nothing else'.

Arguably (in terms of influence on policy outcomes), the aggregate of chequebook participation is the more important influence within democracy and therefore offers a greater overall contribution to remedying any democratic deficit. This sort of participation is not spontaneous, but reflects, in Schier's (2000) terms, targeted *activation* strategies rather than mobilization and he (2000: 43) sees activation as the 'unsavoury' offspring of mobilization: 'Those who respond to activation strategies are often an unrepresentative lot.' For Schier, the term 'mobilization' has been used in too loose a manner. He regards it as an inclusive term signalling that the involvement of the *entire set* of potential participants is sought.[1] *Segmented mobilization,* or his preferred term *activation,* involves targeting a specific subset of potential participants who are most likely to join. It reflects the more efficient use of organizational resources permitted via modern technology and communication systems. When Anglo American parties made their appeals in the 19th century they hoped to mobilize a broad spectrum of the public. Today, political organizations seek to target specific audiences and mobilize relatively smaller numbers around a niche issue.

Accordingly, the use by groups of a particular recruiting strategy may influence the nature, as well as scale, of overall participation. The direct mail/face-to-face recruiting tools are certainly viewed as 'suspect' by those with bottom–up expectations. However, activation offers a range of attributes. Most of the literature on the consequences of this type of proactive recruitment relates to Direct Mail – largely because it is longer established. Generally, however, the strictures over Direct Mail apply equally to face-to-face or Internet recruiting techniques. The critiques are essentially of group-initiated recruitment mechanisms. While research on the implications of support activation finds a range of consequences, often they are seen as problematic (see Godwin, 1988a; Godwin and Mitchell, 1984; Hayes, 1986; Jordan and Maloney, 1997; Knoke, 1981; Mundo, 1992; Rothenberg, 1992). (The scattergun style of criticism means there is inconsistency – thus proactively recruited supporters are charged with being both extreme – and disinterested.)

Member extremism?

Godwin (1992: 4) quotes Broder (1979) who suggested that direct mail and single-issue political action groups lead to 'political extremism' among those participating. He also cites Bell (1975) and Teeter (1978) arguing that direct mail and associated citizen action groups were fragmenting further the dangerously fractured political party structure. Moreover Godwin (1988a: 22) notes that the negative style of communication used in group recruitment (and maintenance) may encourage intolerance, reducing the opportunity for compromise and replacing reason with fear. Schier (2000: 35–36) argues that activation strategies tend to use negative tones (see Chapter 4) and thereby dissuade those on the margins of civic life from participating: 'Activation perpetuates and reinforces these differences within the public. By preaching to potential converts, campaigns and groups help to set limits on mass involvement in politics.'

Godwin and Mitchell's (1984: 837) survey showed that 'direct mail recruits are less committed to the pluralist ideals of moderation and compromise'. Godwin's (1988a: 59) survey of members found that 'marketing attracts two different kinds of people, and social networks reach still another'. One half of direct mail recruits, the passive ones, 'are not as committed to the political cause as other recruits, and they have less political interest, knowledge, and experience'. The other half of the direct mail recruits held more extreme ideological views, while those recruited through social networks are in between the two types of direct mail members. The social network group 'care more about the political goals and ideals of their group than the passive direct-marketing recruits, but they are less extreme in their attitudes and behaviours than the direct-marketing members who joined solely for political purposes' (Godwin, 1988a: 59). That some are (comparatively) extremist may be the factor that makes them available for recruiting, but it is also argued that the stream of one-sided information for direct marketing recruits may make them less tolerant of opposing ideas. In fact Schumpeter (1943: 263) anticipated such potential problems associated with supply-side recruitment and retention:

> The ways in which issues and the popular will on any issue are being manufactured is exactly analogous to the ways of commercial advertising. We find the same attempts to contact the subconscious. We find the same techniques of creating favourable and unfavourable associations...We find the same evasions and reticences and the same trick of producing opinion by reiterated assertion...all these arts have infinitely more scope in the sphere of public affairs than they have in the sphere of private and professional life.

Intransigent groups?

If direct mail recruits are less tolerant than traditional members, Godwin (1988a: 49) suggests this may produce a reluctance to compromise at the top of the groups, and dissatisfaction at the bottom – as recruits can become alienated from the political system. Participation limited *solely* to cheque-writing means the individual does not engage in listening to different viewpoints and Godwin suggests that direct mail–dependent groups need to 'stress conflict and extremism in their political tactics'. In response to the nature of their membership base groups may be steered away from the more traditional 'lobbying behind the scenes'. As Godwin (1992: 318) concluded there was

> a strong association between the degree to which an organization depends on direct mail and the probability that it will choose highly visible and emotional issues . . . the generation of resources by direct marketing may force group leaders to pursue issues and tactics different from those of other interest groups. Direct-mail groups chose issues that would gain the most attention from the media.

Murphy and Bendell (1997: 230) also note that a vibrant membership is assisted by front-page conflict – not quietly efficient policy influence.

Apolitical and apathetic?

Hayes (1986: 137), Mundo (1992: 18) and Putnam (2000: 160) suggest (that the most successful) large organizations are concerned with national issues, lack local- or regional-level chapter/branches (or these are in decline) and therefore offer few, if any, real opportunities for member interaction. Godwin and Mitchell (1984: 837) argue that a national focus, largely without a regional or local base, reduces a group's ability to organize their members for local battles or to secure action when necessary:

> When interests supported by voluntary associations based on direct mail face opposing interests based on social network or institutional organizations, the direct mail interests have an easier time winning at the national level and in the short run. At the local level, and in the long run, interests supported by social network associations have the advantage.

However, as argued in earlier chapters, groups need not fit into the extremes of these categories. Groups have realized that different potential members are attracted by different roles within the organization.

Topolsky (1974) and Sinclair (1982) criticized direct mail for soliciting low-activity participation which otherwise would have had a richer content if direct mail did not provide an easier and less time-consuming alternative. Similarly Maarek (1995: 160) asserts that

> The citizen, reached at his own home, and performing his political action from there, sometimes tends to feel that he has already performed his civic duty by mail, and gets less involved later: he might not even think it necessary to go to the polls on election day.

Maarek (1995: 161) also claims that direct marketing has only a short-term impact as recruits feel comparatively unattached, and unable to influence the organizations. The individual 'soon grows weary of the appeal, or turns to other new and more enticing ones that reach him [*sic*] in a similar manner'.

Leader dominated?

Godwin and Mitchell (1984: 836) noted how direct mail–based members may give political freedom and advantages to the group leaders because 'they contribute without meddling in the association's business' and 'depend for information about the organization on the materials the leadership sends them, and therefore may be more easily manipulated'. There are information asymmetries that leaders can and do exploit. Members in such circumstances can be persuaded (or manipulated) into believing that the leadership course of action – policy and strategy – is the only, or the best, course. This also means that members can exercise only two of Hirschman's (1970) three options – *loyalty* or *exit* – they do not have a *voice*. In short, the main assumption is Schumpeterian: there is of a high level of political incompetence among the public. Accordingly, it would be better for Schumpeter if individuals reacted to decisions made by a leadership that enjoys a relatively wide discretionary governing (and manipulation) power (see Katz, 1997: 51–53). As is set out later such a worldview is anathema to the participatory optimists who drive the expectation that groups are key participatory venues.

Less loyal and committed?

There is a general suspicion that 'recruited' members are less attached to their organizations than their more committed co-members that actively sought involvement (i.e. joined on their own initiative). In an interview, a Friends of the Earth staff member said, 'we lose them [direct mail and direct dialogue recruits] more than any other kind of supporter'. Activation-based membership groups may not have the socio-psychological, perhaps more stable, support built up through solidary activities – meeting, friendships, and so on – upon which to call and sustain long-term support and activity. Godwin and Mitchell (1984: 830) refer to McCarthy and Zald's (1977) work: 'when the members of a social influence association do not interact with one another, as is the case with direct mail recruits, they stress purposive rather than solidary incentives. This shortage of solidary incentives can reduce members' loyalty to the association'. As noted above activation may also affect the ability of groups to mobilize for political intervention. Knoke's (1981: 142) study of membership commitment within voluntary organizations led him to conclude that attachment is influenced by the structure of the organization, and he analysed three aspects of voluntary organizations: centralization of decision-making; pattern of communication; and total amount of influence. Commitment was seen as being about members' willingness to participate, remain, accept organizational goals, and express positive regard or loyalty. The opposite of this was detachment or 'organizational alienation'.

Knoke (1981: 142) explained: 'Detachment from a voluntary association expresses a sense of personal remoteness from the collectivity and feelings of inability to influence organizational activities and policies.' The conclusion was that those organizations where members have 'weak control over collective policy' will experience 'high levels of organizational detachment' among their members (Knoke, 1981: 142–143). Knoke (1981: 154–155) argued that centralization is also a potential problem: the 'less conducive the structural opportunities are for exercising [upward] control, the less supportive and more cut off the members feel'. Organizations with this type of structure and membership need not fail, but 'should a crisis erupt over the policy direction taken by leaders, these organizations may find themselves without a reservoir of loyalty that could see them through the turmoil'. He (1981) cites Knoke and Wood (1981) who found membership support enhanced by associational systems which promoted organizational democracy. Members' commitment increased with their integration into structure and they were also less likely to feel detached.

Jordan and Maloney (1998: 406) noted a *revolving door* problem: public interest groups with proactive recruiting face high membership turnover (see also Jordan and Maloney, 1997: 220–226). Johnson's (1998: 45) study of environmental groups in the US found that while the cost of membership was low, the average retention rate was 70%: groups therefore needed to replace 30% of support each year just to maintain themselves. Similarly Bosso (1995: 114) contended that

> Drop-out rates are high in large part because most members are little but passive check writers, with the low cost of participating often translating into an equally low sense of commitment, particularly when most large organizations give members little if any direct input into policy making or governance.

Groups such as Common Cause and Zero Population which relied upon direct mail to recruit their members suffered 'volatile swings and permanent downturns' (Godwin, 1988a: 66). Jordan and Maloney's (1998: 407) survey of FoE in the UK found that only 35% of those who joined in 1991 rejoined in 1992 and the Amnesty dropout rate was 40% after the first year. Godwin and Mitchell's study of five environmental groups found (1984: 834, 836) that direct mail recruits 'have shorter tenure'.

Some proactive organizations work hard to simplify joining – i.e. members have easy and cheap entry. The lack of deep commitment from many members make exit more likely. This can be related to the type of benefits groups offer. Direct mail groups, or protest businesses, offer expressive benefits, but this reward may have a finite shelf. Jordan and Halpin (2004) found that a shift in the nature of incentives on offer – from expressive to material – sharply reduced a group's membership turnover.

Johnson (1998: 41) argues that for many membership may be short-lived because 'the expressive joy of membership is fleeting. People tend to feel that they have 'done their part' by joining, or perhaps they are distracted by other activities (and uses for their money)'. So they fail to renew.

Group system bias?

One final criticism of the consequences of proactive recruiting was advanced by Bosso (1995: 114) relating to the significant costs associated with direct mail. The prospective mailing 'can cost hundreds of thousands of dollars, even assuming a group already has a mailing list from which to work'. Accordingly, poorer groups will be less able to use such methods (see also O'Shaughnessy, 1990: 93), so the richer ones will do better. Thus interest group competition can be *further* skewed.

In the UK organizations such as FoE and Greenpeace have, to a certain extent, flourished at the expense of *both* smaller and/or more local environmental groups (e.g. the Conservation Trust). The success of the large can be costly for the small. The shift to large-scale groups, with less participatory overtones, could be reducing the democratic contribution of the group sector as a whole. In 2004, the head of research at the National Council for Voluntary Organizations (NCVO) argued that big brand charities were squeezing out the local and 'political support for the sector also seems largely to translate into more funding for the big few... at the expense of smaller organizations... We should not hesitate to celebrate the effectiveness of the large charity names, but the increasing monopolisation of resources by a few organizations must be addressed' (*Times*, 19 July 2004).

Maarek (1995: 161) sums the disadvantages of direct mail recruitment:

> Direct marketing presents an... insidious risk for the normal functioning of the political sphere: it gives considerable leeway to the organization making use of it, meaning political party headquarters or political action committees. The power of influence it gives to the respondent to such appeals is much weaker than what it would be by going through traditional channels of political activism, within which the relatively democratic process allows individual action to acquire greater significance.

In similar vein, Putnam (2000: 160) argues:

> It is not that direct-mail organizations are morally evil or politically ineffective. It may be more efficient technically for us to hire other people to act for us politically. However, such organizations provide neither connectedness among members nor direct engagement in civic give-and-take, and they certainly do not represent 'participatory democracy'.[2]

A more group-friendly interpretation

Anticipatory internal democracy?

Most scholars quoted above also see positive group attributes, and a far less hostile interpretation of the implications of group-led recruiting can be assembled. Many groups and parties take great care to try and prevent supporters/members from taking the exit decision by engaging in internal polling (and other opinion-gathering methods) to help shape policies. Accordingly, the supporters can be seen to shape group agendas by the 'law of anticipated reactions'. So there is a sort of group account-ability by anticipation. Luttbeg and Zeigler (1974: 209) maintained that while many interest groups do not have formal 'consultative mechan-isms, leaders and followers exist in a functionally democratic relation-ship. That is to say, leaders are limited by the followers' expressed or latent values and expectation' (quoted in Luttbeg, 1974: 6). In a similar vein, Truman (1951: 156) argued that 'The attitudes present in the membership define the tasks of the leaders, and the internal political life of the groups is made up of a continuous effort to maintain leaders and followers in some measure of harmonious relationship.' Many organ-izations take great care to avoid members taking the *exit* decision. The threat of exit may actually have a significant impact on limiting leader-ship discretion.

Accordingly, it is not in the interest of supporter/member-financed groups to ignore supporters/members. Large-scale groups without any 'local chapter' structure may use surveys of membership to gauge opinion on certain themes, issues or general policy direction. John Gottschalk, a director of the National Wildlife Federation, stated that 'Our relationship with the bulk of the membership is very tenuous. It probably doesn't exist except in an almost imaginary way. We know from time-to-time pretty much what's going on because we do profes-sionally managed surveys to get their opinions on a variety of issues' (quoted in Shaiko, 1999: 76). Rothenberg (1992: 10) observed that Common Cause gave top priority to electoral finance at the behest of it membership, via polls of members' interests. In the UK, the RSPB maintains that it makes policy through 'proper, structured, unsolicited surveying, which allows us to make the right decisions' (*Daily Telegraph*, 23 April 1994). In 1992, it contacted its members to discover if a strategy of widening the group's appeal as a broad environmental group could be pursued without eroding the traditional 'bird' constituency: group leaders anticipated potential exit. The former director of RSPB, Baroness Young, summarized the organization's perspective:

> We have always regarded ourselves not as an organization that is run by its membership but an organization supported by its members. Our role is to say, 'right, what needs to happen for the conservation of our environment and *how can we sell it to people?* . . . [but] we will not actually get into a policy area unless we have got a clear 'bird route' through it. So we will not, for example, pick up a general pollution issue if it is not a pollution issue that has a major bird impact. That is the way we keep our agenda reasonably tight . . . but it also gives

us our legitimacy with our membership in getting into these wider areas (quoted in Rawcliffe, 1998: 229–230) (emphasis added).

Baroness Young unequivocally argues that the public policies which organization tries to shape have to be 'sold' to the membership/supportership. Her remarks also imply that it is not internal *voice* that is feared, but simply *exit*: the organization works hard to find a 'bird angle'. To a certain extent there is also an ersatz democracy: predicated on the choice to participate or not; or *which* group to support. There is limited expectation of democratic vitality within groups, but there may be democracy in the choice between groups.

Appropriate not apathetic

Given that (say) the environmental movements in the US and Britain have been transformed into professional, bureaucratic organizations staffed by professional economists, lawyers and scientists and supported by sophisticated fund-raising departments and management structures, the useful role of 'members' may be different from that envisioned in the 'little democracy' perspective. Bosso (2003: 410) notes: 'It may be cynical to say so, but what use are "members" when lawyers, scientists, and policy experts are far more valuable in day-to-day policy debates... The emergence of "virtual membership" via the Internet only reinforces the perspective that members *as such* are little more than organizational wallpaper, a collective backdrop for professional advocacy.' The low participation supporter is thus perhaps an organizational strength for some groups (see Fisher, 2006).

Expanded pool of participants

There is evidence offsetting the rather negative interpretation of the supply-side style recruiting as summarized in the previous section. Godwin (1988a: 48–49, 1992: 314–317) notes that while critics assume that members recruited by social networks are more tolerant, 'the direct-mail recruit typically belongs to several organizations with similar ideologies and goals'. The new technology and techniques may enable greater organizational reach, albeit not offering participation in the traditional format. Despite the well-known bias in participation towards the educated and more affluent, Godwin (1988a: 50) notes that 'Direct marketing may overcome these biases because it need not rely on existing social network ties to recruit participants. If individuals have telephones, televisions, and postal addresses, direct-marketing techniques can reach them.' While many citizens with these modern 'essentials' may lack the disposable income to indulge their political interests – many groups offer very low-cost involvement at a low-cost price (i.e. special membership/supportership rates for the unemployed, students, pensioners, etc.).

Rosenstone and Hansen (1993: 26) argue that direct mobilization can create 'opportunities for political action that citizens would not have otherwise'. Thus people get to hear about organizations that otherwise would not be considered – and/or they are given an easy joining opportunity. O'Shaughnessy and Peele (1985: 119) observed how direct mail 'gives ease of entry to the political process, since a recipient only has to return the reply card to become involved'.

Expanded political agenda

Godwin (1992: 324) concludes that the mechanism of allowing supporters to contribute financially has permitted the effective articulation of views that might otherwise have not made it onto the agenda:

> [D]irect marketing has brought more but not different participants into interest group politics, and it has increased public attention on social and moral issues such as the environment and abortion. Direct marketing has allowed citizens from Los Angeles to Boston and Seattle to Miami to pool their resources in support of cleaner air, abortion legislation, and school prayer.

Depersonalization as an advantage

Ewing Cook similarly argued that individuals may in fact *value the impersonal nature* of participation that direct mail offers them. Her survey of group members found that

> for most people, their affiliation with a public interest group is not a matter of great significance. Although most members seem to appreciate the opportunity to contribute to groups that promote their causes, relatively few members are active in the organizations or appear to devote much attention to the groups' activities. For the many nonactivists, *the impersonal nature of the groups seems to be an advantage* in that it allows members to send in a check instead of allotting much of their own time and effort to influencing public policy. It may be that the $15 or $20 fee for membership in public interest groups is, for most people, a real bargain: in exchange citizens get the opportunity to soothe their consciences about not making a

bigger personal commitment to political participation (Ewing Cook, 1984: 427).

As noted in Chapter 4 some groups specifically encourage minimalistic participation and solely seek to attract financial supporters rather than members with a policy role. This circumvents the problems that may be associated with internal democracy and policy interference. Organizations with active internal 'noise' about group direction may be distracted from policy impact. As Cigler and Loomis (2002: 24) argue, the 'real' cost of support has fallen as discretionary incomes have grown: membership of groups such as PETA and Common Cause is no longer a 'luxury'. 'For a $15–$25 membership fee, people can make an "expressive statement" *without incurring other organizational obligations*' (emphasis added). The italicized section is important: it suggests that participation rights are not being denied to frustrated members and that a 'lack' of such rights may not be itself an important or pivotal (dis)incentive. Shallow, contribution-based participation may be *precisely* what is wanted. Richardson (1995: 135) argues significantly that credit-card participation could be a form of 'surrogate activism in which individuals support a particular cause – often single issue – but leave the formulation and delivery of the campaign to organizational professionals or to the few genuine activists within the organization'. Tasks are 'contracted out' by the supporters to the staff. 'Contracting out' may not necessarily lead to social alienation, intolerance and distrust (Maloney, 1999). Conover *et al.* (2002: 60) note:

> Philosophers accord deliberation a special place in democratic theory. And they envision citizens who accord deliberation a special place in their lives. But in fact, the citizens of modern liberal states have neither a special time nor a special place for the practice of democratic discussion . . .

In parallel, the argument is that the public may not value group participation to the extent that participatory optimists assume.

Therefore the fears of the direct marketing critics that this type of participation frustrates members or makes them less open to the needs of others are not confirmed. Godwin (1988a: 64) found that the longer individuals remained members of a direct marketing organization, the less alienated and aggressive they became. He (1992: 317–318) concluded that 'It would appear that even checkbook participation reduces political alienation, as contributors believe their contributions

Table 7.1 Loyalty: Direct mail and direct dialogue

	Direct mail (%) $n = 29$		Direct dialogue (%) $n = 12$	
	Yes	No	Yes	No
Less loyal than the average supporter	17	83	31	69
Less active than the average supporter	23	77	29	71
Less financially giving than the average supporter	21	79	8	92

make a difference. This, in turn, reduces the support for aggressive political participation.'

A study (survey of 4800 recruits) by Sargeant and Jay (2004) found that despite the growing media suspicion about face-to-face fund-raising, the donors expressed high levels of satisfaction. Lapsers tended to have financial pressures rather than disillusion. Nonetheless, they recorded attrition rates of over 50% for some non-profit organizations between years one and two. There were no significant differences between active and lapsed donors in terms of gender or income, but active recruits had an older mean age (by seven years) and also donated to other causes. As usual in terms of (public) interest group mobilization there was a strong bias towards women (64:36) and high annual income (27% over £40,000 per annum).

The campaign group leaders (in our 2002 sample) using direct mail and direct dialogue were asked if they found these supporters to behave in a different way, or if these supporters tended to be 'less loyal' than the members recruited through other means. Only a minority of group leaders agreed with that proposition (Table 7.1 above).

Interest groups, political linkage and social capital

Participation is widely seen both as beneficial for individuals in a developmental way and as a functional policy-making necessity. 'More is better' is the formula – for two main reasons. First, better policies emerge in the areas where groups are active: more informed (and workable) outcomes and greater legitimacy are attached to the end product. As Foley and Edwards (1988: 10) argue, a 'healthy democracy demands representation in terms of competing interest groups and interpretations of the public good, not just via the weak recourse of the individual vote for catchall parties – or, as is increasingly the case in the United States, "partyless" personalities'.

Secondly, there is the J. S. Mill proposition that 'better democrats' may be produced via their experiences within groups: participation in organizations helps individuals develop the individual's civic and political skills and orientations. As Putnam (1993: 89–90) argues,

> Civil associations contribute to the effectiveness and stability of democratic government, it is argued, because of their 'internal' effects on individual members... Internally, associations instil in their members habits of co-operation, solidarity, and public-spiritedness... Participation in civic organizations inculcates skills of co-operation as well as a sense of shared responsibility for collective endeavours...

Pollock (1982) distinguishes between *intentional mobilization* that reflects deliberate group stimulus, and *unintentional* that reflects the general, indirect effect of increasing political skills (quoted in Leighley, 1996: 448). The social capital interpretation assumes that unintentional mobilization/activation 'works' but the evidence is slight. Warren (1996: 241) sets out the normative assumption that participation is developmental:

> Theories of radical democracy hold that if individuals were more broadly empowered, especially in the institutions that most directly affect their everyday lives, their experiences would have transformative effects. Individuals would become more public spirited, more tolerant, more knowledgeable, more attentive to the interests of others and more probing of their own interests. And institutions that make collective decisions in radically democratic ways will tend to generate new forms of solidarity, cooperation and civic attachment.

Sanders (1997: 347) points out, 'When democratic theorists suggest remodelling our politics, it is in the direction of making them more deliberative.' The deliberative 'turn' has built on the participatory turn and perceives active involvement as a requirement of a good citizen. (Oscar Wilde's alleged answer to the why he was not a socialist was, 'I prefer to keep my evenings free.') Arguably, this belief has prompted some of the optimism that growing group numbers have something (loosely) to contribute to educative opportunities. Querying this assumption is, of course, at the centre of this book.

Internal effects have been a core concern for many social capital researchers. However, interest group scholars are also aware of this aspect of group life.[3] The 'schools of democracy' proposition has been summarized by Cigler and Joslyn (2002: 7):

> Citizens learning by experience in associational settings, both political and non-political, are said to acquire transferable skills, as well as behaviour patterns and orientations, *i.e.* 'habits of the heart' in Tocqueville's words, essential for a democratic polity.

Putnam (2000: 350–353) acknowledged that there is a *dark side* to group involvement. The *darkness* is likely to be more prevalent in organizations that generate *bonding* (as opposed to *bridging*) social capital: that is where involvement takes place in homogenous and/or hierarchical settings and where strong anti-views breed intolerance and distrust. Thus, it is important to note that internally democratically structured organizations, with a highly responsive leadership, may in their external societal impact be highly undemocratic and uncivic. As Lipset (1983: 432–433) highlighted:

> An organization under direct membership control may become irresponsible from either the vantage point of its need or those of society. The members may want their 'selfish' objectives pursued even if achieving them will hurt others or endanger the organization... [The] integration of members within a trade-union, a political party, a farm organization, a professional society, may increase the chances that members of such organizations will be active in the group and have more control over its policies. But extending the functions of such organizations so as to integrate their members may threaten the larger political system because it reduces the forces making for compromise and understanding among conflicting groups... It should be obvious that I do not advocate dictatorship in private organizations. But it may be necessary to recognize that many organizations may never fulfil the conditions for a stable internal democracy and still contribute in important ways to the democratic process in the total society, by providing a secure base for factionalism and real vested interests at the same time that they limit individual freedom within the organization and allow a degree of autonomy of action for both leaders and the organization which may undermine social values. This is another case of the incompatibility of values where they have contradictory consequences. There is no simple

answer that can resolve these problems of democracy in modern society.

Some interest group scholars also see problems with the optimistic 'line' that internally groups are providers of democratic opportunities. Many contemporary groups operate a minimalist democracy. Shaiko (1999: 21) argues that in the Public Interest Group sector arguments about internal democracy are all but redundant: 'Even in the most structurally representative organizations, bureaucratization of the leadership infrastructure is an organizational fact of life.' He quotes Moe (1980b: 259–260):

> the degree of internal democracy can be treated, from a pluralist standpoint, as something that does not really affect the more fundamental congruence between group goals and member goals – since congruence is guaranteed by the pluralist logic of membership. If individuals join (quit) interest groups because they agree (disagree) with their policies, then the question of oligarchy is in some sense beside the point.

Democracy is thus provided by the choice to participate or not; or *which* group to support. In this perspective financial support should not be conflated with active participation, especially when assessing the social capital potential of organizations. For many citizens writing the name of the organization on the cheque and signing it is the start and end of their involvement. But should this actually count as participation?

Realistically there may have to be a limited expectation of democratic vitality *within* groups, but there may be democracy in the choice between groups. The notion of a market for democratic choice 'fits' the interest group system better than the party. The prospective environmental supporter/member faces a significant choice between types of environmental groups. As Bosso (1991: 167) highlights,

> To the Greens (i.e. in his sense direct action groups), the major environmental groups have become just another set of lobbyists, and those holding 'deep ecology' values are just as unlikely to find common ground with their more mainstream brethren as they are to have trust in corporate or government leaders. The difference is one of values: mainstream environmentalists see their roles as ones of competitors in interest group politics; Greens shun institutional approaches for a fundamental reconfiguration of social values and behavior. *For the*

mainstream groups the issues are political; for the Greens the issues resolve around lifestyle . . . (emphasis added).

The list of choice factors can be extended (more generally) to issues such as group size; the degree of institutionalization of internal democratic practices; the promotion of 'sectional' interests or collective causes – beyond the membership; or financial or political independence of the organization and so on.

A persistent problem for polyarchies as they aspire to democratic status is that of equality: those whose predisposition is stimulated into *action* (loosely defined) are drawn from a relatively small subset of the public. It is an activity for the resource-rich – money, skills, relatively high educational attainment, confidence, high levels of internal and external political efficacy,[4] and sometimes time (but not always, because in many instances the people apparently with the least disposable time participate more in politics than those with the most) – predominate. The consequence of skewed participation was highlighted by Dahl (1996: 351):

> If some citizens are organized in associations and some are not, then the interests of the organized will almost certainly be taken more fully into account than the interests of the unorganized. Sometimes, in fact, the interest of the unorganized will be almost entirely neglected in political decisions.

Verba and Nie (1972), Parry *et al.* (1992) and many others have found that the standard (SES) model of participation holds; consequently policies may be skewed in favour of 'the particular participant groups and away from the more general "public interest" ' (Verba and Nie, 1972: 342). Group representativeness is further compounded by the fact that these standard (SES) model participators tend to hold multiple member-ships. More public interest groups need not necessarily mean greater citizen participation, it may mean more of the same. The proliferation of groups does not necessarily increase competition. The lesser (or non) involvement of many in society has been well documented over many years. Most famously, Schattschneider (1966: 35) argued that

> The flaw in the pluralist heaven is that the heavenly chorus sings with a strong upper-class accent . . . Pressure politics is a selective process ill designed to serve diffuse interests. The system is skewed, loaded, and unbalanced in favor of a fraction of a minority.

But the problem may be less severe than it appears. Though much of this participation is *by* or *of* a class, it is not necessary *for* that class. The important notion is the *group as surrogate*. Groups act on behalf of citizens that lack the resources. From this perspective even *biased groups* should not simply be tolerated within a democratic system – they may be integral to it. For example, some public interest group members may be drawn from a group of relatively wealthy citizens seeking to remedy a pressing social problem (faced by a disadvantaged social group). The alleged pathology of unrepresentativeness, and of a decline in civic and political involvement, requires more examination than the headlines suggest. While the empirical evidence identifies the 'negative' aspects of skewed involvement it also highlights more 'positive' biases. First, there may be redistributive or progressive elements to skewed involvement. Many resource-rich citizens may patronize causes that poorer citizens support. For example, in the environmental area many relatively poor citizens have strong pro-environmental attitudes, but may not afford the indulgence of membership (see Jordan and Maloney, 2006). The contribution of their wealthier co-citizens ensures that this interest is represented. The analogy is akin to business travellers subsidizing the airfare costs in economy.

Secondly, there is also a bias towards increased political knowledge and tolerance among participators. As Verba *et al.* (1995: 507, 529) note, while the resource-rich are the most involved these

> activists... are better informed and more tolerant of unpopular opinions. Thus, while the process exacerbates political inequality, it may enhance the quality of political discourse and democratic governance... (these citizens) conform to participatory democratic notions of the good citizen. And a participatory system that overrepresents their interest also overrepresents the politically informed and tolerant.

The supply-side sees similar outcomes based on role differentiation in which members use the group to act on their behalf. This supply-side participation is different from, rather than in contradiction to, other forms. Katz (1997: 72) argued that

> political activity is more common than the figures for any one action imply. Participationist democracy does not require that everyone participate in every decision, merely that everyone participate regularly in some area and that all people can participate fully in

any area in making decisions that affect themselves and their community.

Dalton (1996) argues that increasing political sophistication and awareness has led to a growth in *cognitive mobilization* – which has decreased the *costs* associated with political information (e.g. the growth of media coverage, especially television of politics), and increased citizens' abilities to process political information. He (1996: 63–64) further maintains that increasing political sophistication does not imply a growth in the level of all forms of political activity; it *may actually contribute to the changing nature of participation.* However, while Dalton (1996: 64) argues that 'the activity of citizen lobbies, single-issue groups and citizen-action movements may well be increasing in all advanced industrial democracies'. However, it is not necessarily the case that 'The new style of citizen politics . . . make(s) greater demands on the participants.' Chequebook participation does not lead to an increase in direct democracy–type activities. Chequebook participation can be seen as increasing the number of participators, but reducing the amount of participation. Individuals see their cheque writing as patronage of a good cause, with no further demand on their time being required.

However many public interest group supporters/members also support other groups, vote regularly, sign petitions, and can arguably be presented as being very politically active – certainly in contrast to the large bulk of the population who do no more than vote on a regular/irregular basis. Parry *et al.* (1992: 428) argued that 'One may vote and support a political party and thereby seek to influence policy. For most people, however, action beyond that is best taken nearer home. It is about the local environment, housing or transport.'[5] If Parry *et al.*'s (1992) argument is extended to the interest group system – empirically the likelihood of an individual joining a group rather than a party is much greater. Accordingly, joining a chequebook group does not preclude one from being more active in other areas. Individuals may be *participatory dualists* – subcontracting national issues to chequebook groups active in regional and national capitals, and taking part locally in formal and informal organizations.[6]

Finally, chequebook participation may be limited, but it is purposive: that is 'it reflects some degree of unhappiness with the way things are' (Salisbury, 1992: 216). It is purposively directed at funding protest, even if not about directly joining in the protest. Chequebook participation may be seen as rational in the sense of objective and outcome. Cheque writers may see little utility in personally taking to the streets and may realize that the only prospect for a successful outcome is to fund a group.

Group activity judged against the participatory ideal

The overall evaluation of the contribution of modern group life of course depends on the criteria brought to the process. The discontent within the political science community with electorally based democratic opportunities at least dates from Pateman's *Democracy and Participation* (1970) that articulated a participatory ideal. That was the occasion for a step change in the level of discontent with vote-based democracy: participation and 'deliberation' (ideally small-scale) were seen as superior democratic forms. This redirection was reinforced in Barber's *Strong Democracy: Participatory Politics for a New Age* (1984). He defined *strong democracy* as a 'politics in the participatory mode: literally, it is self government by citizens rather than representative government in the name of citizens... Participatory politics deals with public disputes and conflicts of interest by subjecting them into a never ending process of deliberation, decision, and action.'

The deliberative tide surged around 1990. Gutmann and Thompson (2004: vii) note that 'No subject has been more discussed in political theory in the last two decades than deliberative democracy.' While Dryzek (2000: 1) argued:

> Deliberation as a social process is distinguished from other kinds of communication in that deliberators are amenable to changing their judgements, preferences, and views during the course of their interactions, which involve persuasion, rather than coercion, manipulation, or deception. The essence of democracy itself is now widely taken to be deliberation, as opposed to voting, interest aggregation, constitutional rights, or even self-government.

As argued above, the belief in the redemptive qualities of interest group membership make sense if they are seen as part of a syndrome of beliefs that are well debated in Hood's discussion of the egalitarian form of public management. Hood (2000: 122) notes an egalitarian approach to organizations that involve three closely interrelated elements: 'group self-management, control by mutuality, and maximum face-to-face accountability'. These expectations are precisely those that characterize social movement observers. Perhaps they do not reflect objective differences between social movement and interest group scholarship – more of a normative preference. Hood (2000: 122) notes:

egalitarian norms of organization . . . involve relatively weak formal leadership and rely heavily on communal "participative" decision-making involving most or all of the members . . . (such structures) can only continue to exist if the people they contain share beliefs and values that make the structure work.

This conclusion is arguing that much of the weight placed on the interest group system in terms of delivering for democracy is actually by observers who want decision-making to be bottom–up, active and deliberative. Hood (2000: 124) notes a wish in egalitarian management to 'limit the difference between top officeholders and the rank-and-file in organizations'. This of course is precisely the ambition of some who placed democratic potential on groups – and who therefore dislike the protest business tendency. Hood (2000: 11) argues that 'In other words, cultural dynamics work by mutual antagonism among opposites seeking to blame the adherents of alternative ways of life for the social ills they are held to create.' Those dissatisfied with the 'democratic malaise' that is often associated with electoral and party aspects of politics may in their reaction exaggerate the participatory nature of modern associations. Finally, in Chapter 6 Hood points out:

> When things go wrong in public management [substitute democracy] . . . egalitarians tend to see the root of the problem as self-serving behaviour of those at the top of big organizations. From this perspective, it is the gulf between the amoral and manipulative 'executive suite' level of big corporate structures and the virtuous but oppressed organizational rank-and-file or surrounding community that corrupts the whole structure and leads to fiascos. So egalitarian recipes for better public management [read democracy] normally consist of more group participation to limit the large-scale errors and damaging power-plays that conventional hierarchist organization is believed to foster.

Groups do involve large numbers (but as Olson pointed out, certainly nowhere near the numbers who share their views), but their role is a shadow of that sought by the egalitarians. In summary, the role of modern groups may well fall very short of the aspirations of the participatory optimists. Not for them chequebook participation. But to the extent that groups provide limited participation but on a large-scale; activate support by individuals for collective ends (however hard Olson showed it would be); provide a policy expertise that is a more realistic challenge to government than offered by Oppositions or the unorganized public, these are all merits. For all but the utopians and participatory evangelists.

This work accepts the proposition of Rosenstone and Hansen (1993: 228) that few people spontaneously take an active part in public affairs, but instead are engaged through politicians, families and friends and groups in getting them involved. As they hinted (1993: 234) changes in technology and society were weakening parties and had 'promoted interest groups and encouraged them to mobilize'. But it may be a less satisfactory form of engagement than some imagined.

Notes

1. Looking for democracy: The democratic contribution of membership-based interest groups

1. Academically associations (interest groups) are very much *in vogue*, albeit often with snazzy new neologisms – (new) social movement organizations, non-governmental organizations, civil society organizations, etc.). As Grant (2002: 5) points out the unquestioning acceptance of the (newly fashionable) term 'civil society' conjoined with the new intellectual associations of the term, has lead to a positive bestowal of legitimacy on what were once seen as interest groups. The democratic credentials of associations in the interest group guise were seen as deficient. However, a group in civil society robes appears more (normatively) wholesome and attractive.

2. The Directory of British Associations (CBD, 2006) '... includes information on national associations, societies, institutes and similar organizations in all fields of activity which have a voluntary membership'.

3. Of course, the key issue for scholars such as Putnam is not simply the density of the associational universe, but how many members are active? And the levels of their involvement?

4. In Walker's (1991) terminology a citizen group is open to all – unlike many other definitions of groups that require certain professional or occupational credentials. This is potentially a wider scope than the public interest group notion.

5. Browne (1995: 15–17) notes an advocacy explosion in recent years citing a 700% increase in groups between 1947 and 1984.

6. Governments are also keen to support much voluntary association (and specifically interest group) activity. Schudson (1998: 278) cites evidence showing that in 1981 the federal government spent $46 billion 'in support' of non-profit institutions: this sum represented some 38% of revenues of those bodies.

7. Berry (1984: 460) says the trends are independent but the growth of groups has benefited from party decline. In his view the alienation of the public from government both weakened the parties and gave groups an opportunity to expand their role.

8. Putnam (1995b: 664) defines social capital as '... the features of social life – networks, norms, and trust – that enable participants to act more effectively to pursue shared objectives'.

9. The Report of the Rowntree Power Inquiry, *Power to the People* (2006) also stressed the 'myth of apathy' – arguing that the decline is in the area of electoral and formal politics rather than in general.

10. In the 1945–2005 period, the highest General Election turnout was in 1950 (83.9%) and the lowest in 2001 (69.4%).

11. Mueller (1999: 172) echoed Madison's concern when he argued that special interest groups can '... be effectively reined in only by abandoning democracy itself, because their activities are absolutely vital to the form'.

12. While Rousseau argued that associational life prevented the general will from emerging and argued generally against partial interest groups. He did have a 'last resort' position close to that of Madison: 'If, then, the general will is to be truly expressed, it is essential that there be no subsidiary groups within the state, and that each citizen voice his own opinion and nothing but his own opinion... where subsidiary groups do exist their numbers should be made as large as possible and none should be more powerful than its fellows' (cited in Hampsher-Monk, 1992: 187).

13. J S Mill advises against schemes that require 'exalted' principles of conduct (see Pateman, 1970: 29).

14. Rousseau said, '... are the people of England free only once every five years when choosing whom they will be subservient to?'

15. While groups are expected to be internally democratically pure, for many years political parties have not met such standards. For example, in the classic UK studies of political parties over the last 40 years (e.g. McKenzie, 1964 and Minkin, 1980) found that in spite of formal structural differences between the two governing parties – Labour and Conservative – there was little difference in the actual responsiveness of leaders. Both parties were leader dominated.

16. The distinction between individuals and businesses is a little blurred when it comes to organizations representing small businesspeople, builders, the professions and farmers.

17. Demonstrating representativeness is not always as straightforward as it might appear. Even those groups that mobilize relatively large numbers of citizens, might not be so significant or representative when put in context. For example, Cupps (1977: 485–486) quotes Rep. Edith Green as pointing out that in 1974 while Common Cause had around 300,000 members the average congressional district had, at least, a 500,000 population: '... how representative is a group with fewer members than an average district? I have serious reservations about... these groups that cloak themselves in the mantle of the public good and actually represent only the views of a relatively few people'.

18. The broad interpretation of the interest group term is compatible with the influential systems approach developed by Easton (1953) in which it is the fact that organizations make demands that is important – not differences between organizational forms. Easton (1953: 173) observed that the process approach revealed the role of groups in policy-making. Though he noted that not all groups were interest groups, '*Even governmental institutions are now customarily treated in this context as a species of interest groups*' ... (emphasis added).

19. Heinz *et al.* (1993: 29) note that, 'For years scholars presumed that interest groups meant voluntary associations, Truman's (1951) magisterial work deals entirely with such organizations, and they are the focus of Mancur Olson (1965) and those who have followed his lead. Most of the abundant case studies of interest group activity also examine groups whose members choose, more or less freely, to support the group'. It was such an approach that yielded the *voluntary, democratically accountable and individual-based*

image of interest groups outlined above. They go on to note the transformation of the field of inquiry, 'Subsequently, the analysis of interested activity was *explicitly extended to include organizations that had long been active in seeking to advance their interests*... business corporations, universities, state and local governments' (emphasis added). This book reverts to the earlier interpretation. This extension of the scope of coverage in the policy field is sensible in its own context, but it reads oddly for those who see the interest group issue as being about mobilizing individuals for collective action (or even the creation of 'organizations of organizations'). Often the expansion in definitional scope is simply ignored.

20. These distinctions were first set out in a paper by Jordan *et al.* (1992). Gray and Lowery (1996: 12) address this problem by using the term *interest organization*, 'Interest group, however, is fundamentally misleading as a characterization of what we study. As Salisbury (1984) pointed out... most interest organizations are not membership *groups*, representing individuals banded together to influence government policy, but institutions, such as banks, industrial firms, universities, local governments, or hospitals'. Their data reported that scarcely over one-fifth (22.8%) of registered lobbying organizations in the states were membership-based groups. Our term 'pressure participant' combines with interest groups and policy participant and maps on to associations and institutions.

21. The interest groups marketplace is awash with competitor organizations all chasing the same Dollar, Pound or Euro. In order to be successful groups attempt to occupy a particular niche position in distinction to their competitors. In many instances, this market niche leads the organization to seek a narrow membership. The more 'exclusive' membership may be attracted to the group because it is *purer* than some large-scale organization that may have to make internal (and external) compromises to aggregate interests, or maintain an advantageous position in the policy-making process.

22. As Dunleavy (1991: 54) has noted, public choice accounts tend to perceive 'group joining as a one-off problem'. In fact, the rejoining decision often appears to 'undo' the initial decision to join.

23. A caveat regarding local chapters and branches is that even where these exist and a small percentage of members are active (e.g. Friends of the Earth or Greenpeace) some local groups are merely affiliated to the national group via the brand logo, there is no mechanism for local group members to become involved in national policy formulation. In groups such as Amnesty International (British Section) there are greater opportunities for membership input into policy decisions.

24. From the 426 groups classified as campaigning organizations in the Directory 73 provided no information on membership size. While the overall response rate is a healthy 57%, the apparent response rate in the sub categories is higher than would be the case if we were able to classify the 73 non-respondents. Seven groups refused to provide membership data in our survey.

25. In 2003 the Council for the Protection of Rural England changed its name to the Campaign to Protect Rural England.

26. The interviews were conducted by Dr Jennifer Lees-Marshment, who also contributed to early drafts of the questionnaire. Emma Clarence was Dr Lees-Marshment's replacement as Research Fellow on the ESRC project.

She also contributed to the development of the questionnaires and efficiently coordinated the logistics of the data collection and oversaw data inputting.

27. The questionnaire asked: 'In the last 12 months have you:

- been a member of this type of organization (in other words you have paid a membership fee if it is required)
- participated in an activity arranged by this type of organization
- donated money as an individual to this type of organization
- done voluntary or unpaid work for this type of organization?'

It also established environmental attitudes. Respondents were asked to indicate their level of agreement with:

- 'Protecting the environment is so important that environmental improvements must be made regardless of costs.'

28. This generated 746 members and 1391 nonmembers (in the concerned category). Data protection legislation required respondents to express their willingness to be re-contacted. This step led to exclusions: 574 (77%) members and 926 (67%) 'nonmembers' agreed to participate in our study. This data protection filter may have introduced a bias but the rates of refusal at that stage were broadly similar. Subsequent checking found that 74 respondents, who initially designated themselves as members, now indicated that they had no current or previous relationship with an environmental organization and a further six were untraceable, deceased or abroad. The 'switchers' were also excluded. Thus, the effective '*n*' for the member survey fell to 494 and 359 usable responses were received (73%). Similar checks on non-members found 132 respondents indicating that they *had* some form of relationship with an environmental organization and were removed from that population, and a further 22 were ineligible. Accordingly the number of potential non-members fell to 772 and we received 389 responses (50%).

2. The collective action paradox: What incentives induce participation? Olson defied?

1. The free-rider problem was anticipated by Hume in 1793 in arguing that government should provide public goods such as bridges because individuals deriving benefit from a public good will otherwise leave the cost of provision to others (see Stroup, 2000: 485).
2. Dahl (1961: 279) suggested, 'Instead of seeking to explain why citizens are not interested, concerned and active, the task is to explain why a few citizens *are*.' Dahl raises the key puzzle for social science that Olson ignored. He (1961: 283) noted that participation may be a minority activity, but it was disproportionately followed by the 'better-off'. If participation is 'irrational' (Olson) why does education and income increase such irrationality?
3. Of course one can resist the notion of rationality present in that formulation.

4. Berry (1997: 71) says only 17% of AARP members were mainly concerned about issues affecting the elderly: access to the selective benefits of membership were more important.

5. Self-interested motivations underlying some contemporary involvement represent participation that is a long way from the readings of the past. For example, Rousseau perceived *non*-self-interested participation as crucial – the selfish participant was seen as democratically defective as the non-participator. However, in discussions of the political involvement of citizens, group-based participation is commonly regarded as important and valuable. If Olson correctly identified that the motivation for participation is merely material self-interest, then some of the democratic benefits of group participation are severely reduced.

6. As Walker (1991: 41–42) put it, 'Thousands of Americans were descending on Washington at that time to press claims of all sorts on the government, just as scholars were elaborating theories about why they should never be expected to mobilize.' Wilson (1995) noted that 'More voluntary associations existed even in 1965, when Olson, wrote, than one would have predicted knowing only that people are rationally self-interested. And within a very few years, their number grew exponentially.'

7. Downs accepted non-economic reasons for voting.

8. Hay (2004: 44) quotes Dunleavy (1991: 3): 'someone behaves "rationally" if they optimize their preferences in a consistent fashion, however ill-advised we may judge their preferences to be'. This is a more relaxed line than that by Olson and others who assume that rational behaviour must fit their (externally imposed) expectation.

9. Olson (1965: 60) argued that it is 'important to distinguish between the obstacles to group-orientated action that are due to a lack of group consensus and those that are due to a lack of individual incentives'.

10. An organization such as the Automobile Association will attempt to influence the political process on behalf of 'members' – but few would sensibly assume that members join *for* that service. The phenomenon of pseudo groups – for example health clubs, etc. – are muddying the mud in this area.

11. But what Green and Shapiro (1994) regard as 'large' would be dismissed by Olson as simply residual exceptions.

12. This point assumes that the democratic contribution of groups lies in their opportunities for individual participation rather than their agenda-setting and policy-influencing role.

13. In 2002 Greenpeace was advertising an apparent selective incentive – that members could have a PVC free credit card. In reality, however, this was a greater benefit to Greenpeace than the recipient as the group received £10 for every individual who signed up for a card triggered and a share of the spent on the card.

14. Wilson (1995) notes that groups (e.g. Rotary) feel a need to 'cloak' the quest for interpersonal rewards by a more serious intent such as assisting educational or poverty projects. At the least, the members feel the 'good works' justify the more personal benefit they might get through social networks.

15. The concept of purposive incentives has been the most criticized component of Clark and Wilson's model, largely for its 'fuzziness'. Teske (1997: 65)

argues that 'There is no clear consensus on the meaning of "purposive incentive"... and in general the lack of definitional clarity is skated over to allow scholars to get on with empirical analyses.' He cites a variety of definitions. For example, Berry (1984) sees purposive incentives as 'ideological or issue-oriented goals that offer no tangible benefit', while Moe (1980b) claims that they have something to do with one's 'values'. However, Teske (1997: 66) argues that the main problem with the discussion of purposive incentives in the interest group literature is that the concept was devised before the publication of Olson's seminal volume and hence it was not directly concerned with the free-rider problem: 'interest group scholars... see it through an Olsonian prism, but it was not created to test Olsonian hypotheses'. He (1997: 69) argues that the purposive category was not created to account for the paradox of collective action: 'they [Clark and Wilson, 1961] did not yet share the concerns of the post-Olson world and did not think of collective action as paradoxical. In short, the concept of purposive incentives was not developed to resolve the paradox of collective action, but, rather, to help develop a theory of internal organizational dynamics.'

16. The indifferent voter would still be indifferent after the event – the committed voter might be full of self-blame. Of course, in the group, as opposed to the electoral situation, the possibility of identifying 'near win' situations is less common than in elections. In elections one can say '5 more votes would have made a difference'. It is less easy to say that a group with 80,000 members would have had (more) success with 80,001 members. But in two ways this can be reconstructed as actually increasing the value of the minimax regret idea in group behaviour. Since group successes are rarely win/lose like elections it can be surmised that a larger group might get 'more' than a smaller. Thus joining might increase the reward. Secondly, since one is rarely able to say with precision what threshold is vital in group size, then the possibilities of regret can be almost endless.

17. This chapter repeatedly makes a simple point because it seems neglected. That some people join because of their commitment to collective goals is not sufficient to undermine Olson. His point is that the vast bulk would NOT join. The joiners are his exceptions.

18. In a sense the lower rate of group membership than general election voting means Olson seems a better guide to group (in)activity than voting – and of course the measure of group membership is usually financial – suggesting some congruence with Olson. Another comparison between the group and voting cases is that generally the paradox is treated more seriously in the group context. In the voting field it is so large that it seems to inhibit contemporary discussion.

19. Sen (1978) famously charged that at the heart of economic models was the 'self seeking egoist'. He complains that if rational choice is simply about consistent preference ordering then a person is 'rational' in a limited sense of having no inconsistencies. But Sen goes on to identify the purely economic man as 'a bit of a fool [and]... indeed close to being a social moron'.

20. However, while selective incentives may not be the main driver of support for public interest groups, it can be a part of the mechanics of translating

a general sympathy into active support. For example, *The British Sociological Association* underpinned a recruiting drive in 2004 with the very Olsonian incentive that members received Marks and Spencer vouchers for introducing a new member. This reflects on both recruiting and contemporary sociology.

21. In fact, there may be two subgroups of 'wide'. The narrower might still see the individual as 'selfish'. Thus Barry in *Sociologists, Economists and Democracy* (1970) suggests that an altruistic contribution might be compelled by a wish to avoid the guilt of not contributing to such an organization. The donor is thus acting selfishly, or at least self-interestedly, but not economically rationally. Such a scenario identifies non-economical support to altruistic organizations but in a way that retains some kind of personal cost–benefit reasoning.

22. His explanation of the success of veterans' organizations is that they succeeded by supplying 'social benefits' – 'The veteran gets not only the physical facilities of the club, but also comradeship and recognition of his wartime service by joining a veterans' organization . . . In addition, the American Legion offers group insurance benefits to members. All of these social and other benefits go only to those who join; they provide selective incentives.' However, he pointed out that a veteran's bonus would be paid to all veterans whether or not they are in membership. If this was the result of the political power of the lobbies it is a by-product of the selective social and economic services.

23. Opp (1999: 183) maintains that his expanded RCT version does not.

24. Verba *et al.* (2000: 264) argue that their data demonstrates that 'Narrow versions of rational choice that specify self-interested ends (using any limited notion of self-interest) could not explain the wide variety of citizens activity . . . If, however, we admit a large number of other kinds of motivations, then measurement of desires or beliefs about how acts will satisfy these desires becomes very difficult. Indeed it is hard to delineate what actions would not be rational. In sum, a narrow version of rational actor theory when applied to preferences or benefits is testable but wrong. A broader version allowing multiple and varied preferences and benefits is the opposite.'

25. In fact Olson was proposing his own circularity: those who joined groups did so because they obtained advantages not available through not joining. Udehn (1996: 243) quotes Barry (1970: 33–37) who pointed out: 'Obviously, the constant danger of "economic" theories is that they can come to "explain" everything by re-describing it. Theory then fail to be any use in prediction that one thing will happen rather than another. Thus if an organization maintains itself, we say "it must have provided selective incentives", and this is bound to be true since whatever motives people had for supporting it are called "selective incentives".' The problem for Olson was that his link between incentive type and mobilization appeared defective: mobilization without selective material benefit appeared too common. Other types of joining were simply bundled up as 'irrational'.

26. Dunleavy (1991: 43) also notes the problem of what he neatly calls 'bolt on' modifications to Olson's work. He points out that huge numbers of people

do join large interest groups in contradiction of formal, economic rationality. But as he says the modifications fail to keep the core proposition by
Olson intact.

3. Making interests: Creating members?

1. Truman's (1951: 33) famous definition was, ' "interest group" refers to any
   group, that, on the basis of one or more shared attitudes, makes certain
   claims upon other groups . . . '
2. Rothenberg's (1992) 'experiential' interpretation better fits this version.
   Group joiners can test their attitudes against the experience of the group.
3. This thesis profoundly influenced subsequent literature on environmentalism (see, for example, Dalton, 1994; Kanji and Nevitte, 1997;
   Rohrschneider, 1988, 1993; Worcester, 1995).
4. Inglehart's postmaterialist thesis is not the only theory purporting a relationship between environmentalism and broader changes in peoples' values
   or core beliefs. See also Kitschelt (1989, 1990).
5. The idea that a link exists between environmentalism and class is by no
   means universally accepted. van Liere and Dunlap (1980) examined evidence for such a link using various indicators of environmental concern
   including the perception that environmental problems are serious support
   for government efforts to protect the environment and participation in
   pro-environmental behaviour. They concluded that their evidence 'provides
   very weak support for the assertion that social class is positively associated
   with environmental concern'.
6. Downs 1972 article 'Up and Down With Ecology' predicted that public
   attention on topics did not endure indefinitely but rather would be subject
   to the dictates of a systematic 'Issue Attention Cycle'.
7. The social construction explanation for the emergence of environmentalism has faced mounting criticism, most notably from realists (see
   Cudworth, 1999; Martell, 1994 as cited in Cudworth, 1999: 9; Dunlap
   and Catton as cited in Burningham and Cooper, 1999: 229). The realist
   critique is grounded in two related core beliefs: first that non-social
   phenomenon have causal efficacy, and second that it should be possible
   to make objective claims about their efficacy (Burningham and Cooper,
   1999: 229).
8. Szerszynski (1991) notes that the 'cultural logic' whereby certain framing
   of environmental issues engage powerfully with existing discourses
   on society must be the subject of future research on environmental
   attitudes.
9. The idea of *agenda setting* was popularized by Cobb and Elder in an article in
   1971. In their book in 1972, *Participation in American Politics: The Dynamics
   of Agenda Building*, they defined an issue as 'a conflict between two or
   more identifiable groups over procedural or substantive matters relating
   to the distribution of positions or resources'. In creating a public reaction
   it appears important to construct a conflict so that 'sides can be joined'. Like
   the framing discussion, with which it overlaps, the core idea is that public
   views can be shaped by group skill.

10. Zald (1996: 262) terms framing as 'the specific metaphors, symbolic in representation and cognitive cues used to render or cast behaviour in an evaluative mode and to suggest alternative forms of action'.

4. The business of building group membership

1. Kitschelt (1992: 22) argues that the mass media has an important impact on the internal democratic structures of left libertarian movements and parties. He maintains that the direct democracy which previously existed in these organizations has been replaced by 'liberal democratic institutions with personal representation inside small-framework parties that attract few members... the importance of the mass media and campaign technology in the electoral competition has rendered mass party organizations and organized democracy irrelevant'. Kitschelt (1992: 23) concludes that direct democratic procedures have been replaced by 'liberal mechanisms of individualistic representation and entrepreneurship'.

2. Johnson (1995: 15) shows that the direct mail strategy in the US is particularly associated with the largest groups. Six out of the seven largest groups in his sample of environment groups used direct mail. Cohen (1995: 176) notes that Amnesty USA sends out 11 million direct mail letters every year.

3. Jordan and Maloney (1997: 170) quoted Steve Sawyer, former Executive Director of Greenpeace USA, 'The nature of the central ideological debate within Greenpeace is: do we approach direct action as a political tool or as a marketing trademark?' Similarly we cited Berry (1984: 82), 'For some interest group leaders, then, it may not be the mix of benefits they offer, but how aggressively they market their organizations, which make the crucial difference.'

4. His examples are from the environmental field.

5. The six cities were: Aalborg (Denmark), Aberdeen (UK), Bern (Switzerland), Enschede (the Netherlands), Mannheim (Germany) and Sabadell (Spain).

6. Edwards (2004: 194) found that (in the Netherlands) only 10% of the membership of the Association of Women's Interests were connected to the Internet. At the other end of the spectrum the group 45% of Wise Old Women Amsterdam (WOUW) membership had Internet access.

7. The professionalization of this world has seen launch of dedicated journals such as *Interactive Marketing*.

8. Roberts and Berger (1989: 228–230) note that direct mail planners can follow the AIDA model: Attention; Interest; Desire; Action.

9. Johnson (1995: 19) reports one group's entrepreneur as speaking from 'the literature on direct marketing, where the critical concepts are *investment* and the *lifetime value* of a member'. He quotes the respondent describing the group's objective in using (even though it lost many in its first year) direct mail campaign to attract members as follows: 'It is like a sort of capital investment. You put your money in an it comes out eventually, over time... You know, its fairly simple, and a lot more secure than a lot of the kinds of investments that people make all the time... like the stock market and that kind of stuff.'

10. Including age, educational attainment, geographical location, lifestyle, previous record in responding to mail shots, specific magazine subscriptions,

etc. As Gosden (1985: 83) explains, those who have responded to a previous mail shot 'are more apt to respond to something else by mail . . . They are the customers of someone who sells by mail. There is a better chance they will respond to you than non-mail order respondents . . . the fact they respond to mail is a more important selection criteria than any other factor'. Gosden (1985: 85) further observed, 'donors to one cause are more likely to give to another cause'.

11. In addition the format of the request can be varied to suit the values of the organization and recipient. Godwin (1992: 310) describes how 'the Republican National Committee sends engraved invitations in mailings requesting donors to pledge $1,000, whereas Environmental Action, a left-wing environmental group, uses recycled paper and asks for $35'.

12. There are, however, potential limits to the success of this strategy. Jordan *et al.* (1994: 556) noted how Greenpeace UK surveyed its lapsed members and found many felt because of 'doom fatigue': '[m]embers apparently became disillusioned by the scale and long term nature of the environmental problems which the group attempted to deal with. [G]roups like Greenpeace and FoE have changed tack by switching their membership strategies to concentrate on delivering solutions rather than emphasis problems'.

13. Kawashima (2004: 9) quotes the Chief of the World Council of Whalers – 'whales are an issue du jour, a convenient means of accomplishing larger organizational ends; whales are their cash cows . . . ' – and Komori Shigeki of WWF Japan, 'The anti-whaling campaign is important for fund raising for environmental organizations. It brings money.'

14. Kawashima (2004: 13) cites Kojima (1993) who described the activities of Greenpeace in following the Japanese whaling ship Nisshin Mara. Greenpeace attached a long banner to the starboard of the whaling ship *which could not be read from the Nisshin Mara*. This detail neatly makes the point that the banner was the backdrop to the publicity Greenpeace sought rather than directed at the immediate events.

15. E-marketing is no doubt the next evolutionary stage in recruitment. According to the *Guardian*, 'Homelessness charity Centrepoint is planning to launch an e-marketing campaign in the autumn to tackle the problem of an ageing donor base.' Developing from this technique it described how Centrepoint is hoping to build on this younger supporter base through a range of initiatives including cold and warm e-mailings. The charity recently appointed direct marketing agency Whitewater to help develop its e-marketing strategy. Centrepoint direct marketing manager Cathy Gale says e-marketing is a cost-effective way of reaching a wider audience and offers a fast way of communicating with potential or existing supporters: 'It's cheap, which is the key thing. Our marketing budget isn't huge and we have to maximise return on our investment.'

5. Understanding joining – and not joining

1. The *Sunday Times* (2 March 2003) reported that 'charities and campaigning groups are operating more and more like multinationals . . . To meet this challenge they are looking to recruit big international players, many from the private sector, to fill newly created top management roles . . . One of

the best examples of a sector-switcher is Paul Steele, who was appointed chief operating officer of WWF...He was chief executive of the Virgin Trading Company, senior vice-president of sales, marketing and IT with Hilton Hotels, and held various senior roles with Pepsi-Cola International.'

2. Greenpeace treats new members to a welcome programme that sends a welcome pack then follows up with other information allowing the recruit to select different styles of relationship. As established in Chapter 4 new technology permits groups to target members more individually. One group referred to its new computer package (Razor's Edge), 'we can do so much more: we can manipulate the data much better than we could before...the old system was really unsophisticated, there's mot much you could have done with it, but with the new system we can get all sorts of different types of mailing to different types of (sub) groups'.

3. The *Sunday Telegraph* (18 August 2002) reported a problem in the number of nuns coming forward in the US, which has led to focus groups campaigns to recruit. After a television reference during the Oprah Winfrey Show the website of the Adrian Dominican nuns in Michigan got 4000 hits on the following week compared to the usual 150: supply-side salvation. And of course if you do not actually want to join, donations are tax deductible: 'The Adrian Dominican Sisters have been ministering to others for more than a century. Our donors provide major support for our life and mission. Please print this form out from one of the links below and send it along with your contribution to: Adrian Dominican Sisters, 1257 East Siena Heights Drive, Adrian, Michigan 49221-1793. Make checks payable to the Adrian Dominican Sisters. Gifts are tax-deductible as specified in the tax code.'

4. Bosso (2003: 408–409) further notes that 'Even Common Cause – which by itself has generated as much theoretical work on interest groups as the city of New Haven did on power structure research in the 1960s – has evolved into a professional advocacy organization that happens to "sell" the cause of good government to willing consumers.'

5. Jordan and Maloney's (1997) study of lapsed FoE members received a disturbingly high number of calls from respondents denying they were lapsed. FoE confirmed that the individuals' membership had in fact not been sustained. But these were often supporters who gave money on an irregular basis though they still *perceived themselves* to be fully paid-up supporters who had made a donation and intended to do so again at some point. (Some 'lapsed' members actually made financial contributions that were well in excess of the supporter fees.) They were not, in their own minds, members who became non-members. In a(n accidental) way this refers neatly back to Truman (1951: 158): 'Membership...should not be understood narrowly as including only those who pay dues to a formal organization. These "fellow travellers" who share the attitudes characteristic of an interest group must also be reckoned in some degree as participants in it.'

6. Our questionnaire went to the Royal British Legion (Scotland) with 77,090 members reported in the CBD Directory. The Earl Haig Fund shares staff with the Legion and the Chief Executive responded as the Earl Haig Fund representative. The main activity of the fund is a poppy sale when 10,000 collectors will raise about £1.5 million. This is a clear case where the large figure reported were supporters rather than members *per se*.

In many ways the Royal British Legion/Earl Haig overlap is analogous to other organizations that have distinct sub-identities (e.g. Greenpeace has four distinct companies registered with Companies House). The Earl Haig response clearly stated that it was a supporter-based organization without formal membership and acting on behalf of non-members. However the Royal British Legion (Scotland) is a member-based organization with a selective incentive structure. Nonetheless the Chief Executive (of both organizations) reported the 'importance of listening and acting on what the membership has to say'. In our view this is an accurate account by the Chief Executive of a blurred position not a confused one. The two organizations have an overlapping scope. It is not an embarrassment for empirical research to have to deal with these practical problems: they illuminate aspects about organizations that would not otherwise be discovered.

7. Its website says, 'The National Pensioners Convention (NPC) is Britain's biggest pensioner organization representing over 1000 local, regional and national pensioner groups with a total of 1.5 m members.'

8. The NSPCC is not a simple membership body but a complex organization (18,000 staff in 2005) delivering services, lobbying and raising funds. It raised £21.3 million in 2000/2001 via 200 Community appeals, branches, 17,000 Community appeal volunteers, payroll giving, legacies, online shopping, an affiliated credit card, share donation scheme, etc.

9. See Table 1.1 for Sampling Procedures and Response Rates.

10. The 'ns' were 54 small, 68 medium, 9 large and 374 ALL groups.

11. It is worth noting that the question of why people join is of importance only for leaders in so far as it helps them determine successful strategies for gaining and retaining members. The *political* significance of high membership density and the financial resources that the organization gains are the same *regardless* of *why* members actually support the organization.

12. But the number of groups is small (11).

13. This section summarizes the findings in Jordan, G and Maloney, W A (2006).

14. Eurobarometer 51.1 (1999) suggested 66% of UK population thought the environment was an 'immediate and urgent problem'.

15. Concern and knowledge of the group can be related. Concern may be the result of 'framing' by the group.

16. In fact Sabatier (1992: 105) points out that Olson assumed that policy preferences were randomly scattered among members and non-members 'because support for collective goods is, in his view, irrelevant to the decision to join . . . '. This article assumes that Olson's free-riding explanation is best tested comparing members with pro-group views with non-members with pro-group views. This exercise *deliberately excludes non-members with policy preferences inconsistent with the group.* Such non-members are not seen as free-riding.

17. *Members* are compared with *environmental non-members* (as opposed to those not in any membership) to provide a particularly interesting contrast. *Environmental non-members* are already members of other (non-environmental) organizations. Why do they not join groups in this sector?

18. The **Resources** and **Recruitment** headings are self-explanatory. Others were constructed as follows.

Commitment. *Pro-environmental attitudes* – respondents were asked to assess the balance between environmental improvement and economic growth; and the prevention of industrial pollution and its impact on prices. *Material sacrifice* – members and non-members were asked about their willingness to donate part of their income to prevent environmental pollution; tax hypothecation (i.e. to pay higher taxes if the money was used to prevent environmental pollution); and if government should reduce environmental pollution without them having to pay. *Environmental action* – respondents were asked how often they recycled glass, tins, plastic and newspapers; made a special effort to buy organically grown fruits and vegetables; and used public transport instead of own vehicle.

Efficacy. *Organizational effectiveness* – asked members and non-members how effective they believed that environmental groups were at protecting the environment at the local, national and international level; raising public awareness of environmental issues; influencing the behaviour of ordinary people; influencing government policy and preserving habitats for animals. *Efficacy of participation* – respondents were asked how *effective in terms of influencing decisions in society it would be to*: donate money to groups/organizations or simply to be a member of an interest group, undertake voluntary work in organizations; be active within a political party; participate in campaigns and public demonstrations; take part in acts of civil disobedience; and attend a meeting or a rally.

Material self-interest – members were asked if they would be *more or less likely to continue to support an environmental organization* 'if it reduced the resources used for core activities (e.g. campaigning, conservation, etc.) to increase the amount of benefits/services available to members'. Environmental non-members were asked if they *would be more or less likely to join* under the same circumstances.

6. The social capital and democratic potential of campaigning organizations

1. The European Social Survey reported the figure as 6%.
2. The Liberal Democrats membership currently stands at 76,023 and the Greens circa 5000.
3. The Eurobarometer reported that 56% of UK citizens were organizational members.
4. If motoring organizations are included in estimates of political involvement then analogously purchasers of goods and services from mutual and friendly building societies and insurance companies can be added. Indeed many motoring organizations are simply service providers and the relation is simply market-like. This is why Pattie *et al.* (2004) exclude these involvements from their estimates.
5. Based on an estimated UK adult population of 44 million.
6. The question asked was – 'In the last 12 months have you: been a *member* of this type of organization (in other words, have you paid a membership fee

if required); *participated in an activity* arranged by this type of organization; *donated money* as an individual to this type of organization'.

7. The Eurobarometer reported that 58% of UK citizens had donated money to an organization.

8. Conceivably some of this 25% were *animal welfare* contributions, rather than *animal rights*.

9. 92% of small, 93% of medium and 100% of large and 66% of ALL groups stated that they attempted to influence policy outcomes.

10. Nonetheless groups can excise categories of members: size is not an absolute benefit. The Ramblers Association in 1987/1988 wrote off about 4% of their membership (1000 members) because the costs of servicing them were less than the income (Law, 2000: 282).

11. Data on activities in political parties in the UK in the 1990s highlighted low levels of participation. Seyd and Whiteley (1992: 88) and Whiteley *et al.* (1994: 246) found that 36% of Labour Party members and 66% of Conservative Party members had not attended a Party meeting in the previous year (Seyd and Whiteley, 1992: 234; Whiteley *et al.*, 1994: 258). However, when they cast their net a little wider than attending meetings in the previous 12 months, to ask questions about activity over the last five years a different picture emerged – but dependent on a very weak test. By such a standard they found relatively high levels of activity within the Labour Party at election times compared to the Conservatives (and group members generally). For example, 57% of Labour Party members claimed to have frequently 'delivered party leaflets during an election' (an additional 26% stated that they engaged in this activity rarely or occasionally). 36% of members also said that they 'canvassed voters on behalf of the party' frequently (31% said they did this rarely or occasionally). Only 22% of Conservative party members delivered leaflets frequently (17% rarely or occasionally) and 10% canvassed voters frequently (15% rarely or occasionally) (Seyd and Whiteley, 1992: 234; Whiteley *et al.*, 1994: 258).

12. It is important to note that 50% of those groups with memberships/supporterships in excess of 50,000 did not have any internal elections. The corresponding figures for the other sub-categories were 30% (1000–50,000 members/supporters), 20% (under 1000 members/supporters) and 5% (ALL groups).

7. Reinforcing polyarchy: What groups do for democracy?

1. Schier (2000: 24) identifies three large factors accounting for the decline of widespread mobilization strategies in favour of activation strategies: '(1) the decline of party influence in the electoral process and among voters, (2) the proliferation of interest groups since 1960, and (3) transformations in the technology of politics . . .'.

2. Many parties have increasingly adopted similar professionalized recruiting methods to in effect enlist supporters rather than grass-roots members. Farrell and Webb (2000: 122) note parties have 'centralized and professionalized' and are marketing supportership via a full-time professional staff. Dalton and Wattenberg (2000: 283) lament: 'The shift from 'selling' to 'marketing' parties

as diminishing the 'parties' function in representing the citizenry'. Scarrow (2000: 83) argues that the recruitment of supporters – instead of members – may not destabilize representative democracy or undermine 'enduring party systems'. It may however, 'lead to fundamental changes in the ways that parties link citizens to their political elite'.

3. Truman (1951: 138) noted that 'the significance of the "democratic mold" . . . is of fundamental importance in the process of group politics. It has a profound relationship to the problem of unity – not only the cohesion of the particular association, but as well the unity of the society of which it is a part. Associations, in our culture are expected to be "democratic" '.

4. Internal efficacy relates to an individual's ability to both comprehend and participate in politics. External efficacy is a belief that through their action they can actually influence policy outcomes.

5. Parry *et al.* (1992: 429–430) point out that this is not unproblematic: 'the relative lack of citizen participation in national-level issues means that there is a significant arena where the ordinary person makes little direct impact'. Thus the allocation of resources still remains in the hands of the political elite, with the public influencing policy outputs through voting for political packages at election time.

6. In fact, an analogous situation can be found in the relationship between activists in *conventional* and *unconventaional* politics. Jenkins (1995: 19) cites work by Barnes and Kasse (1979) and Herring (1989), which found that those who were active in unconventional politics were simultaneously active in protest politics.

References

Allen, M (1997), *Direct Marketing* (London: Kogan Page).

Almond, G and Verba, S (1963), *The Civic Culture. Political Attitudes and Democracy* (Boston: Little, Brown and Company).

Baer, D L and Bositis, D A (1993), *Politics and Linkage in a Democratic Society* (Englewood Cliffs, N.J.: Prentice Hall).

Barber, B (1984), *Strong Democracy* (Berkeley: University of California Press).

Barnes, S and Kasse, M (1979), *Political Action* (California: Sage).

Barnett, A and King, J (1989), Confidential Coordinator's Report, 12 January, quoted in Evans, M (1995).

Barry, B (1970), *Sociologists, Economists and Democracy* (London: Collier-Macmillan).

Bauman, Z (1991), *Modernity and Ambivalence* (Oxford: Polity Press).

Baumgartner, F R (2005), 'The Growth and Diversity of US Associations, 1956–2004: Analyzing Trends using the Encyclopedia of Associations', Working paper, 29 March 2005.

Baumgartner, F R and Jones, B D (1993), *Agendas and Instability in American Politics* (Chicago: University of Chicago Press).

Beck, U (1992), *Risk Society: Towards a New Modernity* (London: Sage).

Beer, S (1982), *Britain Against Itself: The Political Contradictions of Collectivism* (New York: Norton).

Bell, D (1975), *The Cultural Contradictions of Capitalism* (London: Heinemann).

Berry, J (1977), *Lobbying for the People* (Princeton, N.J.: Princeton University Press).

Berry, J (1984), *The Interest Group Society* (Glenview, Ill.: Scott, Foresman/Little Brown).

Berry, J (1993), 'Citizen Groups and the Changing Nature of Interest Group Politics in America', *The Annals, AAPSS*, vol. 528: 30–41.

Berry, J (1994), 'An Agenda for Research on Interest Groups', in W Croty, M Schwartz and J Green (eds) *Representing Interests and Interest Group Representation* (Lanham, Maryland: University Press of America).

Berry, J (1997), *The Interest Group Society* (3rd edition) (New York: Longman).

Berry, J (1999), *The New Liberalism: The Rising Power of Citizen Groups* (Washington, D.C.: Brookings Institution Press).

Berry, J, Portney, K and Thomson, K (1993), *The Rebirth of Urban Democracy* (Washington, D.C.: Brookings Institution Press).

Birkland, T A (1997), *After Disaster: Agenda Setting, Public Policy and Focusing Events* (Washington, D.C.: Georgetown University Press).

Blumer H (1948), 'Public Opinion and Public Opinion Polling', *American Sociological Review*, vol. 55: 542–555.

Blyth, M M and Varghese, R (1999), 'The State of the Discipline in American Political Science: Be Careful What You Wish For?', *British Journal of Politics and International Relations*, vol. 1, no. 3: 345–365.

Bosso, C (1988), 'Transforming Adversaries into Collaborators', *Policy Sciences*, vol. 21: 3–22.

Bosso, C J (1991), 'Adaptation and Change in the Environment Movement', in A J Cigler and B A Loomis (eds) *Interest Group Politics* (3rd edition) (Washington, D.C.: Congressional Quarterly Press).

Bosso, C J (1995), 'The Color of Money: Environmental Groups and the Pathologies of Fund Raising', in A J Cigler and B A Loomis (eds) *Interest Group Politics* (4th edition) (Washington, D.C.: Congressional Quarterly Press).

Bosso, C J (2003), 'Rethinking the Concept of Membership in Nature Advocacy Organizations', *The Policy Studies Journal*, vol. 31, no. 3: 397–411.

Bosso, C J (2005), *Environmenal Inc.: From Grassroots to Beltway* (Lawrence, Kans.: University of Kansas Press).

Brechin, R and Kempton, W (1994), 'Global Environmentalism: A Challenge to the Post-Materialist Thesis?', *Social Science Quarterly*, vol. 75, no. 2: 245–269.

Brittan, S (1973), *Capitalism and the Permissive Society* (London: Macmillan).

Broder, D (1979), 'Let 100 Single Issue Groups Bloom', *Wahsington Post*, 7 January, C1, C2.

Brookes, S K, Jordan, A G, Kimber, R H and Richardson, J J (1976), 'The Growth of the Environment as a Political Issue in Britain', *British Journal of Political Science*, vol. 6, no. 2: 245–255.

Browne, W P (1995), *Cultivating Congress* (Lawrence, Kans.: University of Kansas Press).

Burningham, K A and Cooper, G (1999), 'Being Constructive: Social Constructionism and the Environment', *Sociology*, vol. 33, no. 2: 297–316.

Butler, D and Kavanagh, D (1992), *The British General Election of 1992* (London: Macmillan).

Buttel, F H and Taylor, P J (1992), 'Environmental Sociology and Global Environmental Change: A Critical Assessment', *Society and Natural Resources*, vol. 5: 211–230.

CBD (1998), *Directory of British Associations and Associations in Ireland* (Kent: CBD Research).

CBD (2006), *Directory of British Associations and Associations in Ireland* (Kent: CBD Research).

Cammisa, A M (1995), *Governments as Interest Groups: Intergovernmental Lobbying and the Federal System* (Westport, Conn.: Praeger).

Chaskin, R J (2003), 'Fostering Neighborhood Democracy: Legitimacy and Accountability Within Loosely Coupled Systems', *Nonprofit and Voluntary Sector Quarterly*, vol. 32, no. 2: 161–189.

Chong, D (1991), *Collective Action and the Civil Rights Movement* (Chicago: University of Chicago Press).

Chong, D (2000), *Rational Lives: Norms and Values in Politics and Society* (Chicago: University of Chicago Press).

Cigler, A J and Hansen, J M (1983), 'Group Formation Through Protest', in A J Cigler and B A Loomis (eds) *Interest Group Politics* (1st edition) (Washington, D.C.: Congressional Quarterly Press).

Cigler, A J and Joslyn, M R (2002), 'The Extensiveness of Group Membership and Social Capital: The Impact of Political Tolerance Attitudes, *Political Research Quarterly*, vol. 55, no. 1: 7–25.

Cigler, A J and Loomis, B A (1986), 'Introduction: The Changing Nature of Interest Group Politics', in A J Cigler and B A Loomis (eds) *Interest Group Politics* (2nd edition) (Washington, D.C.: Congressional Quarterly Press).

Cigler, A J and Loomis, B A (1991), 'Introduction: The Changing Nature of Interest Group Politics', in A J Cigler and B A Loomis (eds) *Interest Group Politics* (3rd edition) (Washington, D.C.: Congressional Quarterly Press).

Cigler, A J and Loomis, B A (1995), 'Contemporary Interest Group Politics: More Than "More of the Same" ', in A J Cigler and B A Loomis (eds) *Interest Group Politics* (4th edition) (Washington, D.C.: Congressional Quarterly Press).

Cigler, A J and Loomis, B A (eds) (2002), *Interest Group Politics* (6th edition) (Washington, D.C.: Congressional Quarterly Press).

Cigler, A J and Nownes, A J (1995), 'Public Interest Entrepreneurs and Group Patrons', in A J Cigler and B A Loomis (eds) *Interest Group Politics* (4th edition) (Washington, D.C.: Congressional Quarterly Press).

Clark, P B and Wilson, J Q (1961), 'Incentive Systems: A Theory of Organizations', *Administrative Science Quarterly*, vol. 6: 129–166.

Cobb, R W and Elder, C D (1972), *Participation in American Politics: The Dynamics of Agenda Building* (Baltimore, Md.: John Hopkins University Press).

Cohen, S (1995), *Denial and Acknowledgement* (Jerusalem: Center for Human Rights, The Hebrew University of Jerusalem).

Collard, D (1978), *Altruism and Economy: A Study of Non-Selfish Economics* (Oxford: Martin Robertson).

Conover, P J and Gray, V (1983), *Feminism and the New Right: Conflict Over the American Family* (New York: Praeger).

Conover, P J, Searing, D D and Crewe, I M (2002), 'The Deliberative Potential of Political Discussion' *British Journal of Political Science*, vol. 32, no. 1: 21–62.

Converse, P E (1964), 'The Nature of Belief Systems in Mass Publics', in D Aapter (ed.) *Ideology and Its Discontents* (Glencoe, Ill.: Macmillan).

Cotgrove, S (1982), *Catastrophe of Cornucopia* (New York: John Wiley and Sons).

Crenson, M A and Ginsberg, B (2002), *Downsizing Democracy: How American Sidelined Its Citizens and Privatized Its Public* (Baltimore, Md.: John Hopkins University Press).

Cudworth, E (1999), 'The Structure/Agency Debate in Environmental Sociology: Towards a Structural and Realist Perspective', *Social Politics Paper no. 4* (London: University of East London).

Cupps, D S (1977), 'Emerging Problems of Citizen Participation', *Public Administration Review*, September/October: 478–487.

Dahl, R A (1956), *A Preface to Democratic Theory* (Chicago: University of Chicago Press).

Dahl, R A (1961), *Who Governs?: Democracy and Power in an American City* (New Haven: Yale University Press).

Dahl, R A (1984), *Modern Political Analysis* (Englewood Cliffs, N.J.: Prentice Hall).

Dahl, R A (1989), *Democracy and Its Critics* (New Haven: Yale University Press).

Dahl, R A (1996), *Toward Democracy: A Journey. Reflections: 1940–1997 Volume One* (Berkeley: Institute of Governmental Studies Press, University of California, Berkeley).

Dalton, R J (1994), *The Green Rainbow: Environmental Groups in Western Europe* (New Haven: Yale University Press).

Dalton, R J (1996), *Citizen Politics: Public Opinion and Political Parties in Advanced Industrial Democracies* (2nd edition) (New Jersey: Chatham House).

Dalton, R J (2006), *Citizen Politics: Public Opinion and Political Parties in Advanced Industrial Democracies* (4th edition) (Washington, D.C.: Congressional Quarterly Press).

Dawes, R M and Thaler, R H (1988), 'Anomalies: Cooperation', *Journal of Economic Perspectives*, vol. 2, no. 3: 187–197.

Dalton, R J and Wattenberg, M P (eds) (2000), *Parties Without Partisans: Political Change in Advanced Industrial Democracies* (Oxford: Oxford University Press).

Dearing, J W and Rogers, E M (1996), *Agenda Setting* (Thousand Oaks: Sage).

Dees, J G, Emerson, J and Economy, P (eds) (2001), *Enterprising Nonprofits: A Toolkit for Social Entrepreneurs* (New York: John Wiley and Sons).

Downs, A (1957), *An Economic Theory of Democracy* (New York: Harper and Row).

Downs, A (1972), 'Up and Down With Ecology – The "Issue Attention Cycle"', *Public Interest*, vol. 28, no. 1: 38–50.

Dryzek, J S (2000), *Deliberative Democracy and Beyond: Liberals, Critics, Contestations* (Oxford: Oxford University Press).

Dunlap, R E (1991a), 'Trends in Public Opinion Towards Environmental Issues: 1965–1990', *Society and Natural Resources*, vol. 4: 285–312.

Dunlap, R E (1991b), 'Public Opinion and Environmental Policy', in J P Lester (ed.) *Environmental Policy and Politics* (London: Duke University Press).

Dunleavy, P (1991), *Democracy, Bureaucracy and Public Choice: Economic Explanations in Political Science* (Hemel Hempstead: Harvester Wheatsheaf).

Easton, D (1953), *The Political System: An Inquiry into the State of Political Science* (New York: Alfred A Knopf).

Edwards, A (2004), 'The Dutch Women's Movement Online: Internet and the Organizational Infrastructure of a Social Movement', in W van de Donk, B D Loader, P G Nixon and D Rucht (eds) *Cyberprotest: New Media, Citizens and Social Movements* (London: Routledge): 183–206.

Elster, J (1983), *Sour Grapes* (Cambridge: Cambridge University Press).

Elster, J (1993), *Political Psychology* (Cambridge: Cambridge University Press).

Entman, R M (1996), 'Reporting Environmental Policy Debate: The Real Media Biases', *Press/Politics*, vol. 1, no. 3: 77–92.

Evans, M (1995), *Charter 88: A Successful Challenge to the British Political Tradition?* (Aldershot: Dartmouth).

Euchner, C E (1996), *Extraordinary Politics: How Protest and Dissent are Changing American Democracy* (Boulder, Colo.: Westview Press).

Eurobarometer 51.1(1999), *Environmental Issues and Consumer Associations*, April–May 1999 (Brussels: EU Commission).

Ewing Cook, C (1984), 'Participation in Public Interest Groups', *American Politics Quarterly*, vol. 12: 409–430.

Eyerman, R and Jamison, A (1991), *Social Movements: A Cognitive Approach* (Cambridge: Polity Press).

Farrell, D M and Webb, P (2000), 'Political Parties as Campaigning Organizations', in R J Dalton and M P Wattenberg (eds) *Parties Without Partisans: Political Change in Advanced Industrial Democracies* (Oxford: Oxford University Press).

Ferejohn, J A and Fiorina, M (1974), 'The Paradox of Not Voting: A Decision-Theoretic Analysis', *American Political Science Review*, vol. 68: 525–535.

Fevre, R, Chaney, P, Williams, C and Betts, S (2004), 'Social Capital and the Participation of Marginalized Groups in Government', ESRC End of Award Report.

Finkel, S E and Opp, K D (1991), 'Party Identification and Participation in Collective Political Action', *Journal of Politics*, vol. 53, no. 2: 339–371.

Fisher, D R (2006), *Activism, Inc.: How the Outsourcing of Grassroots Compaigns is Strangling Progressive Politics in America* (Stanford: Stanford University Press).

Foley, M and Edwards, B (1988), 'Beyond Tocqueville: Civil Society and Social Capital in Comparative Perspective, *American Behavioral Scientist*, vol. 42, no. 1: 5–20.

Foley, M W and Edwards, E B (1996), 'The Paradox of Civil Society', *Journal of Democracy*, vol. 7, no. 3: 38–52.

Frazer-Robinson, J (1999), *It's All About Customers: The Perfect Way to Grow Your Business Through Marketing, Sales and Service* (London: Kogan Page).

Fukuyama, F (1995), *Trust: The Social Virtues and the Creation of Prosperity* (London: Hamish Hamilton).

Gais, T L, Peterson, M and Walker, J L (1984), 'Interest Groups, Iron Triangles, and Representative Institutions in American National Government', *British Journal of Political Science*, vol. 14, no. 2: 161–186.

Gamson, W A and Modigliani, A (1989), 'Media Discourse and Public Opinion on Nuclear Power: A Constructionist Approach', *American Journal of Sociology*, vol. 95, no. 1: 1–37.

Geller, L K (1998), *Direct Marketing Techniques: Building Your Business Using Direct Mail and Direct Response Advertising* (Boston: Thomson).

Gerring, J (2001), *Social Science Methodology* (New York: Cambridge University Press).

Godwin, R K (1988a), *One Billion Dollars of Influence* (Chatham House, N.J.: Chatham House).

Godwin, R K (1988b), 'The Structure, Content and Use of Political Direct Mail', *Polity*, vol. 20: 527–538.

Godwin, R K (1992), 'Money, Technology, and Political Interests: The Direct Marketing of Politics', in M P Petracca (ed.) *The Politics of Interests: Interest Groups Reformed* (Boulder, Colo.: Westview Press).

Godwin, R K and Mitchell, R C (1982), 'Rational Models, Collective Goods and Nonelectoral Political Behaviour', *Western Political Quarterly*, vol. 35: 161–192.

Godwin, R K and Mitchell, R C (1984), 'The Implications of Direct Mail for Political Organizations', *Social Science Quarterly*, vol. 65: 829–839.

Gosden, F F Jr. (1985), *Direct Marketing Success: What Works and Why* (New York: John Wiley and Sons).

Grant, W (2000), *Pressure Groups and British Politics* (Basingstoke: Macmillan).

Grant, W (2001), 'Pressure Politics: From "Insider Politics" to Direct Action', *Parliamentary Affairs*, vol. 54: 337–348.

Grant, W (2002), 'Civil Society and the Internal Democracy of Interest Groups', Paper for PSA Conference, Aberdeen, April.

Grant, W (2005), 'Pressure Politics: A Politics of Collective Consumption', *Parliamentary Affairs*, vol. 58: 366–379.

Gray, V and Lowery, D (1996), *The Population Ecology of Interest Representation: Lobbying Communities in the American States* (Ann Arbor: University of Michigan Press).

Green, D P and Shapiro, I (1994), *The Pathologies of Rational Choice Theory* (New Haven: Yale University Press).

Guber, D (1996), 'Environmental Concern and the Dimensionality Problem: A New Approach to an Old Predicament', *Social Science Quarterly*, vol. 77, no. 3: 644–662.

Guth, J L, Green, J C, Lyman, A K and Smidt, C E (1995), 'Onward Christian Soldiers: Religious Activist Groups in American Politics', in A J Cigler and B A Loomis (eds) *Interest Group Politics* (4th edition) (Washington, D.C.: Congressional Quarterly Press).

Gutmann, A and Thompson, D (2004), *Why Deliberative Democracy?* (Princeton, N.J.: Princeton University Press).

Hall, P A (2002), 'Great Britain: The Role of Government in the Distribution of Social Capital', in R D Putnam (ed.) *Democracies in Flux: The Evolution of Social Capital in Contemporary Society* (Oxford: Oxford University Press).

Hampsher-Monk, I (1992), *A History of Modern Politcal Thought: Major Political Thinkers from Hobbes to Marx* (Oxford: Blackwell).

Hannigan, J A (1995), *Environmental Sociology: A Social Constructionist Perspective* (1st edition) (London: Routledge).

Hannigan, J A (1999), *Environmental Sociology: A Social Constructionist Perspective* (2nd edition) (London: Routledge).

Hansen, J M (1985), 'The Political Economy of Group Membership', *American Political Science Review*, vol. 79: 79–96.

Hardin, G (1995), *The Immigration Dilemma: Avoiding the Tragedy of the Commons* (Washington, D.C.: Federation for American Immigration Reform).

Hardin, R (1979), 'Comments', in C Russell (ed.) *Collective Decision-Making* (Baltimore, Md.: John Hopkins University Press).

Hardin, R (1995), *One for All: The Logic of Group Conflict* (Princeton, N.J.: Princeton University Press).

Hardin, R (1997), 'Theory on the Prowl', in K R Monroe (ed.) *Contemporary Empirical Theory* (Berkeley and Los Angeles: University of California Press).

Hardin, R (2003), 'The Free Rider Problem', in E N Zalta (ed.) *The Stanford Encyclopaedia of Philosophy* (summer 2003 edition), http://plato.stanford.edu/archives/sum2003/entries/freerider/ (accessed 16 July 2004).

Hay, C (2004), 'Theory, Stylized Heuristic or Self-Fulfilling Prophecy? The Status of Rational Choice Theory in Public Administration', *Public Administration*, vol. 82, no. 1: 39–62.

Hayes, M T (1986), 'The New Group Universe', in A J Cigler and B A Loomis (eds) *Interest Group Politics* (2nd edition) (Washington, D.C.: Congressional Quarterly Press).

Hechelman, J and Whapales, R (2003), 'Are Public Choice Scholars Different', *PS Political Science and Politics*, vol. XXXVI, no. 1: 797–799.

Heclo, H (1978), 'Issue Networks and the Executive Establishment', in A King (ed.) *The New American Political System* (Washington, D.C.: American Enterprise Institute).

Heinz, J P, Laumann, E O, Salisbury, R H and Nelson R L (1993), *The Hollow Core: Private Interests in National Policy Making* (Cambridge, Mass.: Harvard University Press).

Herring, E P (1929), *Group Representation Before Congress* (Washington, D.C.: The Brookings Institution).

Hirschman, A O (1970), *Exit, Voice and Loyalty: Responses to Decline in Firms, Organizations and States* (Cambridge, Mass.: Harvard University Press).

Hirschman, A O (1982), *Shifting Involvements* (Princeton, N.J.: Princeton University Press).

Hirschman, A O (1986), *Rival Views of Market Society and Other Essays* (New York: Viking).

Hood, C (2000), *The Art of the State: Culture, Rhetoric and Public Management* (Oxford: Clarendon Press).

Hudson, W E (1995), *American Democracy in Peril: Seven Challenges to America's Future* (Chatham House, N.J.: Chatham House).

Imig, D (1994), 'Advocacy by Proxy: The Children's Lobby in American Politics', Paper prepared for the Annual meeting of the APSA New York.

Inglehart, R (1971), 'The Silent Revolution in Europe: Intergenerational Change in Post-Industrial Societies', *American Political Science Review*, vol. 65: 991–1017.

Inglehart, R (1977), *The Silent Revolution* (Princeton, N.J.: Princeton University Press).

Inglehart, R (1990), *Cultural Shift in Advanced Industrial Democracies* (Princeton, N.J.: Princeton University Press).

Inglehart, R (1995), 'Public Support for Environmental Protection: Objective Problems and Subjective Values', *PS Political Science and Politics*, vol. 28, no. 1: 55–72.

Inglehart, R (1997), *Modernization and Postmodernization: Cultural, Economic and Political Change in 43 Societies* (Princeton, N.J.: Princeton University Press).

Inhaber, H (1992), 'Of NIMBYs, LULUs and NIMTOOs', *Public Interest*, vol. 107: 52–64.

Jamison, A (1996), 'The Shaping of the Global Environmental Agenda: The Role of NGOs', in S Lasch, B Szerszynski and B Wynne (eds) *Risk, Environment and Modernity* (London: Sage).

Jenkins, J C (1995), 'Social Movements, Political Representation, and the State: An Agenda and Comparative Framework', in J C Jenkins and B Klandermans (eds) *The Politics of Social Protest: Comparative Perspectives on States and Social Movements* (Minnesota: UCL).

Jennings, M K (1999), 'Political Responses to Pain and Loss. Presidential Address, American Political Science Association, 1998', *American Political Science Review*, vol. 93, no. 1: 1–13.

Johnson, E (1995), 'How Environmental Groups Recruit Members: Does the Logic Still Hold Up?', Paper presented at the Annual Meeting of the American Political Science Association, Chicago, 2 September 1995.

Johnson, E (1998), 'Interest Group Recruiting: Finding Members and Keeping Them', in A J Cigler and B A Loomis (eds) *Interest Group Politics* (5th edition) (Washington, D.C.: Congressional Quarterly Press).

Jones, B (1994), *Reconceiving Decision Making in Democratic Politics* (Chicago: University of Chicago Press).

Jones, B and Baumgartner, F (2005), *The Politics of Attention* (Chicago: University of Chicago Press).

Jordan, G (2001), *Shell, Greenpeace and the Brent Spar* (Basingstoke: Palgrave).

Jordan, G and Halpin, D (2004), 'Olson Triumphant? Recruitment Strategies and the Growth of a Small Business Organisation', *Political Studies*, vol. 52, no. 3: 431–449.

Jordan, G and Maloney, W A (1996), 'How Bumble Bees Fly: Accounting for Public Interest Participation', *Political Studies*, vol. 44, no. 4: 668–685.

Jordan, G and Maloney, W A (1997), *The Protest Business: Mobilizing Campaign Groups* (Manchester: Manchester University Press).

Jordan, G and Maloney, W A (1998), 'Manipulating Membership: Supply Side Influences Over Group Size', *British Journal of Political Science*, vol. 28, no. 5: 389–409.

Jordan, G and Maloney, W A (2006), 'Letting George Do it: Does Olson Explain Low Levels of Participation?', *Journal of Elections, Public Opinion and Parties*, vol. 16, no. 2 (July): 115–140.

Jordan, G, Halpin, D and Maloney, W A (2004), 'Defining Interests: Disambiguation and the Need for New Distinctions', *British Journal of Politics and International Relations*, vol. 6, no. 2: 1–18.

Jordan, G, Maloney, W A and McLaughlin, A M (1992), 'What is Studied when Pressure Groups are Studied?', *British Interest Group Project, Working Paper Series no. 1* (Aberdeen: British Interest Group Project, University of Aberdeen).

Jordan, G, Maloney W A and McLaughlin, A M (1994), 'Interest Groups: A Marketing Perspective on Membership', in P Dunleavy and J Stanyer (eds) *Contemporary Political Studies: Proceedings of the Annual Conference of the Political Studies Association*, Swansea March 29–31.

Kanji, M and Nevitte, N (1997), 'Environmental Support, Concern and Action: An Exploratory Crossnational Analysis', *International Journal of Public Opinion Research*, vol. 9, no. 1: 66–76.

Katz, R S (1997), *Democracy and Elections* (New York: Oxford University Press).

Kawashima, M (2004), 'Is Anti-whaling a Protest Business? An Aspect of Environmental Organizations' "Save the Whale campaign" ', *The Essex graduate Journal of Sociology*, February 2004, vol. 4: 5–17.

Kitschelt, H (1989), *The Logics of Party Formation: Ecological Politics in Belgium and West Germany* (Ithaca: Cornell University Press).

Kitschelt, H (1990), *Beyond the European Left: Ideology and Political Action in the Belgian Ecology Parties* (Durham: Duke University Press).

Kitschelt, H (1992), 'Social Movements, Political Parties, and Democratic Theory', *The Annals, AAPSS*, vol. 528: 13–29.

Knoke, D (1981), 'Commitment and Detachment in Voluntary Associations', *American Sociological Review*, vol. 46: 141–158.

Knoke, D (1988), 'Incentives in Collective Action Organizations', *American Sociological Review*, vol. 53: 311–329.

Knoke, D (1990), *Organizing for Collective Action: The Political Economies of Associations* (New York: Aldine de Gruyter).

Kriesi, H (2006), 'Organizational Resources: Personnel and Finances', in W A Maloney and S Roßteutscher (eds) *Social Capital and Associations in European Democracies: A Comparative Analysis* (London: Routledge).

Kuhn, T (1970), *The Structure of Scientific Revolutions* (2nd edition) (Chicago: University of Chicago Press).

Lansley, J (1996), 'Membership Participation and Ideology in Large Voluntary Organizations: The Case of the National Trust', *Voluntas*, vol. 7, no. 3: 221–240.

Law, P (2000), *The Long-Run Development of Environmental Interest Groups in Britain: Two Case Studies*, PhD London School of Economics.

Lawson, K (1980), 'Political Parties and Linkage', in K Lawson (ed.) *Political Parties and Linkage: A Comparative Perspective* (New Haven: Yale University Press).

Lawson, K (1988), 'When Linkage Fails', in K Lawson and P Merkl (eds) *When Parties Fail: Emerging Alternative Organizations* (Princeton, N.J.: Princeton University Press).

Lawson, K and Merkl, P (1988), 'Alternative Organizations: Environmental, Supplementary, Communitarian, and Antiauthoritarian', in K Lawson and P Merkl (eds) *When Parties Fail: Emerging Alternative Organizations* (Princeton, N.J.: Princeton University Press).

Leadbetter, C (2004), *Learning About Personalisation* (London: DEMOS).

Leighley, J E (1995), 'Attitudes, Opportunities and Incentives: A Field Essay on Political Participation', *Political Research Quarterly*, vol. 48, no. 2: 181–209.

Leighley, J (1996), 'Group Mobilization and Political Participation', *The Journal of Politics*, vol. 58, no. 2: 447–463.

Levine, C H and Thurber, J A (1986), 'Reagan and the Intergovernmental Lobby: Iron Triangles, Cozy Subsystems, and Political Conflict', in A Cigler and B Loomis (eds) *Interest Group Politics* (2nd edition) (Washington, D.C.: Congressional Quarterly Press).

Lindblom, C E (1988), *Democracy and Market System* (Oxford: Oxford University Press).

Lippmann, W (1925) *The Phantom Public* (NY, Harcourt: Brace and Co).

Lipset, S M (1983), *Political Man: The Social Bases of Politics* (Surrey: Heinemann Educational Books).

Loomis, B A (1983), 'A New Era: Groups and the Grass Roots', in A J Cigler and B A Loomis (eds) *Interest Group Politics* (1st edition) (Washington, D.C.: Congressional Quarterly Press).

Loomis, B A and Cigler, A J (1991), 'Introduction: The Changing Nature of Interest Group Politics', in A J Cigler and B A Loomis (eds) *Interest Group Politics* (3rd edition) (Washington, D.C.: Congressional Quarterly Press).

Lowe, P and Goyder, J (1983), *Environmental Groups in Politics* (London: Allen & Unwin).

Lowe, P and Morrison, D (1984), 'Bad News or Good News: Environmental Politics and The Mass Media', *Sociological Review*, vol. 32, no. 1: 75–90.

Lowe, P and Rüdig, W (1986), 'Review Article: Political Ecology and the Social Sciences – The State of The Art', *British Journal of Political Science*, vol. 16: 513–559.

Lowe, P, Murdoch, J and Norton, A (2001), *Professionals and Volunteers in the Environmental Process* (Newcastle: Centre for Rural Economy).

Luttbeg, N R (1974), *Public Opinion and Public Policy, Models of Political Linkage* (Ithaca: F E Peacock).

Maarek, P J (1995), *Political Marketing and Communication* (London: John Libbey).

Mabbott, J D (1958), *The State and the Citizen* (London: Arrow Books).

Macnaghten, P and Urry, J (1998), *Contested Natures* (London: Sage).

McCarthy, J and Zald, M (1973), *The Trend of Social Movements in America* (Morristown: General Learning Press).

McConnell, G (1969), 'The Public Values of the Private Association', in J R Pennock and J W Chapman (eds) *Voluntary Associations* (New York: Atherton Press).

McFarland, A S (1984), *Common Cause* (Chatham House, N.J.: Chatham House).

McKenzie, R (1964), *British Political Parties* (2nd edition) (London: Mercury).

Madison, J ([1787] 2003), 'The Federalist Paper no. 10', in V Hodgkinson and M W Foley (eds) *The Civil Society Reader* (Lebanon, N.H.: Tufts University Press), 70–75.

Mair, P (2005), 'Democracy Beyond Parties', Center for the Study of Democracy, Paper 05'06 (California: University of California, Irvine).

Majeska, K (2001), 'Understanding and Attracting Your "Customers" ', in P Economy (ed.) *Enterprising Nonprofits: A Handbook for Social Entrepreneurs* (New York: John Wiley and Sons).

Maloney, W A (1999), 'Contracting Out the Participation Function: Social Capital and Checkbook Participation', in J W van Deth, M Maraffi, K Newton and P Whiteley (eds) *Social Capital and European Democracy* (London: Routledge).

Maloney, W A (2007), 'Interest Groups, Social Capital, and Democratic Politics', in D Castiglione, J W van Deth and G Wolle (eds) *Handbook of Social Capital* (Oxford: Oxford University Press).

Maloney, W A and Roßteutscher, S (2005), 'Welfare Through Organizations', in S Roßteutscher (ed.) *Democracy and the Role of Associations* (London: Routledge), 89–112.

Mansbridge, J J (1990), 'The Rise and Fall of Self-Interest in the Explanation of Political Life', in J J Mansbridge (ed.) *Beyond Self-Interest* (Chicago: University of Chicago Press).

Martell, L (1994), *Ecology and Society: An Introduction* (Cambridge: Polity Press).

Marwell, G and Ames, R E (1981), 'Economists Free Ride, Does Anyone Else? Experiments on the provision of public good, IV', *Journal of Public Economics*, vol. 15: 295–310.

Michalowitz, I (2004), 'Analysing Structured Paths of Lobbying Behaviour: Why Discussing the Involvement of "Civil Society" Does not Solve the EU's Democratic Deficit', *European Integration*, vol. 26, no. 2: 145–170.

Michels, R ([1915] 1959), *Political Parties: A Sociological Study of the Oligarchical Tendencies of Modern Democracy* (New York: Dover).

Minkin, L (1980), *The Labour Party Conference: A Study in the Politics of Intra-Party Democracy* (Manchester: Manchester University Press).

Mitchell, R C (1979), 'National Environmental Lobbies and the Apparent Illogic of Collective Action', in C Russell (ed.) *Collective Decision-Making* (Baltimore, Md.: John Hopkins University Press).

Moe, T M (1980a), 'A Calculus of Group Membership', *American Journal of Political Science*, vol. 24: 593–632.

Moe, T M (1980b), *The Organization of Interests* (Chicago: University of Chicago Press).

Moore, W H (1995), 'Rational Rebels: Overcoming the Free-Rider Problem', *Political Research Quarterly*, vol. 48, no. 2: 417–454.

Mueller, J (1992), 'Democracy and Ralph's Pretty Good Grocery: Elections, Equality, and Minimal Human Being', *American Journal of Political Science*, vol. 36, no. 4: 983–1003.

Mueller, J (1999), *Capitalism, Democracy and Ralph's Pretty Good Grocery* (Princeton, N.J.: Princeton University Press).

Muller, E N and Opp, K-D (1986), 'Rational Choice and Rebellious Collective Action', *American Political Science Review*, vol. 80: 471–487.

Mundo, P A (1992), *Interest Groups: Cases and Characteristics* (Chicago: Nelson Hall).

Murphy, D and Bendell, J (1997), *In the Company of Partners* (London: The Policy Press).

Nagel, J (1987), *Participation* (New Jersey: Prentice-Hall).

Norris, P (2002), *Democratic Phoenix: Reinventing Political Activism* (Cambridge: Cambridge University Press).

O'Shaughnessy, N J (1990), 'The Peevish Penmen: Direct Mail and US Elections', in N J O'Shaughnessy (ed.) *The Phenomenon of Political Marketing* (London: Macmillan).

O'Shaughnessy, N and Peele, G (1985), 'Money, Mail and Markets: Reflections on Direct Mail in American Politics', *Electoral Studies*, vol. 4, no. 2: 115–124.

Odegard, P H (1928), *Pressure Politics: The Story of the Anti-Saloon League* (New York: Columbia University Press).

Oliver, P (1993), 'Formal Models of Collective Action', *Annual Review of Sociology*, vol. 19: 271–300.

Olson, M (1965), *The Logic of Collective Action* (Cambridge, Mass.: Harvard University Press).

Olson, M (1971), *The Logic of Collective Action* (2nd edition) (Cambridge, Mass.: Harvard University Press).

Olson, M. (1979), 'Epilogue: Letter to Denton Morrison', *Research in Social Movements, Conflicts, and Change*, vol. 2: 149–150.

Olson, M (1982), *The Rise and Decline of Nations: Economic Growth, Stagflation and Social Rigidities* (New Haven: Yale University Press).

Opp, K-D (1986), 'Soft Incentives and Collective Action: Participation in the Anti-Nuclear Movement', *British Journal of Political Science*, vol. 16: 87–112.

Opp, K-D (1999), 'Contending Conceptions of the Theory of Rational Action', *Journal of Theoretical Politics*, vol. 11, no. 2: 171–202.

Parry, G, Moyser, G and Day, N (1992), *Political Participation and Democracy in Britain* (Cambridge: Cambridge University Press).

Pateman, C (1970), *Participation and Democratic Theory* (Cambridge: Cambridge University Press).

Pattie, C, Seyd, P and Whiteley, P (2004), *Citizenship in Britain: Values, Participation and Democracy* (Cambridge: Cambridge University Press).

Petracca, M (1991), 'The Rational Choice Approach to Politics: The Challenge to Normative Democratic Theory', *Review of Politics*, vol. 53: 289–319.

Pierce, J C, Steger, M-A E, Steel, B S and Lovrich, N P (1992), *Citizens, Political Communication, and Interest Groups: Environmental Organizations in Canada and the United States* (Westport, Conn.: Praeger).

Protess, D and McCombs, M (eds) (1991), *Agenda Setting* (New Jersey: LEA).

Putnam, R D (1993), *Making Democracy Work* (Princeton, N.J.: Princeton University Press).

Putnam, R D (1995a), 'Bowling Alone: America's Declining Social Capital', *Journal of Democracy*, vol. 6, no. 1: 65–78.

Putnam, R D (1995b), 'Tuning In, Turning Out: The Strange Disappearance of Social Capital in America', *PS: Political Science and Politics*, vol. XXVIII, no. 4: 664–683.

Putnam, R D (2000), *Bowling Alone: The Collapse and Revival of American Community* (New York: Simon and Schuster).

Putnam, R D and Goss, K A (2002), 'Introduction', in R D Putnam (ed.) *Democracies in Flux: The Evolution of Social Capital in Contemporary Society* (New York: Oxford University Press), 3–19.

Rauch, J (1994), *Demosclerosis: The Silent Killer of American Government* (New York: Times Books).

Rawcliffe, P (1992), 'Swimming with the Tide – Environmental Groups in the 1990s', *ECOS*, vol. 13, no. 1: 2–9.

Rawcliffe, P (1998), *Environmental Pressure Groups in Transition* (Manchester: Manchester University Press).

Richardson, J J (1995), 'The Market for Political Activism: Interest Groups as a Challenge to Political Parties', *West European Politics*, vol. 18, no. 1: 116–139.

Richardson, J J and Jordan, A G (1979), *Governing Under Pressure* (Oxford: Martin Robertson).

Riker, W H and Ordeshook, P C (1968), 'A Theory of the Calculus of Voting', *American Political Science Review*, vol. 62, no. 1: 25–42.

Riker, W H and Ordeshook, P C (1973), *An Introduction to Positive Political Theory* (Englewood Cliffs, N.J.: Prentice Hall).

Roberts, M L and Berger, P D (1989), *Direct Marketing Management* (Englewood Cliffs, N.J.: Prentice Hall).

Rochefort, D and Cobb, R (1994), *The Politics of Problem Definition* (Lawrence, Kans.: University of Kansas Press).

Rohrschneider, R (1988), 'Citizens Attitudes Towards Environmental Issues: Selfish or Selfless', *Comparative Political Studies*, vol. 21: 347–367.

Rohrschneider, R (1993),'Environmental Belief Systems in Western Europe: A Hierarchical Model of Constraint', *Comparative Political Studies*, vol. 26, no. 1: 3–29.

Rosenblum, N (1998), *Membership and Morals: The Personal Uses of Pluralism in America* (Princeton, N.J.: Princeton University Press).

Rosenthal, A (1998), *The Decline of Representative Democracy: Process, Participation, and Power in State Legislatures* (Washington, D.C.: Congressional Quarterly Press).

Rosenstone, S J and Hansen, J M (1993), *Mobilization, Participation and Democracy in America* (New York: Macmillan).

Rothenberg, L S (1988), 'Organisational Maintenance and the Retention Decision in Groups', *American Political Science Review*, vol. 82: 1129–1152.

Rothenberg, L S (1992), *Linking Citizens To Government* (New York: Cambridge University Press).

Rowntree Power Inquiry (2006), *Power to the People Report* (Joseph Rowntree Foundation).

Royal Society for the Protection of Birds (RSPB) (2004), *Introducing the RSPB* . . . http://www.rspb.org.uk/Images/Introducing%20the%20RSPB_tcm5–58645.pdf (accessed 20 July 2006).

Rucht, D (2004), 'The Quadruple "A": Media Strategies of Protest Movements since the 1960s', in W van de Donk, B D Loader, P G Nixon and D Rucht (eds) *Cyberprotest: New Media, Citizens and Social Movements* (London: Routledge), 29–56.

Ryden, D K (1996), *Representation in Crisis: The Constitution, Interest Groups, and Political Parties* (New York: State University of New York Press).

Sabatier, P A (1992), 'Interest Group Membership and Organization: Multiple Theories', in M Petracca (ed.) *The Politics of Interest* (Boulder, Colo.: Westview Press).

Salisbury, R H (1969), 'An Exchange Theory of Interest Groups', *Midwest Journal of Political Science*, vol. 13: 1–32.

Salisbury, R H (1984), 'Interest Representation: The Dominance of Institutions', *American Political Science Review*, vol. 78, no. 1: 64–76.

Salisbury, R H (1992), *Interests and Institutions: Substance and Structure in American Politics* (Pittsburgh: University of Pittsburgh Press).

Salisbury, R H, Heinz, J P, Nelson, R L and Laumann, E O (1992), 'Triangles, Networks, and Hollow Cores: The Complex Geometry of Washington Interest Representation', in M P Petracca (ed.) *The Politics of Interests: Interest Groups Reformed* (Boulder, Colo.: Westview Press).

Sanders, L (1997), 'Against Deliberation', *Political Theory*, vol. 25: 347–376.

Sargeant, A and Jay, E (2004), 'Reasons For Lapse: The Case of Face-To-Face Donors', *International Journal of Nonprofit and Voluntary Sector Marketing*, vol. 9, no. 2: 171–182.

Scarrow, S E (2000), 'Parties Without Members? Party Organization in a Changing Electoral Environment', in R J Dalton and M P Wattenberg (eds) *Parties Without Partisans: Political Change in Advanced Industrial Democracies* (Oxford: Oxford University Press).

Schattschneider, E E (1942), *Party Government* (New York: Holt, Rinehart & Winston).

Schattschneider, E E (1966), *The Semisovereign People: A Realist's View of Democracy in America* (New York: Holt, Rinehart & Winston).

Schier, S (2000), *By Invitation Only: The Rise of Exclusive Politics in the United States* (Pittsburgh: University of Pittsburgh Press).

Schlozman, K L (1984), 'What Accent the Heavenly Chorus? Political Equality and the American Pressure System', *The Journal of Politics*, vol. 46, no. 4: 1006–1032.

Schlozman, K and Tierney, D (1986), *Organized Interests and American Democracy* (New York: Harper and Row).

Schoenfeld, A C, Meier, R F and Griffin, R (1979), 'Constructing a Social Problem: The Press and The Environment', *Social Problems*, vol. 27, no. 1: 38–61.

Schudson, M (1998), *The Good Citizen: A History of American Civic Life* (Cambridge, Mass.: Harvard University Press).

Schumpeter, J A ([1943] 1994), *Capitalism, Socialism and Democracy* (Introduction by R Swedberg) (London: Routledge).

Schumpeter, J A (1951), *The Theory of Economic Development* (Cambridge, Mass.: Harvard University Press).

Sen, A K (1978), 'Rational Fools: A Critique of the Behavioural Foundations of Economic Theory', in H Harris (ed.) *Scientific Models and Men*, reprinted in J J Mansbridge (ed.) *Beyond Self-Interest* (Chicago: University of Chicago Press). (1990).

Seyd, P and Whiteley, P F (1992), *Labour's Grass Roots: The Politics of Party Membership* (Oxford: Clarendon Press).

Seyd, P, Whiteley, P and Pattie, C (2001), 'The Citizen's Audit', Paper presented at the Elections, Public Opinion and Parties Conference, University of Sussex, September.

Shaiko, R G (1999), *Voices and Echoes for the Environment: Public Interest Representation in the 1990s and Beyond* (New York: Columbia University Press).

Sinclair, B W (1982), 'Political Consultants: The New King-Makers Work Their Magic', *The Washington Post*, 5 June: A–6.

Skocpol, T (1995), *Social Policy in the United States; Future Possibilities in Historical Perspective* (Princeton, N.J.: Princeton University Press).

Skocpol, T (2003), *Diminished Democracy: From Membership to Management in American Civic Life* (Oklahoma: University of Oklahoma Press).

Sorauf, F J and Beck, P A (1988), *Party Politics in America* (6th edition) (Glenview, Ill.: Scott, Foresman).

Spector, M and Kitsuse, J I (1973), 'Social Problems: A Re-Formulation', *Social Problems*, vol. 21, no. 2: 145–159.

Spector, M and Kitsuse, J I (1977), *Constructing Social Problems* (Menlo Park, Calif.: Cummings).

Stern, P, Dietz, T, Kalof, L and Guagnano, G (1995), 'Values, Beliefs and Pro-Environmental Action: Attitude Formation Towards Emergent Attitude Objects', *Journal of Applied Social Psychology*, vol. 25, no. 18: 1611–1636.

Stroup, R L (2000), 'Free Riders and Collective Action Revisited', *The Independent Review: A Journal of Political Economy*, vol. IV, no. 4: 485–500.

Stone, B (1997), *Successful Direct Marketing Methods* (Chicago: NTC/Contemporary Publishing).

Szerszynski, B (1991), *Environmentalism, the Mass Media and Public Opinion* (Lancaster: Lancaster University).

Tarrow, S (1994), *Power in Movement* (1st edition) (Cambridge: Cambridge University Press).

Tarrow, S (1998), *Power in Movements: Social Movements and Contentious Politics* (2nd edition) (Cambridge: Cambridge University Press).

Teske, N (1997), *Political Activism in America: The Identity Construction Model of Political Participation* (Cambridge: Cambridge University Press).

Thomas, C (ed.) (2004), *Research Guide to U.S. and International Interest Groups* (Westport, Conn.: Praeger).

Thomas, G (2005), 'The Qualitative Foundations of a Political Science Methodology', *Perspectives on Politics*, vol. 3, no. 4: 855–866.

Tillock, H. and Morrison, D E (1979) 'Group Size and Contributions to Collective Action: An Examination of Olson's Theory Using Data from Zero Population Growth, *Research in Social Movements, Conflicts and Change*, vol. 2: 131–158.

Tocqueville, A de ([1848] 1966), *Democracy in America*, (ed.) J P Mayer (New York: Harper Perennial).

Topolsky, M (1974), 'Common Cause?', *Worldview*, vol. 17 (April): 35–39.

Truman, D B (1951), *The Governmental Process: Public Interests and Public Opinion* (New York: Alfred A Knopf).

Udehn, L (1996), *The Limits of Public Choice* (London: Routledge).

van de Donk, W, Loader, B D, Nixon, P G and Rucht, D (2004), 'Introduction: Social Movements and ICTs', in W van de Donk, B D Loader, P G Nixon and D Rucht (eds) *Cyberprotest: New Media, Citizens and Social Movements* (London: Routledge), 1–25.

van Liere, K D and Dunlap, R E (1980), 'The Social Bases of Environmental Concern: A Review of Hypotheses, Explanations and Evidence', *Public Opinion Quarterly*, vol. 44: 181–197.

Verba, S and Nie, N (1972), *Participation in America: Political Democracy and Social Equality* (New York: Harper and Row).

Verba, S, Schlozman, K L and Brady, H (1995), *Voice and Equality: Civic Voluntarism in American Politics* (Cambridge, Mass.: Harvard University Press).

Verba, S, Schlozman, K L and Brady, H (1997), 'The Big Tilt: Participatory Inequality in America', *The American Prospect*, vol. 32: 74–80.

Verba, S, Schlozman, K L and Brady, H (2000), 'Rational Action and Political Activity', *Journal of Theoretical Politics*, vol. 12, no. 3: 243–268.

Walker, J (1991), *Mobilizing Interest Groups in America: Patrons, Professions and Social Movements* (Ann Arbor: University of Michigan Press).

Ware, A (1996), *Political Parties and Party Systems* (Oxford: Oxford University Press).

Warren, M (1996), 'What Should We Expect from More Democracy? Radically Democratic Responses to Politics', *Political Theory*, vol. 24: 241–270.

Warren, M (2000), *Democracy and Association* (Princeton, NJ: Princeton University Press).

Webb, P (1994), 'Party Organizational Change in Britain: The Iron Law of Centralization?' in R S Katz and P Mair (eds) *How Parties Organize* (London: Sage).

Whiteley, P F (1995), 'Rational Choice and Political Participation – Evaluating the Debate', *Political Research Quarterly*, vol. 48, no. 2: 211–233.

Whiteley, P, Seyd, P and Richardson, J (1994), *True Blues: The Politics of Conservative Party Membership* (Oxford: Clarendon Press).

Wilson, G K (1990), *Interest Groups* (Oxford: Basil Blackwell).

Wilson, J Q (1995), *Political Organizations* (2nd edition) (Princeton, N.J.: Princeton University Press).

Worcester, R (1995), *Business and The Environment: The Predictable Shock of Brent Spar* (London: MORI).

Wynne, B (1996), 'May the Sheep Safely Graze? A Reflexive View of the Expert-Lay Knowledge Divide', in S Lasch, B Szerszynski and B R Wynne (eds) *Environment and Modernity* (London: Sage).

Yearley, S (1991), *The Green Case: A Sociology of Environmental Issues, Arguments and Politics* (London: HarperCollins).

Zahariadis, N (2003), *Ambiguity and Choice in Public Policy* (Washington, D.C.: University of Georgetown Press).

Zald, M N (1996), 'Culture, Ideology and Strategic Framing', in D McAdam, J D McCarthy and M N Zald (eds) *Comparative Perspectives on Social Movements: Political Opportunities, Mobilizing Structures, and Cultural Framings* (Cambridge: Cambridge University Press).

Zaller, J and Feldman, S (1992), 'A Simple Theory of the Survey Response: Answering Questions versus Revealing Preferences', *American Journal of Political Science*, vol. 36, no. 3: 579–616.

Name Index

Subject Index